Trademark Acknowledgements

The UML logo is a trademark of Rational Software Corporation.

Wrox has endeavored to provide trademark information about all the companies and products mentioned in this book by the appropriate use of capitals. However, Wrox cannot guarantee the accuracy of this information.

Credits

Author
Pierre-Alain Muller

Translator
Jean-Claude Franchitti
thanks to
Daniel Arapu

Editors
Jon Hill
Victoria Hudgson

Development Editor
John Franklin
Managing Editor-Eyrolles
Eric Supice

Technical Reviewers
Ian Clough
Anthony Kesterton

Technical Reviewers
for Eyrolles
Jean-Luc Adda
Jean Bezivin
Jerome Desquilbet
Nathalie Gaertner
Yves Holvoet
Nasser Kettani
Philippe Perrin
Michel Reyrolle
Marie-Christine Roch
Philippe Studer
Christine Trybocki

Cover/Design/Layout
Andrew Guillaume
Graham Butler
for Eyrolles
Francoise Patenotre

Index
Simon Gilks

About the Author

Pierre-Alain Muller is an associate professor of computer science at ESSAIM (Ecole Superieure des Sciences Appliquees pour l'Ingenieur), a school of engineering at Mulhouse, France.

He has over 10 years experience in object modeling, worked for 5 years at the Rational Software Corporation, as a consultant on object methods, and has been involved with numerous OO projects in Europe.

In parallel with his current education and research duties, Pierre-Alain consults on object-oriented modeling, and teaches with Rational. His research interests include object-oriented methods and architectures.

Pierre-Alain Muller received MS and PhD degrees in Computer Science from the University of Haute-Alsace.

Redde Caesari quae sunt Caesaris

The main authors of the UML notation are Grady Booch, Ivar Jacobson and James Rumbaugh. This book makes constant reference to their work and relies heavily upon it.

Going beyond the UML notation, this book describes a management process for object-oriented development projects that is largely inspired by the development process tailored by the consultants of Rational Software Corporation. I am thankful to all of them, and in particular to Philippe Kruchten.

I also thank all the people who proofed the manuscript and generated valuable comments; in particular, Jean-Luc Adda, Jean Bézivin, Jérôme Desquilbet, Nathalie Gaertner, Yves Holvoët, Nasser Kettani, Mireille Muller, Philippe Perrin, Michel Reyrolle, Marie-Christine Roch and Philippe Studer.

I will not forget all the people who influenced the writing of this book, in particular Etienne Morel and Bernard Thirion, as well as Jean-Jacques Bockstaller, Tom Joad, Philippe Laroque, Gérard Metzger, Bernard Monnoye and the few hundred people who attended my training seminars on object-oriented technology. I do not thank Dominique Griesinger.

Finally, I would like to thank Anne, Jonathan, Roxane and Lara for their patience and I dedicate this book to them.

Pierre-Alain Muller

Instant
UML

Pierre-Alain Muller

Wrox Press Ltd.®

Instant UML

© 1997 by Editions, Eyrolles, Paris, France

Printing History:

1997: Original French Edition "Modélisation objet avec UML"
Editions Eyrolles. ISBN 2-212-08966X

1997: English translation and edit
Wrox Press

Published by Wrox Press Ltd. 30 Lincoln Road, Olton, Birmingham, B27 6PA.
Printed in CANADA

ISBN 1-861000-87-1

Foreword

UML is the result of a long process started a couple of years ago by three of the most reputable modeling experts: Grady Booch, Ivar Jacobson, and Jim Rumbaugh. Aware that their respective work represented different aspects of the same problem, they cleverly decided to gather their efforts rather than entering into futile disagreements. Two years of work at Rational Software Corporation and the help of numerous other specialists in the domain have allowed them to define this new approach to object-oriented software modeling. UML is both the synthesis and the natural extension of their respective work.

Based on its standardization by OMG, which should occur during 1997, and given the fact that it has been adopted by the largest players in the software industry (IBM, Microsoft, Oracle, Hewlett Packard, to name only a few of the largest), UML will surely become the standard for modeling the software applications of tomorrow.

Having spent five years at Rational Software in direct collaboration with the gurus in the domain, Pierre-Alain Muller was the person best suited to write this first book on UML. His outstanding competence in the field, along with his excellent training abilities, make this book an extremely valuable guide for all those who strive to understand and apply UML principles when developing their applications.

Etienne Morel
General Manager
Rational France

Table of Contents

Introduction

Instant UML is a book about object-oriented modeling. It describes the use of the UML (Unified Modeling Language) notation, which was put together in response to a request for proposals initiated by the OMG (Object Management Group), in order to define a standard notation for modeling object-oriented applications.

The UML notation represents the state of the art in terms of object-oriented modeling languages. It is the natural evolution of the notations used in the Booch, OMT (Object Modeling Technique) and OOSE (Object Oriented Software Engineering) methods. Therefore, UML has quickly become a de-facto standard among users and with respect to standardization.

Who this Book is for

This book is for anybody who would like to understand and use the object-oriented approach. In particular, it is intended for software professionals who need to make the transition to UML. Reading the book does not require any specific knowledge of object-oriented technology, and only assumes a basic background in software engineering. The book could be used for a graduate level course in software engineering.

The content of the book, its organization, and the level of abstraction retained for the presentation of the UML notation are the result of using object-oriented methods in real projects. The presentation stresses object-oriented modeling (i.e. the analysis and definition of the user's requirements); this is not because design or programming are considered less noble tasks, but simply because software engineers find it much harder to find out what to do, than how to do it.

The book is divided into 5 chapters that can be read almost independently:

- The first chapter presents the need for methods and describes the genesis of the UML unified notation

- The second chapter presents basic object-oriented technology concepts in order to facilitate the reading of the book by beginners

- The third chapter describes UML concepts, using the notation to support the description of the model elements' semantics

- The fourth chapter introduces the basics of object-oriented project management with a description of the development process implied by UML (driven by use cases, architecture-centric, iterative, and incremental)

> The fifth chapter presents a case study: the object-oriented modeling with UML of a system that controls access to a building

The book ends with appendices focusing on the transition to UML and on deployment rules. The appendices are organized as follows:

> A guide to help with the transition from Booch and OMT to UML

> A section on C++ code generation

> A section on Java code generation

> A section on IDL code generation

> A section on Visual Basic code generation

> A section on SQL code generation

The book can be read in a number of different ways, based on the knowledge and the particular focus of the reader:

> The novice reader is invited to read the whole book, in chapter order. This advice also applies to programmers who already know an object-oriented programming language such as C++, but have not followed a formal training course in object-oriented analysis and design.

> The reader who is already quite knowledgeable in a particular modeling method, such as Booch or OMT, can start reading the third chapter directly. However, I recommend these readers to skim the second chapter as well, since experience shows that certain concepts, such as **generalization**, are often misunderstood.

> Software architects, after studying the UML notation in the third chapter, should focus particularly on the fourth chapter which pertains to object-oriented architectures and introduces the '4 + 1' views model.

> Project leaders will find in chapter four all the necessary information needed to put together a development process that is driven by use cases, centered on architecture, iterative, and incremental. It will also be beneficial to them to skim the first chapters in order to read and understand the models.

It is probably worth adding that this book is not...

> ...a formal presentation of object-oriented programming; the book does not describe any particular programming language in detail.

> ...a UML addendum; the book pertains to object-oriented modeling using the UML notation.

What You Need to Use This Book

UML does not require any particular piece of software or programming language, so from that perspective the only things necessary for reading *Instant UML* are a little time and a willingness to learn. However, in order to experiment with the model developed in Chapter 5 (and available for download from the Wrox Press web site), you'll need either Microsoft Visual Modeler or Rational Rose (the demonstration version will suffice).

Tell Us What You Think

We have tried to make this book as accurate and enjoyable as possible, but what really counts is what the book actually does for you. Please let us know your views, whether positive or negative, either by returning the reply card in the back of the book, or by contacting us at Wrox Press using either of the following methods:

e-mail: feedback@wrox.com
Internet: http://www.wrox.com/
              http://www.wrox.co.uk/

Chapter

1

The Genesis of UML

Software engineering has slowly become part of our everyday life. From washing machines to compact disc players, through cash machines and phones, most of our daily activities use software, and as time goes by, the more complex and costly this software becomes.

The demand for sophisticated software greatly increases the constraints imposed on development teams. Software engineers are facing a world of growing complexity due to the nature of applications, the distributed and heterogeneous environments, the size of programs, the organization of software development teams, and the end-users' ergonomic expectations.

To surmount these difficulties, software engineers will have to learn not only how to do their job, but also how to explain their work to others, and how to understand others' work when it is explained to them. For these reasons, they have (and will always have) an increasing need for **methods**.

The days of intuitive programming and programs that 'fall into place' are over. The golden age of mature, reasoned and efficient software engineering has arrived!

Analysis and Design Methods

What is the Purpose of a Method?

A method defines a reproducible path for obtaining reliable results. All knowledge-based activities use methods that vary in sophistication and formality. Cooks talk about recipes, pilots go through checklists before taking off, architects use blueprints, and musicians follow rules of composition. Similarly, a software development method describes how to model and build software systems in a reliable and reproducible way.

In general, methods allow the building of models from model elements that constitute the fundamental concepts for representing systems or phenomena. The notes laid down on musical scores are the model elements for music. The object-oriented approach to software development proposes the equivalent of notes — objects — to describe software.

Methods also define a representation — often graphical — that allows both the easy manipulation of models, and the communication and exchange of information between the various parties involved. A good representation seeks a balance between information density and readability.

Over and above the model elements and their graphical representations, a method defines the rules that describe the resolution of different points of view, the ordering of tasks and the allocation of responsibilities. These rules define a process that ensures harmony within a group of cooperating elements, and explains how the method should be used.

As time goes by, the users of a method develop a certain 'know-how' as to the way it should be used. This know-how, also called experience, is not always clearly formulated, and is not always easy to pass on.

From Functional to Object-Oriented Methods

Although object-oriented methods have roots that are strongly anchored back in the 60s, structured and functional methods were the first to be used. This is not very surprising, since functional methods are inspired directly by computer architecture (a proven domain well known to computer scientists). The separation of data and code, just as exists physically in the hardware, was translated into the methods; this is how computer scientists got into the habit of thinking in terms of system functions.

This approach is natural enough when looked at in its historical context, but today, because of its lack of abstraction, it has become almost completely anachronistic. There is no reason to impose the structure of underlying hardware on a software solution. Hardware should act as the servant of the software that is executed on it, rather than imposing architectural constraints.

More recently, towards the beginning of the 80s, object-oriented methods started re-emerging. History — with a big H — is said to repeat itself. The lesser history of methods repeats itself as well: the paths followed by functional methods and object-oriented methods are similar. To begin with, there was programming, with subprograms and objects as alternatives for the basic elements of structure. A few years later, software scientists pushed the idea of structure towards design as well, and invented structured design in one instance, and object-oriented design in the other. Later again, progress was made in the area of analysis, always using the same paradigm, either functional or object-oriented. Both approaches are therefore able to provide a complete path across the whole software lifecycle.

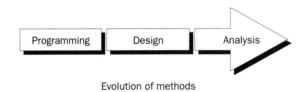

Evolution of methods

The evolution of methods, whether object-oriented or not, always progresses from programming towards analysis.

In practice, the situation is a bit more complex — methods often do not cover the full lifecycle. This results in methods being mixed and matched: method A is used for analysis followed by method B, which is used for the design. As long as it uses a single paradigm — the functional approach or the object-oriented approach — this compartmentalization remains reasonable. Although it may remain understandable, the mixture of paradigms is clearly less reasonable.

Towards the mid-80s, the benefits of object-oriented programming began to gain recognition, and object design seemed like a sensible approach for people who wanted to use an object-oriented programming language such as Smalltalk. However, from the analysis standpoint, the concept of object-orientation was still only vapor and supposition. At that time, corporations had developed a strong knowledge of functional analysis and semantic data modeling methods. Computer scientists were inclined to follow a functional analysis phase with an object-oriented design phase.

This approach has serious drawbacks attached to the paradigm shift. Moving from a functional approach to an object-oriented one requires a translation of the functional model elements into object model elements, which is far from being straightforward or natural. Indeed, there is no direct relationship between the two sets, and it is therefore necessary to break the model elements from one approach in order to create model element fragments that can be used by the other. This paradigm shift, right in the middle of the development effort, can greatly hinder the navigation from the statements of requirements obtained early in the analysis phase, to the satisfaction of those requirements in the design phase. Moreover, an object-oriented design obtained after translation very often lacks abstraction, and is limited to the encapsulation of low-level objects available in the implementation and execution environments. All this implies a great deal of effort in order to obtain results that are not very satisfactory.

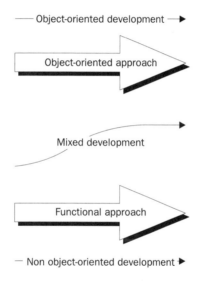

The combination of a functional approach for analysis and an object-oriented approach for design and implementation does not need to exist today, as modern object-oriented methods cover the full software lifecycle.

During the past decade, object-oriented applications — going from requirements analysis to implementation — have been developed in all sectors of programming. The experience acquired on these projects has helped the understanding of how to join together the various activities required to support a fully object-oriented approach. To date, the evolution of these practices is not complete, and there are still a few advocates of the mixed approach, prisoners beneath the weight of their habits. Corporations that are on the brink of the transition to object-orientation should not reproduce this flaw. It is far easier to deploy an approach that is completely object-oriented. In addition, software developed using this approach is simpler, more reliable and more easily adapted to the expectations of its users.

The Proliferation of Object-Oriented Methods

The first few years of the 90s saw the blossoming of around fifty different object-oriented methods. This proliferation is a sign of the great vitality of object-oriented technology, but it is also the fruit of a multitude of interpretations of exactly what an object *is*. The drawback of this abundance of methodologies is that it encourages confusion, leading users to adopt a 'wait and see' attitude that limits the progress made by the methods. The best way of testing something is still to deploy it; methods are not cast in stone — they evolve in response to comments from their users.

Fortunately, a close look at the dominant methods allows the extraction of a consensus around common ideas. The main characteristics of objects, shared by numerous methods, are articulated around the concepts of class, association (described by James Rumbaugh), partition into subsystems (Grady Booch), and around the expression of requirements based on studying the interaction between users and systems (Ivar Jacobson's **use cases**).

Finally, well-deployed methods, such as Booch and OMT (Object Modeling Technique), were reinforced by experience, and adopted the methodology elements that were most appreciated by the users.

Booch and OMT Getting Closer

The second generations of the Booch and OMT methods, called Booch'93 and OMT-2, were far more similar to one another than their predecessors had been. The remaining differences were minor, and pertained primarily to terminology and notation. Booch'93 was influenced by OMT and adopted associations, Harel diagrams and event traces. In turn, OMT-2 was influenced by Booch and introduced message flows, hierarchical models and subsystems, and model components. More importantly, it removed data flow diagrams from the functional model. These were inherited functional baggage and were not well integrated with the overall OMT approach.

By this stage, both methods offered complete lifecycle coverage, but with a notable distinction in focus. Booch'93 focused on implementation, while OMT-2 concentrated on analysis and abstraction. Nonetheless, there were no serious incompatibilities between the two methods.

Object-oriented concepts have a history that is often complex and intricate. The elements presented in the table below emerged from the experience of deploying the various methods, and have influenced the effort to unify the Booch and OMT methods.

Origin	Element
Booch	Categories and subsystems
Embley	Singleton classes and composite objects
Fusion	Operation descriptions, message numbering
Gamma et al	Frameworks, patterns and notes
Harel	Statecharts
Jacobson	Use cases
Meyer	Pre- and post-conditions
Odell	Dynamic classification, emphasis on events

Origin	Element
OMT	Associations
Shlaer-Mellor	Objects' lifecycles
Wirfs-Brock	Responsibilities and collaborations

Unification of Methods

Towards a Unified Modeling Language

The unification of object-oriented modeling methods became possible as experience allowed evaluation of the various concepts proposed by existing methods. Based on the fact that differences between the various methods were becoming smaller, and that the method wars did not move object-oriented technology forward any longer, Jim Rumbaugh and Grady Booch decided at the end of 1994 to unify their work within a single method: the **Unified Method**. A year later they were joined by Ivar Jacobson, the father of **use cases**, a very efficient technique for the determination of requirements.

Booch, Rumbaugh and Jacobson adopted four goals:

- To represent complete systems (instead of only the software portion) using object-oriented concepts
- To establish an explicit coupling between concepts and executable code
- To take into account the scaling factors that are inherent to complex and critical systems
- To creating a modeling language usable by both humans and machines

The authors of the Unified Method rapidly reached a consensus with respect to fundamental object-oriented concepts. However, convergence on the notation elements was more difficult to obtain, and the graphical representation used for the various model elements went through several modifications.

The first version of the description of the Unified Method was presented in October 1995 in a document titled *Unified Method V0.8*. This document was widely distributed, and the authors received more than a thousand detailed comments from the user community. These comments were taken into account in version 0.9, released in June 1996. However, it was version 0.91, released in October 1996, which represented a substantial evolution of the Unified Method.

The main modification was a change in the direction of the unification effort, so that the first objective was the definition of a universal language for object-oriented modeling, and the standardization of the object-oriented development process would follow later. The Unified Method was transformed into UML (the **Unified Modeling Language** for object-oriented development).

9

In 1996, it was clear that UML was perceived as a basic element in the strategy of several large corporations. A consortium of partners was then created to work on the definition of UML version 1.0; it included among others: DEC, HP, i-Logix, Intellicorp, IBM, ICON Computing, MCI Systemhouse, Microsoft, Oracle, Rational Software, TI and Unisys. This collaboration gave birth to the description of UML version 1.0, which was submitted to the OMG (Object Management Group) for their consideration on January 17 1997.

However, UML 1.0 was only one response to OMG's request for proposals for modeling languages. During the course of the next few months, the UML partners collaborated with other respondents, resulting in the production of UML 1.1. This release cleared up some semantics and included some new contributions, and UML was re-submitted to the OMG on September 10, for likely standardization before the end of the year.

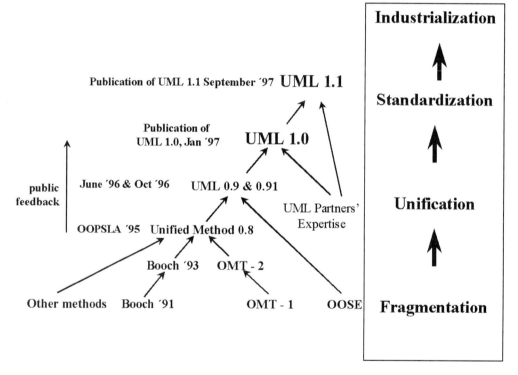

UML's creators take great care to point out that the notation forms an object-oriented *modeling language*, rather than an object-oriented *method*. The comments received about version 0.8 clearly showed that users expected a formalization of the development artifacts rather than the deployment process of such artifacts. Therefore, the UML notation has been designed to serve as an object-oriented modeling language, regardless of the deployment method. The UML notation can therefore replace — without loss of information — the notations of methods such as Booch, OMT or OOSE (Object Oriented Software Engineering, also called Objectory).

UML is not a proprietary notation: it is accessible to everybody — tool manufacturers and training agencies can use it freely. Thanks to its openness, the richness of the notation and the precise definition of the semantics of its model elements, UML is a simple and generic notation that is clearly *not* simplistic.

Model and Metamodel

The initial effort focused on the identification and definition of the semantics of fundamental concepts — the building blocks of object-oriented modeling. These concepts are the artifacts of the development process, and must be exchanged between the different parties involved in a project. To implement these exchanges, it was first necessary to agree on the relative importance of each concept, to study the consequences of these choices, and to select a graphical representation, of which the syntax must be simple, intuitive, and expressive.

To facilitate this definition work, and to help formalize UML, all the different concepts have themselves been modeled using a subset of UML. This recursive definition, called **metamodeling**, has the double advantage of allowing the classification of concepts by abstraction level, by complexity and by application domain, while also guaranteeing a notation with an expressive power such that it can be used to represent itself.

A metamodel describes formally the model elements, and the syntax and semantics of the notation that allows their manipulation. The added abstraction introduced by the construction of a metamodel facilitates the discovery of potential inconsistencies, and promotes generalization. The UML metamodel is used as a reference guide for building tools, and for sharing models between different tools.

A model is an abstract description of a system or a process — a simplified representation that promotes understanding and enables simulation. The term 'modeling' is often used as a synonym of analysis, that is, the decomposition into simple elements that are easier to understand. In computer science, modeling starts with the description of a problem, and then describes the solution to the problem. These activities are called respectively 'analysis' and 'design'.

The form of the model depends on the metamodel. Functional modeling decomposes tasks into functions that are simpler to implement. Object-oriented modeling decomposes systems into collaborating objects. Each metamodel defines model elements, and rules for the composition of these model elements.

The content of the model depends on the problem. A modeling language like UML is sufficiently general to be used in all software engineering domains and beyond — it could be applied to business engineering, for example.

A model is the basic unit of development; it is highly self-consistent and loosely coupled with other models by navigation links. As a rule, a model relates to a specific phase of development, and is built from model elements with their different associated representations.

A model is not directly visible by users. It captures the underlying semantics of a problem, and contains data accessed by tools to facilitate information exchange, code generation, navigation, etc. UML defines several models for representing systems:

- The class model captures the static structure
- The state model expresses the dynamic behavior of objects
- The use case model describes the requirements of the user
- The interaction model represents the scenarios and messages flows

11

- The implementation model shows the work units
- The deployment model provides details that pertain to process allocation

Models are browsed and manipulated by users by means of graphical representations, which are projections of the elements contained in one or more models. Many different perspectives can be constructed for a base model — each can show all or part of the model, and each has one or more corresponding diagrams. UML defines nine different types of diagram:

- Class diagrams
- Sequence diagrams
- Collaboration diagrams
- Object diagrams
- Statechart diagrams
- Activity diagrams
- Use case diagrams
- Component diagrams
- Deployment diagrams

Different notations can be used to represent the same model. The Booch, OMT, and OOSE notations use different graphical syntaxes, but they all represent the same object-oriented concepts. These different graphical notations are just different views of the same model elements, so that it is quite possible to use different notations without losing the semantic content.

At heart, then, UML is simply another graphical representation of a common semantic model. However, by combining the most useful elements of the object-oriented methods, and extending the notation to cover new aspects of system development, UML provides a comprehensive notation for the full lifecycle of object-oriented development.

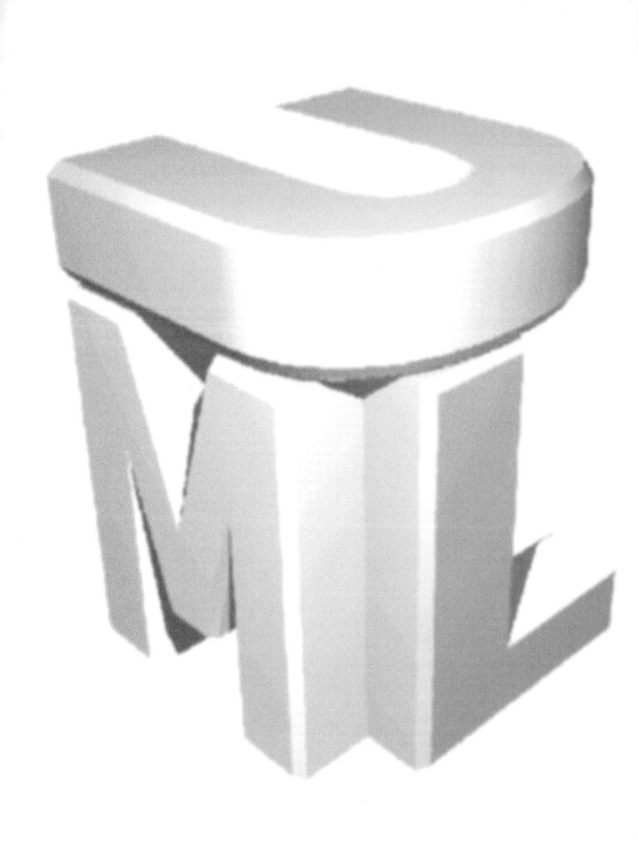

The Object-Oriented Approach

This chapter introduces the main concepts of the object-oriented approach. It is targeted in particular at software engineers who are in transition to object technology. Mastering the ideas presented in this chapter is important in order to enable reading the rest of the book. The examples included provide a step-by-step introduction to some of the basics of the UML notation.

Why the Object-Oriented Approach?

Why is the object-oriented approach so attractive? To answer this question, object-oriented technology experts always point out that the advantages of this approach include:

- The stability of models with respect to real-world entities
- Iterative construction, which is made easier by the weak coupling between components
- The ability to reuse elements across development projects

Some experts also extol the virtues of a model so simple that it requires only five underlying concepts (objects, messages, classes, inheritance, and polymorphism) to express the analysis, design, and implementation of a software application in a uniform fashion. All these points are perfectly accurate, but they are only the consequence of the amazing capacity for integration — for unification — of the object-oriented approach.

In general, any software implementation method must take into account the organization, inter-relationships, and layout of structures in order to obtain the complex macroscopic behavior of the system being created. Any study of the system must therefore take into account the collective organization of its pieces, and lead to a more global view of its components. The study must also progress at different levels of abstraction and, as a result, it should focus on both the details *and* the overall organization.

Consequently, building a software program involves a series of 'divide and reunite' iterations; it is necessary to decompose — to divide — in order to understand, and it is necessary to compose — to reunite — in order to build. This leads to a paradoxical situation, as it is necessary to divide in order to reunite.

In view of this paradox, the decomposition process has traditionally been driven by functional criteria. System functions are identified, then recursively decomposed into sub-functions until simple elements are obtained that can be directly represented using programming languages, with functions and procedures.

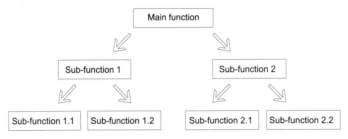

Software architecture implemented in this fashion reflects the system functions. This approach, which is based on function and hierarchy integration mechanisms, only produces satisfactory results when functions have been identified properly and remain unchanged through time. However, given that the functions induce the structure, the evolution of those functions may imply important structural modifications as a result of the static coupling between the architecture and the functions.

The object-oriented approach relies on the rationale of a Cartesian approach, and on a systems-oriented approach that treats a system as an organized entity made of components that can only be defined with respect to one another. It proposes a method of decomposition that is based not only on what the system does, but more importantly, on the integration of what the system is and does.

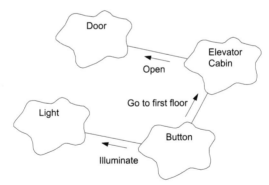

Object-oriented decomposition integrating structure and behavior (Booch notation)

While initially based on using objects as abstractions of the real world, the goal of the object-oriented approach is a model of the static and dynamic properties of the environment in which the requirements are defined. This environment is referred to as the **domain** of the problem. The object-oriented approach formalizes our understanding of the world and the phenomena that occur within it. It also interrelates the problem and solution spaces by preserving the structure and behavior of the system being analyzed. In this approach, functions are represented as types of collaborations between the objects that comprise the system. Coupling becomes dynamic and functional evolution no longer affects the static structure of the software.

When the problem is completely understood, the software system is implemented by creating software representations of the simple elements that were identified using one of the decomposition mechanisms described above. System construction can therefore be seen as a process of integration — a harmonious organization of more basic components aimed at supporting our way of managing complexity by decomposition.

In a unified system, the ability to distinguish components is tied to the way they were integrated in the first place. The power of the object-oriented approach comes from its dual ability to decompose (divide) and recompose (reunite) thanks to the richness of its integration mechanisms, which apply to both the static and dynamic aspects of software. Integration is seen as the fundamental quality of object-orientation; it assures consistency between the components of a software system, within a uniform model that applies to all the phases of the software lifecycle.

The object-oriented approach gets its strength from its ability to reunite what has been separated, to build complex entities from simple ones, and most of all to integrate system components both statically and dynamically.

Objects

An object is an atomic entity, formed from the union of state and behavior. It provides an encapsulation relationship that ensures a strong internal cohesion, and a weak coupling with the outside. An object reveals its true role and responsibility when, by sending messages, it becomes part of a communication scenario.

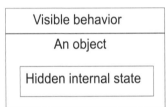

An object contains its own internal state, and a behavior accessible to other objects

The world in which we live is composed of tangible objects of all kinds. The size of these objects varies a lot: some are small, like grains of sand, and others are very big, like stars. Our intuitive perception of what makes an object is based on the concept of mass, that is, a property that characterizes the amount of matter within a body.

To extend this, it is quite possible to define other objects that do not have any mass, such as bank accounts, insurance policies or mathematical equations. These objects correspond to concepts, rather than to physical entities.

Extending the idea further still, objects may belong to 'virtual' worlds (associated with the Internet, for example) in order to create communities of people who are not located in the same geographical area.

Software objects define an abstract representation of real or virtual world entities in order to drive or simulate them. This abstract representation may be thought of as a kind of software mirror, reflecting a simplified image of an object that exists in the world perceived by the user. Software objects, which we will refer to simply as 'objects' from now on, encapsulate a portion of knowledge of the world in which they evolve.

Object technology experts have got into the habit of considering objects as entities with a life of their own, so that they often present them as part of an anthropomorphic vision. As living things, the real world objects that surround us are born, live, and die. Object-oriented modeling allows the representation of the lifecycles of objects by means of their interactions.

In UML, an object is represented as a rectangle; the name of the object is underlined. This diagram represents three objects:

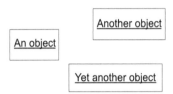

The next diagram represents several bank customers and the accounts associated with each of these clients. The lines that connect these objects represent the links that exist between a particular client and a particular account. The diagram also shows a rectangle with a folded upper right corner: this represents a **note** — an optional, free form piece of information intended for clarification purposes, in order to ease understanding of the diagram. Dashed lines implement the connection of any model element to a descriptive note.

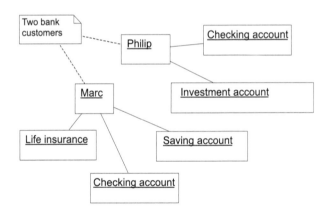

It is often difficult to find a name for every object; this is the reason why the notation supports the specification of a generic name instead of an individual name. This feature makes it possible to talk about objects in general terms while avoiding the proliferation of names like **a**, **b**, **y** or **z** that carry only very approximate semantic content.

The following diagram shows students and professors. The absence of any text preceding the colon before the names indicates anonymous objects of types **Student** and **Professor**.

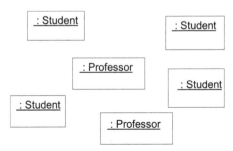

Fundamental Characteristics of an Object

Presenting the fundamental characteristics of an object allows a more formal answer to the recurring question, "But what defines an object?" Every object has the following three characteristics: a **state**, a **behavior**, and an **identity**:

> Object = State + Behavior + Identity

An object must have value over and above being a simple assembly of information or executable code. An object without state or without behavior may just exist, but an object *always* has an identity.

State

The state groups the values of all the **attributes** of an object at a given time, where an attribute is a piece of information that qualifies the containing object. Each attribute may take on a value in a given definition domain. The state of an object, at a given time, corresponds to a particular selection of values from all the possible values of the various attributes.

The following diagram illustrates a car that contains the values of three different attributes: color, mass, and horsepower rating:

The state evolves with time; when a car is being used, the gasoline quantity goes down, the tires wear out, and the passenger compartment temperature changes. Some state attributes may be constant: the brand name of the car, for example, or the country in which it was built. However, as a general rule, the state of an object is variable and may be viewed as the result of its past behavior.

In the following example, a given car is driven for about 60 miles; while it moves, the value that represents the fuel quantity goes down as a function of the distance traveled.

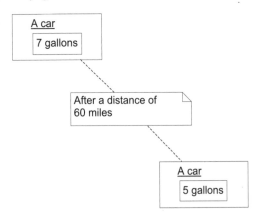

Behavior

The behavior groups all the abilities of an object and describes the actions and reactions of that object. Each individual behavioral component is called an **operation**. The operations of an object are triggered as a result of an external stimulus, represented in the form of a message sent by another object.

In the following diagram, **Operation 1** or **Operation 2** is triggered, depending on the content of the message:

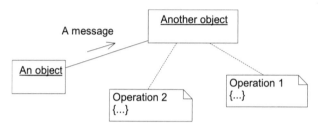

Interactions between objects are represented using diagrams in which interacting objects are joined to each other via solid lines called **links**. The existence of a link indicates that an object knows about or sees another object. Messages navigate along links, usually in both directions. In the following example, object **A** asks object **B** to eat, and object **B** asks object **C** to sleep. This presumes that object **B** has the ability to eat, and that object **C** is capable of sleeping.

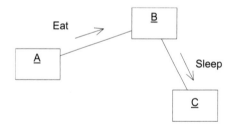

State and behavior are linked; indeed, the behavior at a given time depends on the current state, and the state may be modified by the behavior. It is only possible to land a plane if it is flying, so the behavior **Land** is only valid if the information **InFlight** is true. After landing, the information **InFlight** becomes false, and the operation **Land** no longer makes sense. The following example illustrates the connection between state and behavior.

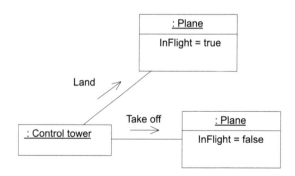

Identity

As well as its state, an object has an identity that characterizes its own existence. The identity makes it possible to distinguish any object in an unambiguous way, and independently from its state. This allows, among other things, the differentiation of two objects for which all attributes have identical values.

Identity is a concept that does not get represented specifically during the modeling phase. Each object implicitly has an identity. During the implementation phase, the identity is often created using an identifier that comes naturally from the problem domain. Our cars all have a plate number, our phones have a calling number, and all of us can be identified using our social security number. This kind of identifier, also called a 'natural key', may be added to the objects' states in order to distinguish them. However, this is only an artifact of implementation, as the concept of identity remains independent of the concept of state.

Implementation Constraints

The concepts of state, behavior, and identity, described in the previous section, are applicable to objects in a very general way that is independent of the implementation environment. However, objects may also possess features that are more to do with the actual implementation of the software, such as program distribution, databases, or multi-language development.

Object Persistence

Persistence refers to an object's ability to transcend time or space. A persistent object saves its state in a permanent storage system to make it possible for the process that created the object to terminate, without losing the information represented by the object. Later, the object may be reconstructed by another process and will behave in exactly the same way as it did in the initial process. Non-persistent objects are said to be transient or ephemeral. By default, objects are not considered persistent.

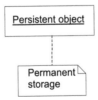

Object-oriented programming languages as a whole do not provide direct support for object persistence. This is unfortunate, and forces users to make use of external means to ensure object persistence. Database vendors provide solutions for object persistence; some are fully object-oriented, others are hybrid.

Broadcasting Objects

The problem of object persistence is closely related to that of migrating objects from one process to another. This similarity arises in the context of sending an object via an arbitrary connection from one address space to another; the operation is very like the storage and reconstruction processes described earlier. Objects do not really travel — the original object is analyzed as it is being sent, the object description is sent via the communication infrastructure, a clone of the object is rebuilt as it is received, and the initial object is deleted. *Star Trek* enthusiasts might compare this with the teleportation mechanism.

21

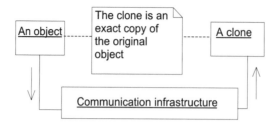

Proxy Objects

Proxy objects provide an alternative to object broadcasting. A proxy object behaves in the same way as the object with which it is synchronized. The client manipulates the proxy as if it were manipulating the remote object. This makes it possible to hide all the communication complexity within the infrastructure of the proxy object.

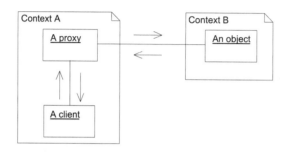

Object Intercommunication

Object-oriented software systems may be viewed as teams of objects that operate in synergy to implement the functionality of the application. At execution time, the objects contribute as a whole to the proper execution of the application. The overall behavior relies on the intercommunication between the objects that make up the application.

As a result, the study of the types of communication between domain objects is of primary importance in object-oriented modeling. As a matter of fact, the main difference between the functional approach and the object-oriented approach resides in precisely this notion, which reduces the coupling between structure and function.

Categories of Behavior

Objects interact to implement the functionality of an application. Based on the nature of these interactions — that is, depending on the direction of the messages being exchanged — it is possible to describe the behavior of the objects in a general way. Three categories of behavior are frequently identified: clients, servers and agents.

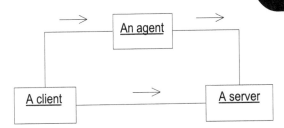

Clients are objects that instigate an interaction. They are generally **active objects** — they own a **thread**, and they are responsible for handing control to other objects.

Conversely, servers *never* initiate an interaction and are always the targets for messages. They are **passive objects** that wait for another object to require their services. In this case, the flow of control is passed to the server by the object that sends the message, and is recovered after execution of the service.

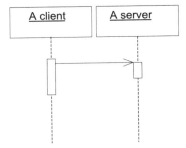

Agents combine characteristics from both clients and servers. These objects have a behavior that is very similar to that of human beings — they can interact with other objects at any time, either on their own or as a result of external motivation.

Agents are the basis for the delegation mechanism that allows an object to behave as a filter in front of another object. Agents dissociate client objects from server objects by introducing an indirection in the message propagation mechanism. This way, a client is able to communicate with a server that it does not know directly and, additionally, the server involved may change between two phases of message passing.

In the following example, the client communicates indirectly with the first server without knowing it, and without knowing that two other servers exist. The routing of messages from the client to the server is performed dynamically by the intermediate agent.

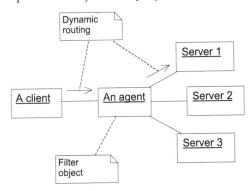

The Concept of Messages

The unit of inter-object communication is called the **message**. The message is the foundation of a communication relationship that dynamically links the objects that were separated by the decomposition process. It allows interaction in a flexible manner, while at the same time being both the coupling agent and the decoupling agent. It is responsible for the delegation of tasks, and guarantees that constraints are satisfied. The message is a dynamic integrator that allows an application's functionality to be built through the collaboration of a group of objects. It reaches its full potential when it is associated with polymorphism and with dynamic linking (defined later in this chapter). As illustrated in the following figure, messages are represented by arrows placed along the links that bind objects together:

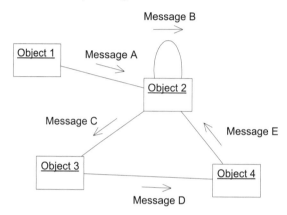

A message combines control flows and data flows within a single entity. The notion of a message is an abstract concept that can be implemented in a number of ways, such as a procedure call, a discrete event, an interrupt, a UDP datagram, a dynamic search, etc.

The following diagram describes a message completely. The simple arrow indicates control flow, and the arrows decorated with small circles indicate data flows.

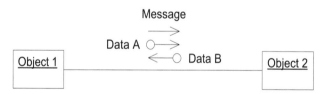

Message Categories

There exist five main message categories:

- Constructors, which create objects

- Destructors, which delete objects

- Selectors, which return all or part of the state of an object

- Modifiers, which change all or part of the state of an object

- Iterators, which visit the state of an object or the content of a data structure that includes several objects

The following example shows a C++ class in which the member functions have been grouped according to the classifications proposed above:

```
class Rabbit
{
public:
   // Constructors
   Rabbit();
   Rabbit(const Rabbit& right);

   // Destructor
   ~Rabbit();

   // Assignment
   const Rabbit& operator=(const Rabbit& right);

   // Equality
   int operator==(const Rabbit& right) const;
   int operator!=(const Rabbit& right) const;

   // Other operations
   void Eat();
   void Sleep();

   // Selectors
   const String Name() const;
   const Int Age() const;

   // Modifiers
   void ChangeName(const String value);
   void ChangeAge(const Int value);

  private:
     String Name;
     Int Age;
  };
```

Message Synchronization Types

The types of message synchronization describe the nature of the communication mechanisms that facilitate passing messages from one object to another. The concept of synchronization is most interesting when several objects become active at the same time, and when it becomes necessary, for example, to protect access to shared objects. The following diagram illustrates a shared object that implements the interface of an input/output device.

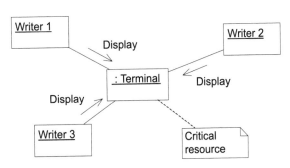

In a purely sequential application, writers communicate with the terminal in turn, and the screen display does not cause any problem. However, as soon as several **Writer** objects can become active simultaneously, the **Terminal** object becomes a critical resource to which access must be protected by the synchronization of message broadcasts.

The concept of synchronization specifies the nature of the communication and the rules that control message passing. There are five main message broadcast categories listed below, of which the first and the last have standard representations in UML, and the others are extensions to it:

- Simple
- Synchronous
- Rendez-vous
- Timed
- Asynchronous

Simple Message Broadcast

This category applies to systems with a single flow of execution, in which only a single object is active at a time. The transfer of control is performed when a message is sent from the active object to a passive object. A simple message broadcast is represented by a simple arrow.

Simple broadcast

Synchronous Message Broadcast

A synchronous message only triggers an operation when the target accepts the message. Once the message is sent, the sender is blocked until the recipient accepts the message. A synchronous message broadcast is represented by an arrow marked with a cross.

Synchronous broadcast

Rendez-vous Message Broadcast

A rendez-vous message only triggers an operation if the recipient has first placed itself in a 'wait for message' mode. This type of synchronization corresponds to a kind of waiting that is the inverse of the mechanism for a synchronous message broadcast. In the case of a synchronous message, the sender agrees to wait; in the case of a rendez-vous message, the recipient agrees to wait. A rendez-vous message broadcast is represented as an arrow that returns to the sender.

Rendez-vous broadcast

Timed Message Broadcast

A timed message blocks the sender for a given period of time while waiting for acknowledgment by the recipient. The sender is freed up if the acknowledgment does not occur within the duration specified in the description of the timed message broadcast. A rendez-vous message broadcast corresponds to the special case of a timed message with a null waiting period. A timed message broadcast is represented by an arrow decorated with a watch, symbolized by a small circle.

Timed broadcast

Asynchronous Message Broadcast

An asynchronous message does not interrupt the sender's execution. The sender sends the message without knowing when or even if the recipient will process the message. From the recipient's standpoint, asynchronous broadcasts can be acknowledged at any time. An asynchronous message broadcast is represented by a half-arrow.

Asynchronous broadcast

The specification of the message synchronization type is often performed at design time — in order to implement mutual exclusion around a critical resource, for example. The following diagram illustrates how various writers communicate synchronously with the terminal. The terminal serializes the requests, and the various writers must wait in turn.

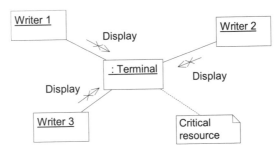

The representation of message synchronization is also useful during analysis, as shown in the following diagram that illustrates a communication by telephone. **Antoine** calls **Marc** on the phone; the communication can only occur if **Marc** picks up the phone. **Antoine** does not wait forever, and may hang up after three rings.

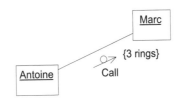

27

Communication in writing conforms to an asynchronous schema. **Gerard** sends a letter to **Bernard**; he does not know when the letter will arrive, or even whether the letter will arrive at all, and he does not wait for **Bernard** to receive it.

Letter via mail

Representation of Interactions between Objects

Objects interact in order to implement collectively the services offered by applications. Interaction diagrams represent objects in relation to one another, and show how they communicate within an interaction. Each interaction has a name and a context in which it is valid that must be specified in textual form. There are two kinds of interaction diagrams: collaboration diagrams and sequence diagrams.

Collaboration Diagrams

Collaboration diagrams are actually just what we have been using in the preceding examples. These diagrams show some objects in a given situation. Objects are represented as rectangles, with links between objects that know about each other — that is, between objects that can interact. Messages exchanged between objects are represented along these links. The sending order of the various messages is shown by a number placed at the head of the message.

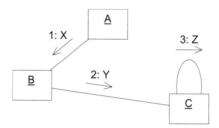

The diagram should be read like this:

> *The scenario starts with an object **A** that sends a message **X** to an object **B**, then object **B** sends a message **Y** to an object **C**, and finally **C** sends a message **Z**. (Message **Z** is a means of notation that represents an activity occurring within object **C**.)*

Collaboration diagrams are particularly suitable for the exploratory phase, corresponding to the search for objects. The placement of objects in the diagram may reflect the spatial layout of objects in the real world, while showing a type of interaction. Object diagrams describe both the static structure (through links between objects), and the behavior (through the broadcast of messages along these links). However, this type of diagram has the usual limitations of graphical representations — it is only possible to display a limited amount of information, and therefore only a small collaboration may be shown. The following diagram illustrates the limitations of a collaboration diagram: a large number of messages render the diagram difficult to understand.

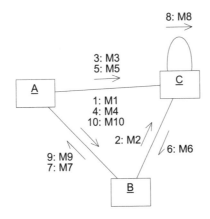

Sequence Diagrams

Sequence diagrams show approximately the same information as collaboration diagrams. However, the focus is on communication rather than spatial structure. A vertical bar represents each object. Time elapses from top to bottom, so message numbering is optional. Moving from one type of diagram to the other is possible automatically, as long as the only information kept pertains to the existence of objects and communication. The collaboration diagram above corresponds to the following sequence diagram:

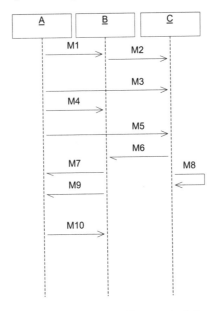

This diagram shows only the message chronology. The vertical bars may be decorated with rectangular stripes in order to show control flow distribution among the various objects, as shown overleaf.

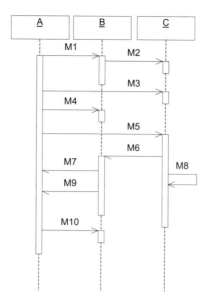

Both kinds of interaction diagram are useful for object modeling. The sequence diagram, given its tabular form, is particularly well suited for the representation of complex interactions. The collaboration diagram is better suited for the discovery of abstractions, as it allows the domain objects to be displayed according to a physical layout, close to reality. In practice, the main domain objects are often represented initially in collaboration diagrams. Then, once the objects are well identified, migrating to sequence diagrams facilitates the representation of interactions in all their complexity.

Classes

The real world is composed of a very large number of interacting objects. These objects result in amalgams, which are often far too complex to be understood as a whole at one time. In order to reduce this inherent complexity — or at least, to master it — and, as a result, to understand the surrounding world, human beings have taken to grouping together similar elements and distinguishing structures at a higher level of abstraction, while ignoring irrelevant details.

The Process of Abstraction

Abstraction corresponds to the ability of human beings to focus their thinking on an element of a representation or a concept, devoting their full attention to it while neglecting all others. The process of abstraction starts with the identification of the common characteristics of a set of elements, and proceeds to the concise description of these characteristics in what is conventionally called a **class**. The abstraction process is arbitrary: it is defined with respect to a particular viewpoint. As a result, a real world object may be seen through different abstractions, which implies that it is important to establish sensible criteria in the application domain of interest.

The class describes the definition domain of a set of objects. Each object belongs to a class. General characteristics are contained within the class, and specialized characteristics are contained in the objects. Software objects are built from the class, via a process referred to as **instantiation**. As a result, any object is an **instance** of a class.

Object-oriented languages make it possible to describe and manipulate classes and their instances. This means that the user can build a software representation of the abstractions on a computer, without having to translate these abstractions into lower level concepts (such as the functions or procedures of programming languages that are not object-oriented).

Object-oriented languages reduce the gap between our way of reasoning (by abstraction) and the language understood by computers, so that it is easier overall to implement an application using an object-oriented language rather than a traditional language, even if the object-oriented approach requires a change in working habits.

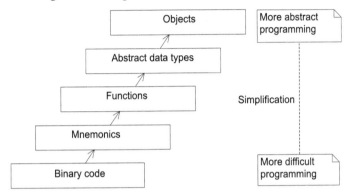

Graphical Representation of Classes

Each class is represented as a rectangle subdivided into three compartments. The first compartment contains the name of the class, the second contains the attributes, and the last contains the operations. By default, attributes are hidden and operations are visible. These compartments may be omitted to simplify the diagrams.

Class name
Attributes
Operations( )

The following examples illustrate the use of classes to describe in a general way some of the objects that surround us.

The **Motorcycle** class contains the attributes **Color**, **Engine size** and **Maximum speed**. The class also groups the operations that are applicable to the instances of the class, which in this case are **Start()**, **Accelerate()** and **Brake()**.

Motorcycle
Color Engine size Maximum speed
Start ( ) Accelerate( ) Brake( )

The set of complex numbers includes numbers that have a real and an imaginary part. Knowledge of the internal representation of the complex number — Cartesian or polar — is not necessary to use the operations described in the following example. The class **Complex number** hides the details of its implementation.

```
┌─────────────────────────┐
│     Complex number      │
├─────────────────────────┤
│ Add( )                  │
│ Subtract( )             │
│ Multiply( )             │
│ Divide( )               │
│ Obtain modulus( )       │
│ Obtain argument( )      │
│ Obtain real part( )     │
│ Obtain imaginary part( )│
└─────────────────────────┘
```

A TV set is a piece of electronic equipment of considerable complexity, but which even very young children may use. The TV set offers a simple abstraction through a few elementary operations, like **Change channel** or **Adjust volume**.

```
┌──────────────────┐
│      TV-set       │
├──────────────────┤
│ Turn on( )        │
│ Turn off( )       │
│ Change channel( ) │
│ Adjust volume( )  │
└──────────────────┘
```

A banking transaction is an abstraction of a non-physical operation that forms an interaction between a customer and a bank. The implementation details of current account transactions, such as withdrawals and deposits, are not known to the customer, who only indicates the account on which he wishes to operate and the transaction amount. The account is another abstraction of the banking domain.

The abstraction hides the complexity of account management so that transactions may be performed simply by the customer, on his own, from an automated teller or from a computer terminal.

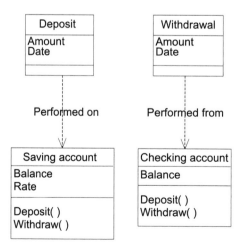

The electronics of integrated circuits exploit the idea of abstraction very successfully. Electronic complexity and internal details are completely hidden from the users of these components. In the case of logic gates, the integrated circuit forms a functional abstraction.

Or {Y=A+B}
A
B
Y( )

All abstract data types manipulated by software engineers are, as their names indicate, abstractions described in terms of operations applicable to values. This type of abstraction usually pertains to design, and never appears during the analysis phase where the term 'collection' is sufficient to designate groups of objects.

List
First( )
Last( )
Add( )
Subtract( )
Cardinality( )

Stack
Stack( )
Unstack( )
Cardinality( )

Binary tree
Left subtree( )
Right subtree( )
In depth traversal( )

Description of Classes

The description of a class is split into two parts:

- The specification of a class, describing the definition domain and the properties of the instances of that class, corresponding to the notion of a type as defined in conventional programming languages

- The implementation of a class describes how the specification is implemented, and contains the bodies of the operations and the data necessary for them to function properly

A class makes a contract with other classes; it agrees to provide the services published in its specification, and the other classes agree not to make use of knowledge other than that described in the specification.

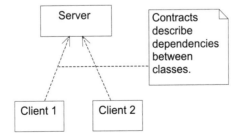

Contracts describe dependencies between classes.

Modular languages allow the separate compilation of the specification and the implementation, so that it is possible first to validate the consistency of the specifications (also called interfaces), and then to validate the implementation at a later stage.

33

In programming languages, the concepts of type, description, and module are integrated in the concept of class to a greater or lesser extent:

- In Ada 95, for example, a class is built explicitly by putting a type (private) along with its operations into a module (package). This approach enables the inclusion of several types within a module to implement, as a result, the equivalent of friend classes in C++.

- Conversely, in C++, the class is implemented directly by a syntactical construct that incorporates the concepts of type, description, and module. The class may be used to obtain a single module by adding the keyword **static** in front of all operations.

- In Java, as in C++, the class is the integration of the concepts of type, description, and module. However, in addition, there exists a more general concept of modules (the package) that may contain several classes.

The split between the specification and the implementation of a class plays a role in escalating the level of abstraction. The notable features are described in the specification, while the details are confined to the implementation. The hiding of implementation details is referred to as **encapsulation**.

Encapsulation has a dual advantage. First, data encapsulated in objects is protected against unexpected accesses — which guarantees its integrity — and second, the users of the abstraction do not depend on its implementation, but only on its specification, which reduces coupling within models.

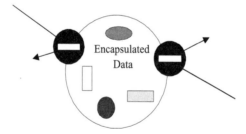

Data encapsulated within an object is not accessible from the outside.

By default, the attribute values of an object are encapsulated within the object and cannot be manipulated directly by other objects. All interactions between objects are performed by triggering the various operations declared in the class specification and accessible by the other objects.

Visibility rules complement, or refine, the concept of encapsulation. Therefore, it is possible to smooth the degree of encapsulation, as well as the degree of protection, to the benefit of particular user-defined classes that are designated in the specification of the server class. The benefit of breaking encapsulation can, for example, reduce the time required to access attributes by making it unnecessary to call selector functions.

The three different encapsulation levels that are currently accepted correspond to those proposed in the C++ programming language:

- The strongest level is called the 'private' level; the private part of a class is completely opaque, and only friends (in the C++ sense) may access attributes located in the private section.

- It is possible to slightly relieve encapsulation by placing some attributes in the 'protected' section of the class. These attributes are then visible both by friends and by the classes derived from the server class. For all other classes, attributes remain invisible.

- The weakest level is obtained by placing the attributes in the 'public' part of the class. This is equivalent to doing away with the concept of encapsulation and making all attributes visible for all classes.

The level of visibility may be specified in the graphical representation of classes using the characters **+**, **#** and **-**, which correspond respectively to the public, protected, and private levels:

Visibility rules
+ Public attribute
# Protected attribute
- Private attribute
+ Public operation( )
# Protected operation( )
- Private operation( )

The example of complex numbers described earlier readily illustrates the benefits of encapsulation. Because the specification of complex numbers — which groups, among others, the addition, subtraction, multiplication and division operations — is not affected at all by changing the internal representation (from the polar notation to the Cartesian notation), the objects that use complex numbers — and which only depend on the specification — are not affected by this change either. The following diagram illustrates the two representations of complex numbers. The public part of the abstraction is identical in both cases, but the private part is different:

Complex number	Complex number
- Modulus - Argument	- Real part - Imaginary part
+ Addition( ) + Subtraction( ) + Multiplication( ) + Division( )	+ Addition( ) + Subtraction( ) + Multiplication( ) + Division( )

Encapsulation reduces coupling within the model, and facilitates modularity and software maintenance. The criteria for encapsulation rest on the strong internal cohesion within a class and the weak coupling between classes. It is not sufficient to obtain a good abstraction, to gather data and to provide operations for reading and writing that data. A class must offer added value on top of the simple gathering of information. This is clearly the case in the **Complex number** class, which provides arithmetic operations.

Relationships Between Classes

The links that connect objects may also be seen, in an abstract way, within the world of classes: for each family of inter-object links, there exists a relationship between the classes of those objects. As every object is an instance of a class, so an inter-object link is an instance of an association between classes.

Association

The association relationship expresses a bi-directional, semantic connection between classes. An **association** is an abstraction of the links that exist between object instances. The following diagram shows objects linked to each other, and their classes associated correspondingly. Associations are represented in the same way as links. The difference between a link and an association is determined according to the context of the diagram:

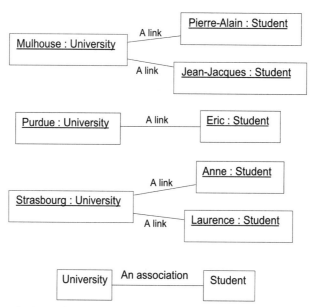

The links between universities and students are all instances of the association between the University and Student classes

It is important to point out that the association relationship is at the same level of abstraction as classes. The association is not contained within the classes, nor is it subordinate to the classes; it reflects a connection that exists within the application domain.

To improve the readability of diagrams, the association may be labeled in an active or a passive voice. In the following examples, the reading direction is specified by the symbols ◄ and ►.

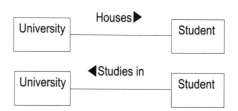

It is possible to specify the **role** of a class within an association: a role name may be specified on either side of the association. The following example illustrates two associations between the **University** class and the **Person** class. The diagram specifies that some people act as students and some other people act as teachers. The second association also bears a role name on the **University** class side to indicate that the university acts as an employer for its teachers. Role naming becomes particularly interesting when several associations connect two identical classes.

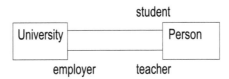

Roles also carry multiplicity information that specifies the number of instances that participate in a relationship. The multiplicity information appears in class diagrams next to the corresponding role. The table below summarizes the most common multiplicity values:

Symbol	Meaning
1	One and only one
0..1	Zero or one
M..N	From M to N (natural integers)
*	From zero to any positive integer
0..*	From zero to any positive integer
1..*	From one to any positive integer

Multiplicity may also be expressed using more complex expressions. By default, there is no correlation between the * values in a single diagram. The following diagram gives an example of representing multiplicity values.

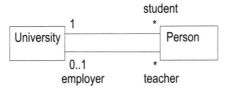

The above diagram may be interpreted in the following way:

A given university groups many people; some act as students, others as teachers. A given student belongs to a single university; a given teacher may or may not be working for the university at a particular time.

Aggregation

An association expresses a kind of coupling between abstractions. The strength of that coupling depends on the nature of the relationship within the problem domain. By default, the association expresses a weak coupling, where the associated classes remain somewhat independent of each other. An **aggregation** is a particular kind of association that expresses a stronger coupling between classes. One of these classes plays a more important role within the relationship than the other class does. Aggregation allows the representation of relationships like 'master and slave', 'all and part of', or 'composed of and components'.

Aggregations represent bi-directional and asymmetric connections. The concept of aggregation is a purely logical one, completely independent of the choice of representation. From a mathematical standpoint, aggregation is a relationship that is transitive, asymmetric, and may be reflexive.

The following example shows how a person can take care of several children. The relationship is asymmetric within the domain of interest: the adult is responsible for the children. The relationship is also reflexive: some people act as parents, and some as children. An aggregation is represented like an association, with an additional small diamond placed next to the aggregate.

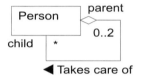

Aggregation facilitates the propagation of attribute values and operations from the aggregate to the components. When the aggregate cardinality is 1, and the deletion of the aggregate would result in the deletion of the components, UML defines an even stronger form of aggregation called **composition**. This is represented by filling in the diamond at the end of the association.

The diagram below demonstrates the example of cars. Each car has an engine that cannot be shared with other cars. The complete deletion of the car results in the deletion of its engine.

A non-reflexive aggregation, in which the multiplicity is 1 on the aggregate side, may be implemented via physical containment.

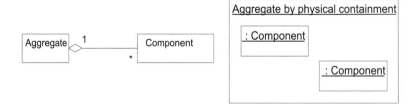

When the multiplicity is greater than 1, the aggregation relationship may be implemented by an idiomatic form of smart pointer: several pointers reference the same object, while synchronizing themselves to de-allocate the object when it is no longer referenced by any pointer.

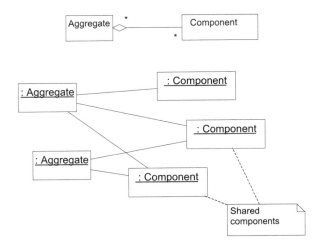

Parallels between Class and Object Diagrams

Class diagrams and object diagrams belong to two complementary views of a model. A class diagram shows an abstraction of reality, focused on expressing the static structure from a general standpoint. An object diagram represents a particular case, a concrete situation at a given time; it expresses both the static structure and a behavior.

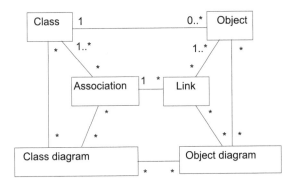

Correspondence between class diagrams and object diagrams.

The following rules govern the transition between the two types of diagram:

- Each object is an instance of a class, and the object's class may not change during the lifetime of the object
- Some classes — abstract classes — may not be directly instantiated
- Each link is an instance of an association
- Links connect objects, associations connect classes

39

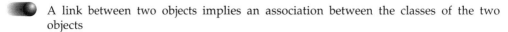 A link between two objects implies an association between the classes of the two objects

A link between two objects indicates that the two objects know about each other and may exchange messages

Object diagrams that contain objects and links are instances of class diagrams that contain classes and associations

Class and object diagrams must be consistent with respect to one another. However, it must be understood that the object-oriented modeling process is not a linear process, and one is therefore not expected to build a diagram of one type, and fully derive the other type from it thereafter. Forcing the creation of a diagram of one type before another limits the freedom of creativity. To make a musical analogy, dissociating the construction of object diagrams from that of class diagrams is equivalent to asking a composer to consider the tone and duration of musical notes separately.

In practice, object and class diagrams are built in parallel, with many comings and goings between the two representations. There is no reason to define classes before objects. It is true that each object is an instance of a class, but the specification of a class may very well occur after that of its objects. The real world that surrounds us contains objects and not classes, so it seems natural to find objects first and then to abstract classes from them. In fact, there is no general rule; in some cases, the class structure is obvious, in other cases, objects are simpler to identify than classes.

Class Hierarchies

Class hierarchies (or classifications) make it possible to manage complexity by ordering objects within trees of classes, with increasing levels of abstraction.

Generalization and Specialization

Generalization and **specialization** are points of view that are based on class hierarchies.

Generalization consists of factoring common elements (attributes, operations and constraints) within a set of classes into a more general class called a **superclass**. Classes are ordered within a hierarchy; a superclass is an abstraction of its subclasses.

Generalization is quite a difficult process, as it requires a good capacity for abstraction. The tuning of an optimal hierarchy is a difficult, iterative process. Trees of classes do not grow from their roots; on the contrary, they are determined from their leaves, since the leaves belong to the real world, while the 'higher' levels are abstractions created to aid organization and understanding.

The following example illustrates a hierarchy of means of transportation. The arrow that represents the generalization between two classes points towards the more general class.

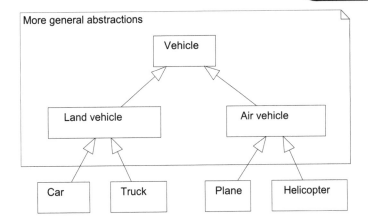

Specialization allows the capture of the specific features of a set of objects that have not been distinguished by the classes already identified. The new characteristics are represented by a new class, which is a subclass of one of the existing classes. Specialization is a very efficient technique for extending a set of classes in a coherent way.

The following example illustrates a partial classification of transmission equipment, according to two large families: continuous and discrete systems. Concrete mechanisms are added to the hierarchy through derivation from the closest parent.

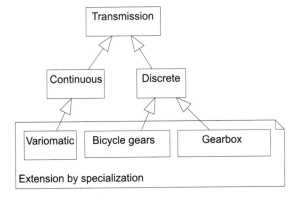

Generalization and specialization are two opposite viewpoints of the concept of classification; they express the direction in which a class hierarchy is extended. In any real application, the two viewpoints are implemented at the same time. Generalization is usually applied once the domain elements have been identified, in order to obtain a detached description of the solutions. Specialization is the basis for programming by extension and reuse. The new requirements are encapsulated within subclasses that extend the existing functionality harmoniously.

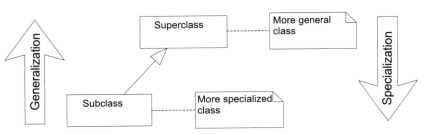

The extension of a class hierarchy requires different qualities and skills from developers, depending on the point of entry into the tree. The identification of superclasses requires above all the capacity for abstraction, while the implementation of subclasses requires mostly a depth of experience in a particular domain.

In fact, the issue is somewhat paradoxical. It is difficult to find superclasses, but programs written using them are simpler to develop. It is quite simple to find subclasses, but more difficult to implement them.

A generalization does not carry any particular name; it always means: 'is one of' or 'is a kind of'. Generalization only pertains to classes, it cannot be instantiated via links, and therefore it does not carry the concept of multiplicity. In the following example, the lion is a kind of carnivorous animal, and it is not possible for a lion to be carnivorous more than once: a lion *is a* carnivorous animal.

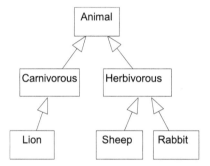

Generalization is a non-reflexive relationship: a class cannot be derived from itself.

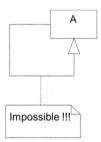

Generalization is an asymmetric relationship: if class **B** is derived from class **A**, then class **A** cannot be derived from class **B**.

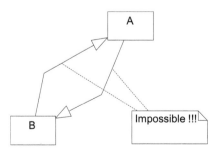

42

On the other hand, generalization *is* a transitive relationship: if class **C** is derived from class **B** which is itself derived from class **A**, then class **C** is also derived from class **A**.

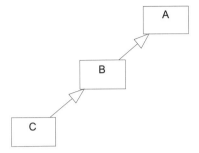

From Sets to Classes

The concept of class is very close to the concept of a set. The specification of a class is an abstract description, analogous to the description of a set. Object instances of a class share its general characteristics, expressed within the class as attributes, operations, and constraints.

These characteristics constitute the **characteristic property** of the set of instances. The characteristic property of a set **X** is denoted $\mathcal{P}(\mathbf{X})$. In the following paragraphs, the term 'characteristic property' is applied directly to the class and not to the set of its instances. The following diagram shows the analogy between a class and a set.

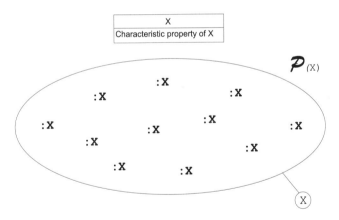

A class gives an abstract description of a set of objects that share common characteristics.

The set **X** may be divided into subsets in order to distinguish, for example, additional features that are only shared by some of the elements of **X**. The diagram on the next page shows two subsets of **X**, the sets **Y** and **Z**. The characteristic properties of sets **Y** and **Z** are extensions of the characteristic property of **X**:

$$\mathcal{P}(X) \subseteq \mathcal{P}(Y) \text{ and } \mathcal{P}(X) \subseteq \mathcal{P}(Z) \text{ and } \mathcal{P}(Y) \cap \mathcal{P}(Z) = \mathcal{P}(X)$$

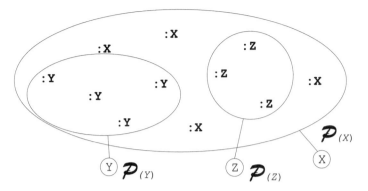

Classes and subclasses are equivalent to sets and subsets. Class generalization corresponds to the inclusion relationship of sets. As a result, objects that are instances of a given class are not only described by the characteristic property of their class, but also by the characteristic properties of all the parent classes of their class. Subclasses may not disown the characteristic properties of their parent classes. The characteristic property of a subclass includes those of all its superclasses. What is true of an object that is an instance of a superclass, is also true of an object that is an instance of a subclass. As for inclusion into sets, generalization organizes objects within a hierarchy of classes. The following diagram shows that there exist two particular kinds of elements of **X**, described respectively by the classes **Y** and **Z**.

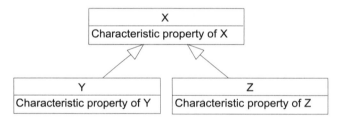

The characteristic property of the subclasses is an extension of the characteristic property of the superclasses.

The next diagram illustrates a concrete example. There are many books around; some are targeted very specifically at children, others are targeted at teaching. The classification is not exhaustive: books that are not targeted at children or teaching are not distinguished, and belong collectively to the class of books. General properties of books, such as the name of the author or the number of pages, are defined in the superclass **Book**. Each subclass takes on these characteristics and may add new ones, such as the age range of the readers in the case of children's books.

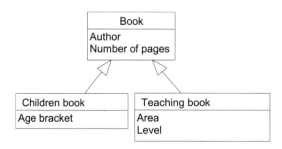

Generalization — in the form referred to as multiple generalization — also exists between unconnected trees of classes. In the following example, class **T** results from the combination of classes **Y** and **Z**.

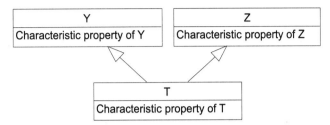

In the world of sets, the above example corresponds to the intersection of two sets that are not subsets of the same superset.

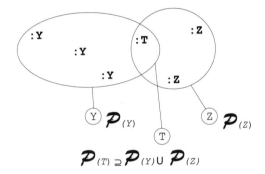

Set representation of multiple generalization between classes without a common ancestor.

The diagram below illustrates a very interesting situation. The sets **Y** and **Z** partition the set **X**, so that objects of set **X** *must* belong to one of its subsets. The characteristic property $\mathcal{P}(\mathbf{X})$ does not describe the elements of **X** directly. $\mathcal{P}(\mathbf{X})$ is an abstract description of the elements of **Y** and **Z**, which is obtained by a factorization operation on $\mathcal{P}(\mathbf{Y})$ and $\mathcal{P}(\mathbf{Z})$.

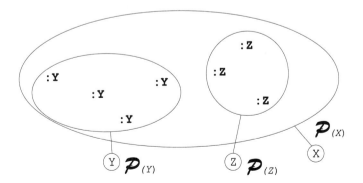

In the world of classes, the above diagram involves an abstract class — a class that does not produce objects directly. It is a more abstract specification of the objects that are instances of its subclasses. The main benefit of this approach is to reduce the level of detail in the descriptions of subclasses. The name of an abstract class is italicized in class diagrams.

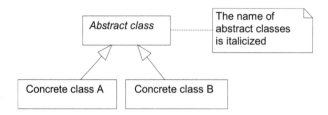

Abstract classes facilitate the implementation of generic software that can be extended easily by subclassing. The set of mechanisms that serves as a skeleton for the functionality of the application is built from general elements supplied by the abstract classes. The specific features and extensions are encapsulated within concrete subclasses.

In the previous example, the subsets **Y** and **Z** are disjoint. In the following example, the intersection of **Y** and **Z** is non-zero and defines the set **T**. **T** groups the set of objects that belong to both class **Y** and class **Z**. **T** is simultaneously a subset of **Y** and **Z**. The characteristic property of set **T** is the union of the characteristic properties of sets **Y** and **Z**, and the characteristic property of **T** itself.

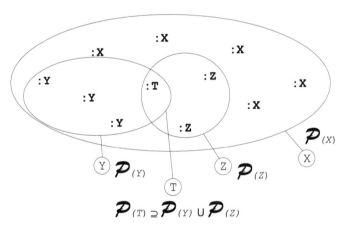

In terms of classes, the above example is represented like this:

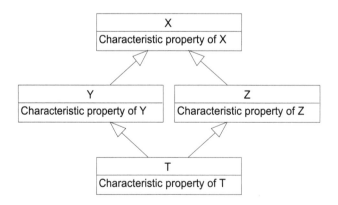

Objects of class **T** are described only once by the characteristic property of **X**. The number of branches of the generalization is not significant for the propagation of characteristic properties, and therefore **T** does not own the characteristic property of **X** twice.

Objects are either instances of a class, or they are not. It is not possible for an object to be an instance of the same class several times.

The Difficulty of Classification

Classification is not always a trivial operation. In fact, the specification of classification criteria is difficult and in some cases impossible. In 1755, long before UML, Jean-Jacques Rousseau, in his work *Discourse on the origin and the foundations of inequality among men*, describes the problem of classification in the following way:

> *At first, each object received a particular name, without thought of genus or species (...). If one elm tree was called A, another elm tree would be called B, as the first idea we get about two things is that they are not the same, and we often need a lot of time to observe what they have in common. As knowledge of more things was acquired, the bigger the dictionary became. The difficulty of all this nomenclature could not be easily addressed because, in order to classify entities under common and generic names, it is necessary to know their properties and differences; it is necessary to have observations and definitions — historical and metaphysical — far better than the men of that time could have.*

Most importantly, classifications must discriminate between objects well. Good classifications are stable and extensible. They may contain exceptions that cannot be classified according to the selected criteria. For example, the giant panda is a member of the bear family, while the panda is closer to raccoons. The platypus belongs to the family of mammals, even though it lays eggs.

Classifications are put together according to criteria that depend on the point of view. Therefore, there is not a single classification, but rather several classifications, each adapted to a particular usage.

As a result, for animals, a number of criteria may be selected:

- The number of legs they have
- The type of food they eat
- The appearance of their skin

The specification of relevant criteria and the order in which they must be applied is not always easy. Once the criteria have been selected, they must be followed in a consistent and uniform way, and in the order specified. The order of application of the criteria is often arbitrary, and leads to a covariant decomposition that translates into isomorphic model elements.

In the following example, the 'number of legs' criterion has been applied before the 'type of food' criterion. Without any additional information, it is very difficult to explain why this choice was made.

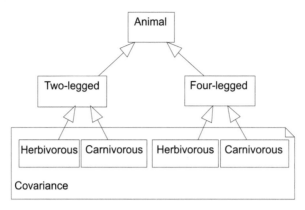

Animals may just as well be specialized first based on the type of food they eat:

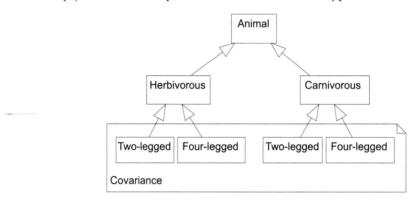

In fact, neither of the previous solutions is satisfactory, as the covariance phenomenon results in multiple maintenance areas within the model.

Multiple generalization provides an elegant solution for building classifications with independent criteria that are difficult to order. The independent criteria specify different dimensions of specialization, and concrete classes are obtained as the cross product of these different dimensions.

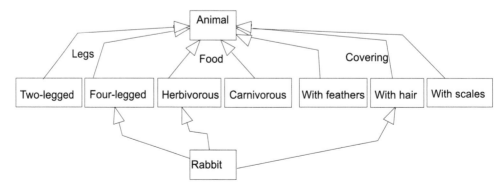

In some cases, the covariance exists due to the nature of the application domain. The following example illustrates this point: an enduro motorcycle rider must have an enduro license, and an off-road motorcycle rider must have an off-road license. This type of covariance is not reducible, as it pertains to two distinct hierarchies.

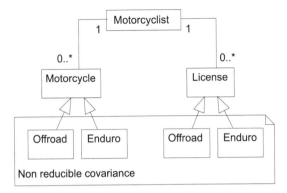

Classifications must also include balanced abstraction levels. In the following example, the decomposition is not performed in a homogenous way. The first two subclasses specialize according to the role of the vehicle, while the third subclass corresponds to motorcycle brands.

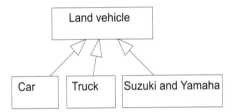

The enumeration of all these brands is not a good idea in any case, since it creates a lot of subclasses. It is preferable to favor the most global criteria, since these will generate the most extensible classes. As a general rule, it is better to limit the number of subclasses at each hierarchical level, in favor of augmenting the number of objects per class and using object attributes in order to specify the objects precisely.

The derivation of too large a number of classes is illustrated in the following example. The color criterion is too precise to determine a class, and it generates too many classes. Finally, given the static link between class and instance, the model does not allow changing the color of a car! The class generation criteria *must* be static. The color must be an attribute of the vehicles, and not a specialization criterion.

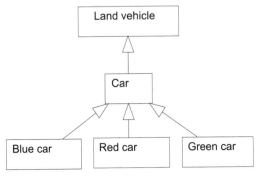

The classical form of generalization relationship for classes introduces a very strong, immutable, static coupling within the model, like the one between an object and its class. From that point of view, generalization is not suitable to represent metamorphosis. The following example does *not* correctly represent the case of the butterfly that moves through the successive stages of being a caterpillar, a chrysalis, and an adult.

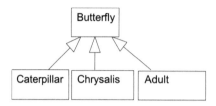

The solution for representing butterflies is to extract the mutable element. In our case, the appearance of a given butterfly is conveyed by a link to a specific object that describes its stage.

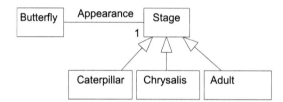

The general approach for making a classification dynamic, as in the case of mutability, is to extract the element or elements subject to specialization. This approach also allows multiple classification, by means of an unlimited multiplicity.

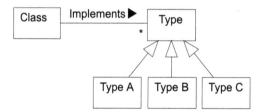

The next diagram shows an example of implementing a classification based on the previous form, but without generalization. A sticker is placed on each book, and the color of the sticker identifies the owner or specifies the topic of the book.

Inheritance

There are many ways to implement classification. In object-oriented programming, the technique used most often relies on **inheritance** between classes.

General Principle

Inheritance is a technique offered by programming languages to construct a class from one or more other classes, sharing attributes, operations and sometimes constraints within a hierarchy of classes. Child classes inherit characteristics from their parent class; the attributes and operations declared in the parent class are accessible in the child class, as if they had been declared locally. Of course, the visibility may be specified in UML by using the public, protected or private symbols, which were discussed earlier in the chapter.

Inheritance is used to satisfy two distinct needs: classification and construction. This ambiguity of the inheritance relationship is the source of many programming inconsistencies. Inheritance is similar to driving a car; one must not veer too much in either direction, or the risk of accident is very high. It is necessary to learn to use inheritance correctly, just as it is necessary to learn how to drive cars.

In programming with an object-oriented language such as C++, classification is very often implemented by an inheritance relationship between the more general and the more specific class. Inheritance propagates the characteristics of the parent class into the child classes, so that several classes may share the same description. From that standpoint, inheritance allows an economical description of a set of classes connected by a classification relationship.

Many programmers perform an amalgam between the concept of classification implied by inheritance, and the virtual composition that results from it. These programmers are mostly looking for economies in the short term; they have got into the habit of integrating components into a composite entity by using the propagation of characteristics implemented automatically by the inheritance relationship. Component construction by inheritance is a perfectly respectable programming technique, as long as it is clearly expressed in the program. When the programmer builds by inheritance, he must indicate that the inheritance relationship is being used for construction and not for classification. The C++ language, for example, makes it possible to distinguish between inheritance for classification purposes and inheritance for construction purposes using the **public** and **private** keywords.

```
class Thing : private Parent_For_Construction,
              public  Parent_For_Classification
{
...
};
```

The distinction must be made visually within class diagrams, as shown in the following example: a semaphore is neither a linked list nor a counter, but it can be built using these two components.

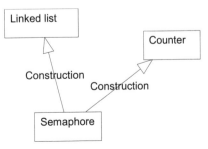

This distinction is basically made during design where, unless otherwise indicated, inheritance represents a generalization relationship rather than a composition relationship.

'Pure' inheritance is marred by implementation contingencies; in particular, inheritance does not perform a union of the properties that characterize classes, but rather a sum of them. As a result, some characteristics may be unduly duplicated within subclasses. Multiple inheritance must therefore be manipulated very carefully, as inheritance implementation techniques may cause name collision problems during the propagation of attributes and operations from parent classes to subclasses.

The following example illustrates a naming conflict that results from a multiple inheritance relationship. The superclasses both define an attribute **A**, so class **z** has two attributes **A**. If **A** represents exactly the same concept in classes **X** and **Y**, there is no reason to propagate two attributes in the subclass. Conversely, if **A** designates two *different* properties, it would be judicious to rename one in order to be able to distinguish them. There are no ready-made answers to this problem: object-oriented languages differ in their method of treating it.

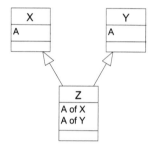

The conflict described above can also appear when the base classes are themselves derived from a common class — this is shown in the diamond generalization pattern below. This time there really are no reasons to duplicate attribute **A** in class **z**, given the fact that attribute **A** is unique in class **T**. Here again, each object-oriented language brings its own solution to this type of problem.

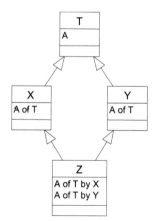

This situation is sufficiently troublesome that some object-oriented languages, such as Java or Ada 95, do not offer multiple inheritance. In practice, multiple inheritance may be used without too much difficulty when its implementation has followed the development of the model from the beginning. On the other hand, multiple inheritance is probably not the way to merge two sets of classes built in a completely independent way. In conclusion, the use of multiple inheritance must be anticipated!

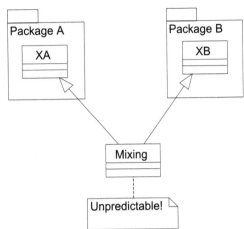

Multiple inheritance is not suited to the construction of a class by mixing several classes coming from packages implemented independently

Delegation

Inheritance is not an absolute necessity and can always be replaced by **delegation**. Delegation has the advantage of reducing coupling within the model: firstly, the client does not know about the server directly, and secondly, the server may be modified along the way. This approach allows the implementation of multiple generalization with languages that only support single inheritance. The following diagram illustrates the delegation mechanism; the client communicates with an interface that propagates questions to one or more delegates.

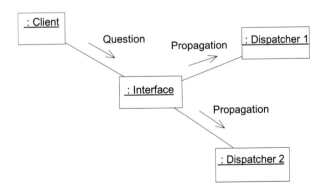

Delegation also allows the bypassing of the covariance problem mentioned earlier, at the cost, however, of the automatic propagation of superclass characteristics to their subclasses. The following diagram illustrates a construction based on delegation that may replace multiple generalization.

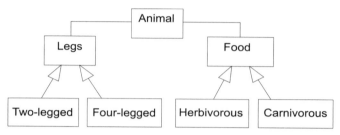

In the X Window System, and more precisely in the 'intrinsics' layer, inheritance is completely simulated by hand, thanks to the implementation of data structures that designate the parent data structures. The following diagrams illustrate Douglas A. Young's example for the implementation of inheritance when building 'widgets'.

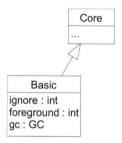

The X Window System is implemented completely in C, without direct support for inheritance. The following diagram illustrates how inheritance is simulated by hand, by incorporating a description of the parent class **CoreClassPart** in the derived class **BasicClassRec**. The **BasicPart** class groups instance variables and contains a reference to the description of the **BasicClassRec** class.

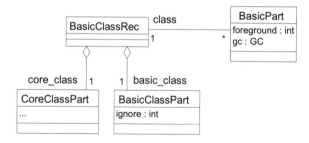

The Substitution Principle

Classification propagates state, behavior and constraints. There are no half measures: all the properties of the parent class are completely valid for the child class. The need to inherit partially is a sign that the inheritance relationship under consideration does not truly implement a classification relationship.

The substitution principle, initially put forward by Liskow, makes it possible to determine whether an inheritance relationship is well-suited for classification. The substitution principle asserts that:

It must be possible to substitute any object instance of a subclass for any object instance of a superclass without affecting the semantics of a program written in terms of the superclass.

The following figure shows a program — represented by a rectangle — which makes reference to objects of the parent class. If the substitution principle is verified, any object instance of class **CP** (the parent class) can be replaced by an object instance of class **CE** (the subclass) without affecting the program written in terms of class **CP**.

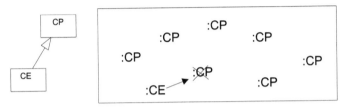

A program written according to
the terms of the parent class

The concept of generalization implies that the characteristic properties of the superclass are included in the characteristic properties of the subclass. However, compilers for some languages are not able to fully verify that this condition is satisfied in the case of inheritance, since the syntax alone is not always sufficient to express the full set of properties. Attributes and operations are propagated automatically, but this is not necessarily the case for constraints. Often, a constraint is translated into a particular kind of code inserted into the implementation of an operation. As object-oriented languages allow the redefinition of operations within subclasses, programmers may unwittingly introduce inconsistencies between the specification of a superclass and its implementation in one of the subclasses. These inconsistencies pertain mainly to constraints expressed programmatically in a non-declarative way. Adhering to the substitution principle guarantees that an inheritance relationship between classes corresponds well to a generalization. Unfortunately, the implementation of the substitution principle is up to the programmer and not up to the compiler and, as the programmer is human, he may make mistakes. If the substitution principle is not satisfied, the polymorphism described in the following section cannot be implemented.

Polymorphism

The term **polymorphism** describes the characteristic of an element that may take on different forms, like water that can be found in either a solid, liquid or gaseous state. In computer science, polymorphism pertains to a concept of type theory, according to which an object name can designate instances of different classes within a single hierarchy.

General Principle

Interactions between objects are written according to the terms of specifications defined not in the objects' classes, but in their superclasses. This enables the writing of more abstract code, detached from the specifics of each class, and also allows mechanisms to be obtained that are general enough to remain valid in the future as new classes are created.

In this case, the term 'polymorphism' refers to operation polymorphism — the ability to trigger different operations in response to the same message. Each subclass inherits the operation specifications of its superclasses, and has the ability to modify the behavior of these operations locally, in order to better take into account the particular features of a given abstraction level. From this point of view, a given operation is polymorphic, since its implementation may take on several forms.

Polymorphism is a decoupling mechanism that acts over time. The benefits of polymorphism are mainly obtained during maintenance. Polymorphism does not influence analysis, but it does rely on analysis: its efficient implementation rests on identifying abstract mechanisms that are applicable in a uniform way to object instances of different subclasses. Analysis must not be thought of in terms of polymorphism, but rather in terms of abstraction. Polymorphism is made possible by a useful side effect of this abstraction.

Application

The following diagram represents a polymorphic collection: the zoo. The zoo contains numerous animals, including lions, tigers, and bears. The name **Animal**, which is known by the **Zoo** class, collectively describes all sorts of animals. Software written at the 'zoo' level of abstraction does not need to know the specific details of each animal.

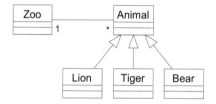

The animals in this example all know how to sleep, but each species has its particular habits. The specification of an animal says that animals can sleep. Subclasses specialize the **Sleep()** operation according to the tastes of each species. The next diagram shows how each animal species usually sleeps:

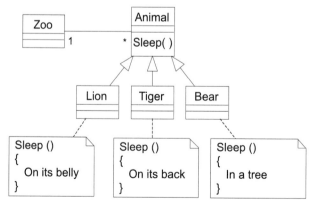

The general mechanisms written according to the specification of **Zoo** do not need to know the particular tastes of each kind of animal in order to invoke the **Sleep()** operation. As a result, at night, the guard walks through the zoo and tells every animal that it is time to sleep.

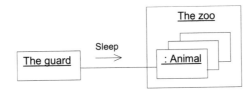

In terms that are closer to computer science, this is equivalent to visiting the **zoo** collection, possibly using an **iterator**, and sending the **Sleep** message to each animal.

An iterator is an object associated to a collection that allows of all its elements to be visited, without exposing its internal structure. The iterator is said to be active when control of the iteration is given to the user via the following four operations:

- **First()**, which takes into account the elements present in the collection at a given time, and moves the iterator to the first of them
- **Next()**, which allows moving to the next element
- **CurrentItem()**, which returns the current element
- **IsDone()**, which is true when all the elements have been visited

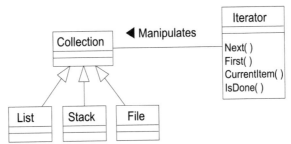

The following code fragment illustrates the use of an iterator on the **zoo** collection. The variable **AnAnimal** is polymorphic: it may contain any of the animals returned by the function **Visit.CurrentItem()**. Sending the **Sleep** message to the animal contained in the variable **AnAnimal** triggers a specific way of sleeping that depends on the animal's subclass.

```
Visit: Iterator;
AnAnimal: Animal; -- polymorphic variable
...
Visit.First(theZoo);
while not Visit.IsDone()
loop
    AnAnimal := Visit.CurrentItem();
    AnAnimal.Sleep();
    Visit.Next();
end loop;
```

The mechanism that makes all animals in the zoo sleep is independent of the animals that are actually in the zoo at a given point in time: the count of each species is not written in the algorithm, which only uses an iterator on a collection. The mechanism is also independent of the specific subclass of the current animal: if new animals are added to the zoo, it is not necessary to modify the code that makes the existing animals sleep, in order to make the newly-arrived animals sleep. The specific features of the new animals are encapsulated in their class, which is added to the model by deriving it from the already existing **Animal** class. To take into account a new animal, it is sufficient to create a subclass, to implement the **Sleep()** operation it inherits, and to recompile as necessary.

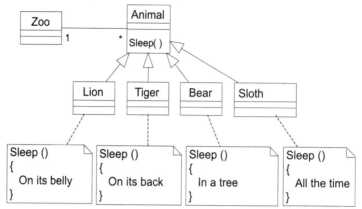

The automatic selection of the correct code is the result of dynamic linking. In traditional programming languages like Pascal, the choice of an operation is a completely static activity that is performed during compilation based on the types of the variables. In programming languages that support dynamic linking, the triggering of an operation requires processing at execution time, in order to retrieve the implementation of the operation that corresponds to the message received. Without dynamic linking, the previous code would need to be transformed in the following way:

```
Visit: Iterator;
AnAnimal: Animal; -- polymorphic variable
...
Visit.First(theZoo);
while not Visit.IsDone()
loop
    AnAnimal := Visit.CurrentItem();

    case AnAnimal.Class()
        When Lion
            -- Sleep on its belly
        When Tiger
            -- Sleep on its back
        When Bear
            -- Sleep in a tree
        When Sloth
            -- Sleep all the time
    end case;

    Visit.Next();
end loop;
```

This solution without dynamic linking has the drawback of introducing several maintenance points in the code. Each time a new animal is added to the zoo, a branch must be added in the **case** statement to account for the specific features of the new animal.

Polymorphism gets rid of these maintenance points and at the same time considerably reduces the use of multiple branch instructions in mechanisms that do not need to know the class of an object explicitly. Operations of type **Class_Of** that return the class of an object, such as the one used in the previous example (**case AnAnimal.Class()**), must always be used carefully, since their use goes against polymorphism. A mechanism written according to the terms of a superclass must be able to ignore the specific details in the subclasses.

The previous example also shows that it is possible to use a statically-linked programming language instead of a dynamically-linked language after object-oriented analysis, but that the implementation effort is greater, since it is necessary to manually organize the triggering of operations.

Taking Advantage of the Substitution Principle

The above example only works if every animal understands the **Sleep** message. The mechanisms that implement polymorphism manipulate objects through the specifications of their superclasses. In the case of a typed language, the compiler can verify statically that the messages will be understood by an object, either because an operation is declared in the class of the object itself, or because that operation is inherited from one of the superclasses. This syntactic verification is not sufficient to guarantee good polymorphic behavior; it is also necessary for the implementations of operations in subclasses to conform to the specifications given in the superclasses, and in particular to the constraints that go along with them. In order for polymorphism to work effectively, it is necessary to satisfy not only the syntax, but also the substitution principle.

The following example illustrates a violation of the substitution principle. The programmer decides to derive the **Ostrich** class from the **Bird** class in order to obtain the feathers and the beak, but fails to respect the specification of the **Fly()** operation by implementing a piece of code that does not make the ostrich fly.

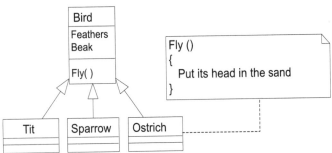

This inconsistency has no consequences as long as nobody writes a general mechanism to manipulate birds. However, as soon as general mechanisms start taking advantage of the specification of the **Bird** class — to make all the types of birds fly in case of danger, for example — the inconsistency introduced into the **Ostrich** class translates at best into an ostrich that gets eaten, and in the worst case into the most catastrophic thing that could happen, in accordance with Murphy's law.

The collaboration diagram overleaf illustrates how a small ostrich may be eaten by a big cat!

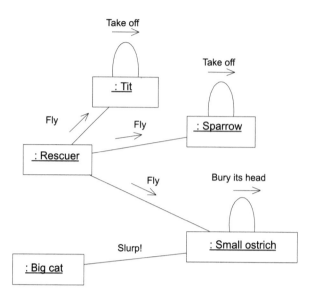

Triggering Operations

This section aims to introduce the general characteristics of the dynamic linking mechanism, independently from the syntactic particulars of programming languages. The different steps in the example show the ways of triggering an operation according to the class of the object that receives the message.

The following class diagram describes the hierarchy of classes that will support this discussion, and shows the definition and the implementations of the **Z()** operation that will be triggered. The abstract classes **I** and **J** cannot be instantiated.

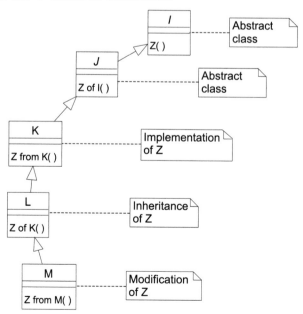

Objects of the **Client** class have polymorphic links to objects of classes **K**, **L** or **M**:

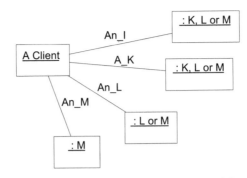

Each object of class **Client** *can communicate with four object instances of the concrete classes* **K**, **L** *or* **M**.

The link **An_I** is polymorphic and can designate an object instance of a concrete class derived from **I** — the subclass **K**, for example. The client can therefore manipulate an object instance of a subclass through the specification of a superclass. All the characteristics of the superclass are applicable to object instances of subclasses. To give an example, the **z** message can be sent to the **A_K** object along the **An_I** polymorphic link.

The code corresponding to operation **z** is searched for at execution time by going down the inheritance tree until the precise class of the object is found. Class **K** implements operation **z**, the message is understood, and the operation implemented in class **K** is executed.

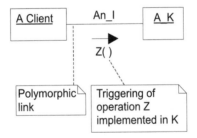

The next example is similar to the previous one. The difference here is that the search is performed one level down in the hierarchy. Since class **L** has not modified the implementation of operation **z**, inherited from class **K**, the same behavior as before is triggered.

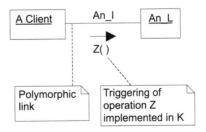

Any intermediate class in the class hierarchy can supply a specification for manipulating the object instances of its subclasses. To this extent, the **An_L** link may be used in a polymorphic way to manipulate object instances of the class **M**. As **M** modifies the **Z** operation, the expression **An_L.Z()** triggers the code implemented in class **M**.

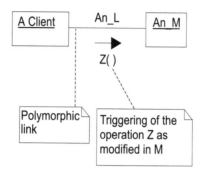

Dynamic linking is only necessary to search automatically for code modified in the subclasses and called from the specification of a superclass. When dynamic linking is not required, it may be advantageous to replace the passing of messages by simple procedure calls that are resolved statically. Languages such as C++ or Ada 95 let the programmer choose the linking strategy on a piecemeal basis, operation by operation and as needed. In Eiffel, the programmer does not need to worry about the linking choice, as the compiler is sufficiently clever to recognize the links that will always be static.

In this final example, linking may be static, partly because the **A_K** link specifies an object of class **K**, and also because the operation **Z** is implemented in that class.

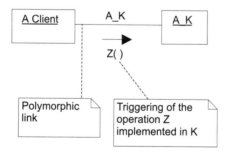

Code that takes advantage of polymorphism is characterized by the near-absence of multiple branch statements (**case**, **switch**). This is due to the fact that branches are implemented implicitly — based on the class of the object receiving the message — when searching for the operation to execute in response to the receipt of a message.

The Influence of Typing

Polymorphism exists in typed environments as well as in untyped environments, but only typed environments guarantee a predictable execution of programs — as long as the substitution principle is respected. The concept of typing makes it possible for the compiler to check statically that all the messages sent to an object will be understood at execution time. In Ada 95, Eiffel, C++ or Java, messages are always understood by the recipient, due to strong typing. In the absence of strong typing, any message can be sent to any object. In Smalltalk, a message may not be understood, and the sender must therefore be prepared for that eventuality. This does not remove any of the virtue of dynamic binding, which is still useful for finding the code that is best adapted to the class. However, unlike typed languages, the search may be unsuccessful.

It is important to not confuse polymorphism with operation overloading, which is sometimes called **ad hoc polymorphism**. Some languages allow the use of the same name to designate a family of operations with different parameter profiles. Overloading is an elegant way to provide the notion of variable signature, without getting caught up in the intricacies of operations with a variable number of parameters (as in C). Overloading is always resolved statically by compilers and has nothing to do with dynamic linking.

Happy parents will recognize the behavior of their children in the following class. The `Eat()` operation is overloaded: it exists in three different forms that can be identified statically by the compiler, according to the signature.

Child
Eat ()   Eat (Slowly : Boolean)   Eat (Slowly : Boolean, Like_A_Pig : Boolean)

Summary

This chapter has explained the reasons for, and benefits of, the object-oriented approach to application design. Basic UML notation has been introduced to illustrate the discussion. Some of the points worth keeping in mind from this chapter are:

- Software objects have state, behavior, and identity. The behavior can depend upon the state, and the state may be modified by the behavior.

- Objects communicate with one another by means of messages, of which there are five main categories: constructors, destructors, selectors, modifiers, and iterators.

- Object interactions can be represented by collaboration diagrams or sequence diagrams. The former are better for showing the physical layout of objects, while the latter better indicate the sequence of interactions.

- Every object is an instance of a class, which has a name, attributes and operations. If two objects are linked, then the classes to which they belong are said to have an association.

- Classes may be placed in hierarchies by means of the generalization and specialization relationships. In object-oriented programming languages, these relationships are usually implemented using inheritance.

- Proper use of inheritance enables polymorphism, which is the ability to implement different responses to the same stimulus, by allowing one object name to designate instances of different classes, according to the context.

The next chapter moves on to expand the UML syntax introduced in this chapter, and covers the UML notation in its entirety.

63

The UML Notation

The UML notation is a fusion of the notations of Booch, OMT, OOSE and others. UML is designed to be readable on a large variety of media, such as whiteboards, paper, restaurant tablecloths, computer displays, black and white printouts, etc. The designers of the notation have sought simplicity above all — UML is straightforward, homogeneous, and consistent. Awkward, redundant and superfluous symbols have been eliminated, in order to favor a better visual rendering.

UML focuses on the description of software development artifacts, rather than on the formalization of the development process itself, and it can therefore be used to describe software entities obtained through the application of various development processes. UML is not a rigid notation: it is generic, extensible, and can be tailored to the needs of the user. UML does not look for over-specification — there is not a graphical representation for all possible concepts. In the case of particular requirements, details may be added using extension mechanisms and textual comments. Great freedom remains for tools to filter the information displayed. The use of colors, drawings, and particular visual attributes is left up to the user.

This chapter gives an overview of the semantics of UML's model elements, and aims to introduce the main concepts of modeling, articulating them in terms of the UML notation. The visual and modeling elements are introduced together, using the UML notation as a foundation for the presentation of their semantics.

UML defines nine types of diagrams to represent the various modeling viewpoints. The presentation order of the various diagrams does not reflect the order of implementation in a real project, but simply follows a textbook approach that attempts to minimize prerequisites and cross-references.

UML Diagrams

A diagram provides the user with the means of visualizing and manipulating model elements. The various types of UML diagrams are presented in the diagram below:

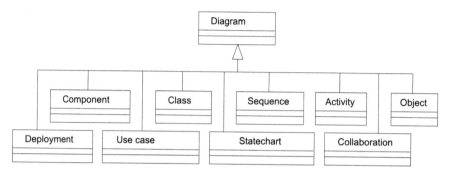

The different types of diagrams defined by UML

A UML diagram contains visual elements that represent model elements coming from different packages — even in the absence of visibility relationships between these packages. (Packages are discussed later in this chapter.)

The diagrams may show all or part of the characteristics of the model elements, with a level of detail that is suitable in the context of a given diagram. Diagrams may also gather together pieces of linked information to show, for example, the characteristics inherited by a class.

Here, in alphabetical order, is a list of the various diagrams:

- **Activity diagrams** represent the behavior of an operation as a set of actions
- **Class diagrams** represent the static structure in terms of classes and relationships
- **Collaboration diagrams** are a spatial representation of objects, links, and interactions
- **Component diagrams** represent the physical components of an application
- **Deployment diagrams** represent the deployment of components on particular pieces of hardware
- **Object diagrams** represent objects and their relationships, and correspond to simplified collaboration diagrams that do not represent message broadcasts
- **Sequence diagrams** are a temporal representation of objects and their interactions.
- **Statechart diagrams** represent the behavior of a class in terms of states*
- **Use case diagrams** represent the functions of a system from the user's point of view

Sequence and collaboration diagrams can be grouped together under the more general title of **interaction diagrams**.

---

*Harel, D. 1987. Statecharts : A Visual Formalism for Complex Systems. Science of Computer Programming vol. 8.

Basic Concepts

It is practical to represent the semantics of UML model elements according to the formalisms of UML itself — the process is known as **metamodeling**. However, this type of recursive representation runs into the 'chicken and egg' problem, especially when you're learning. This is why it is advisable at first to consider all the diagrams in this chapter as examples of the notation, rather than looking for a deep understanding. With this in mind, the metamodel diagrams show simplified views in order to make the text accessible to the largest number of readers possible.

Common Elements

Elements are the building blocks of UML, and comprise model elements and visual elements. Model elements represent abstractions of the system being modeled, while visual elements provide textual or graphical projections that facilitate the manipulation of model elements.

Elements are grouped into packages that contain or reference model elements. A model is an abstraction of a system, represented by a hierarchy of packages.

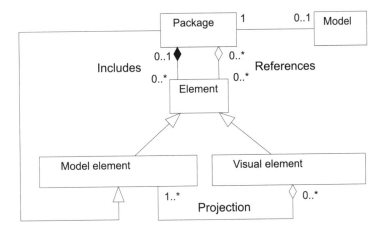

Representation of the two large families of elements that form the content of models.

Common Mechanisms

UML defines a small number of common mechanisms that ensure the notation's conceptual integrity. These common mechanisms comprise **stereotypes**, **tagged values**, **notes**, **constraints**, **dependencies**, and type/instance and type/class **dichotomies**. Each model element has a specification that contains a unique and detailed description of all the characteristics of that element.

Stereotypes, tagged values, and constraints facilitate the extension of UML. Stereotypes specialize metamodel classes, tagged values extend the attributes of the metamodel classes, and constraints extend the metamodel semantics.

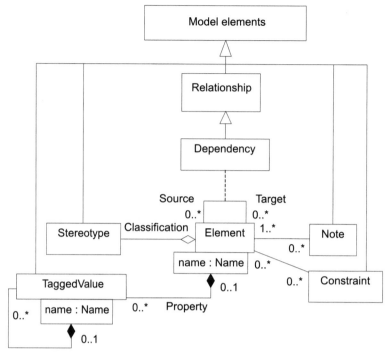

Simplified metamodel representation of common mechanisms.

Stereotypes

Stereotypes are part of the range of extensibility mechanisms provided in UML. Each UML model element may have one or more stereotypes when the basic semantics of the element are not sufficient. A stereotype allows the metaclassification of a UML element. It permits users (methodologists, tool builders, analysts, and designers) to add new model element classes on top of the kernel predefined by UML. Stereotypes also facilitate the unification of related concepts, such as subsystems or categories, that are expressed using packaging stereotypes. Examples of predefined UML stereotypes are «uses» and «extends».

Stereotypes allow the controlled extension of metamodel classes by UML users. An element specialized by a stereotype **S** is semantically equivalent to a new metamodel class, also named **S**. Pushing this concept to its limit, the whole UML notation could have been constructed using the two classes **Thing** and **Stereotype**, all other concepts being derived by stereotyping the **Thing** class.

UML's designers have looked for a balance between the built-in classes and the extensions introduced by stereotypes. Therefore, only fundamental concepts have been expressed as distinct classes. Other concepts that can be derived from these basic concepts have been treated as stereotypes.

Tagged Values

A tagged value is a (name, value) pair that describes a property of a model element. Properties allow the extension of metamodel element attributes. A tagged value modifies the semantics of the element to which it relates.

Notes

A note is a comment attached to one or more model elements. By default, notes do not carry semantic content. However, a note may be transformed into a constraint by using a stereotype and, in that case, it modifies the semantics of the model elements to which it is attached.

Constraints

A constraint is any kind of semantic relationship between model elements. UML does not specify a particular syntax for constraints, other than that they should appear between braces, so they may therefore be expressed using natural language, pseudo-code, navigation expressions, or mathematical expressions. It should be noted, however, that UML 1.1 does *prefer* the use of a constraint language called OCL (Object Constraint Language).

Dependencies

The dependency relationship defines a unidirectional use relationship between two model elements referred to, respectively, as the source and target of the relationship. Notes and constraints may also be the source of a dependency relationship.

Type/Instance and Type/Class Dichotomies

Many model elements present a type/instance dichotomy, in which the type characterizes the essence of the element, and the instance, with its values, is a manifestation of that type. Similarly, the type/class dichotomy corresponds to the split between the specification of an element, which is described by the type, and the implementation of that specification that is provided by the class.

Data Types

The heading 'data types' groups all the abstractions underlying UML. They are not model elements, and therefore they do not have stereotypes, tagged values, or constraints. A primitive type is a data type that has no substructure.

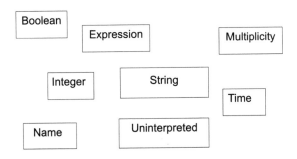

Simplified metamodel representation of some UML data types.

69

The following is a list of UML data types:

- **Boolean**. A Boolean is an enumerated type with the two values **True** and **False**.

- **Expression**. An expression is a character string whose syntax goes beyond the scope of UML.

- **Multiplicity**. A multiplicity is a non-null set of positive integers extended by the character ***** to indicate an unlimited multiplicity. The multiplicity is specified by a comma-separated sequence of integer intervals. For example, intervals of the form **0..1** and **1..10** indicate multiplicities of 0 to 1 and 1 to 10 respectively.

- **Name**. A name is character string that enables the specification of an element. Composite names take the form,

  ```
  simple_name {'.'composite_name}
  ```

  and may be qualified by the name of its containing or referencing package:

  ```
  package_name {'::'simple_name}
  ```

- **Integer** An integer is a primitive type, and an element of the infinite set of positive and negative whole numbers.

- **String**. A string is a primitive type. It is a sequence of characters referred to by a name.

- **Time**. A time is a character string that represents an absolute or a relative duration, whose syntax goes beyond the scope of UML.

- **Uninterpreted**. An uninterpreted type is a 'thing' whose meaning depends on the domain, and which is undefined in UML.

Packages

Packages provide a general mechanism for partitioning models and grouping model elements. Each package is represented graphically by a folder.

Packages divide and organize models in much the same way that directories organize file systems. Each package corresponds to a subset of a model and contains, depending on the model, classes, objects, relationships, components, or nodes, as well as their associated diagrams. (Nodes are discussed towards the end of this chapter.)

Decomposition into packages is not the basis for a functional decomposition; each package is a grouping of elements according to purely logical criteria. The general system layout (the system architecture) is expressed by the hierarchy of packages and by the network of dependency relationships between packages.

The stereotypes «category» and «subsystem» allow distinguishing between packages of the logical view and packages of the implementation view as required. (These views are described in chapter 4.)

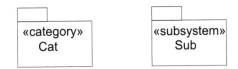

A package defines a namespace, so that two distinct elements contained in two distinct packages may have the same name. A package may contain other packages, with no limitation on nesting levels. A given level may contain a mixture of packages and other model elements, in the same way as a directory may contain other directories and files.

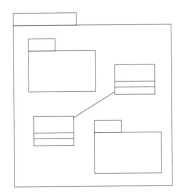

Every element belongs to a package. The package located at the highest level is the root package of the whole model. A class contained within one package may also appear in another package in the form of an imported element, by means of an inter-package dependency relationship.

Imports between packages are represented within class diagrams, use case diagrams and component diagrams, using a stereotyped dependency relationship drawn from the client package to the supplier package.

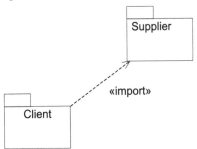

A dependency relationship between two packages means that at least one class in the client package uses the services offered by at least one class in the supplier package. The classes contained within a package are not all necessarily visible outside the package.

The operator **::** allows the specification of a class defined in a context other than the current context. The expression **Zoo::Kangaroo**, for example, refers to the **Kangaroo** class as defined in the **Zoo** package.

A package is a group of model elements, but it is also an encapsulation of these elements. Just like classes, packages have an interface and an implementation. Each element contained within a package has a parameter that indicates whether the element may be seen outside the package. The possible values of that parameter are **public** or **implementation** (private).

In the case of classes, only those marked as public appear in the interface of the package that contains them; they may then be used by class members of client packages. Implementation classes are only usable within the package that contains them.

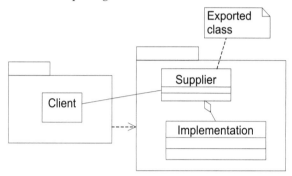

Dependencies between packages result in obsolete relationships between model elements contained within these packages. For reasons that pertain to compilation at the implementation stage, it is strongly recommended to make sure that cross-package dependencies result only in acyclic graphs. The following situation must therefore be avoided:

Similarly, circular, transitive dependencies, like the one illustrated below, should be avoided:

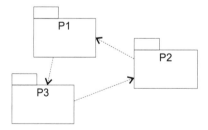

As a general rule, circular dependencies may be reduced by splitting one of the questionable packages into two smaller packages, or by introducing a third, intermediate package.

Some packages are used by all other packages, and group basic classes like sets, lists, files, or error management classes. These packages have a property that identifies them as global packages. It is therefore not necessary to show the dependency relationships between them and their users, limiting the graphical load on the diagram.

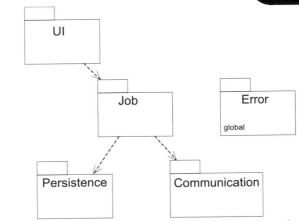

*In order to reduce graphical load, dependencies related to packages that
are visible globally are not represented in diagrams.*

Class Diagrams

Class diagrams express, in a general way, the static structure of a system, in terms of classes
and relationships between those classes. Just as a class describes a set of objects, an association
describes a set of links; objects are class instances, and links are association instances. A class
diagram does not express anything specific about the links of a given object, but it describes, in
an abstract way, the potential links from an object to other objects.

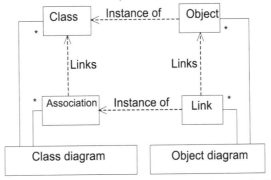

Simplified metamodel showing class diagrams to represent classes and relationships

Classes

Classes are represented by compartmentalized rectangles. The first compartment contains the
class name. The class name must facilitate the understanding of what the class is, not what it
does. A class is not a function; a class is an abstract — condensed — description of a set of
objects from the application domain. The two other compartments contain respectively the class's
attributes and its operations.

```
Class name
```

A class always contains at least its name. When a name has not yet been found, or is not yet selected, it is recommended to show a generic name that is easy to identify, such as **To_Be_Defined**. Class compartments may be suppressed when their content is not relevant within the context of a diagram. Compartment suppression is purely visual; it does not mean that there are no attributes or operations.

```
┌─────────────┐
│ Class name  │
└─────────────┘
```

The rectangle that acts as a symbol for the class may also contain a stereotype and properties. UML defines the following class stereotypes:

Stereotype	Definition
«signal»	A notable event that triggers a transaction within a state machine.
«interface»	A description of visible operations.
«metaclass»	The class of a class, as in Smalltalk
«utility»	A class reduced to the concept of module and which cannot be instantiated

Properties refer to all the values attached to a model element, such as attributes, associations, and tagged values. A tagged value is a (name, value) pair defined by the user; it allows, for example, the specification of code generation, identification, or cross-referencing information.

```
┌──────────────┐    ┌──────────────┐
│  Class name  │    │   Vehicle    │
│ «stereotype» │    │  «utility»   │
│   Property   │    │ State = tested│
│              │    │ Author = pam │
└──────────────┘    └──────────────┘
```

Attributes and Operations

Attributes and operations may be shown exhaustively or non-exhaustively within class compartments. By convention, the first compartment contains the attributes and the second compartment contains the operations.

```
┌─────────────────────────┐
│       Class name        │
├─────────────────────────┤
│ Name : type = initial value │
├─────────────────────────┤
│         Name( )         │
└─────────────────────────┘
```

The syntax used for describing attributes takes the form:

```
Attribute_Name : Attribute_Type = Initial_Value
```

This description can be completed gradually during the transition from analysis to design.

Redundant properties may be specified during the requirements analysis phase. **Derived attributes** offer a solution for allocating properties to classes, while clearly indicating that these properties are derived from other properties that have already been allocated. In the following

74

example, the **Rectangle** class has a **Length** attribute, a **Width** attribute, and a derived attribute **Area** that may be built from the other two attributes.

Rectangle
Length
Width
/Area

Later on, during design, the derived attribute **/Area** will be transformed into an operation **Area()** that will encapsulate the computation of the area. This transformation may, however, be performed without waiting, as soon as the derived nature of the area property has been detected.

Rectangle
Length
Width
Area ( )

The syntax used for the description of operations takes the form:

```
Operation_Name (Argument_Name : Argument_Type = Default_Value,...)
     : Return_Type
```

However, given the length of the specification, the operation arguments may be suppressed in graphical representations.

Visibility of Attributes and Operations

UML defines three visibility levels for attributes and operations:

public — the element is visible to all the clients of the class

protected — the element is visible to subclasses of the class

private — the element is visible only to the class

Visibility information does not always appear explicitly in class diagrams, but that does not mean that visibility is not defined within the model. The visibility level is represented symbolically by the characters **+**, **#** and **-**, which correspond respectively to the levels **public**, **protected** and **private**.

Some attributes and operations may be visible globally, in the entire lexical scope of the class. These elements, also called **class variables** and **class operations**, are represented like objects, with an underlined name. This notation is sensible, since a class variable looks like an object shared by the instances of a class. By extension, class operations are also underlined.

A
+Public attribute
#Protected attribute
-Private attribute
<u>Class attribute</u>
+Public operation( )
#Protected operation( )
-Private operation( )
<u>Class operation( )</u>

75

Interfaces

An interface uses a type to describe the visible behavior of a class, a component (described later in the book), or a package. An interface is a stereotype of a type. UML represents interfaces using small circles connected with a line to the element that supplies the services described by the interface.

Interfaces may also be represented using stereotyped classes; the circle-and-line notation (often called a 'lollipop') is simply an equivalent, alternative notation.

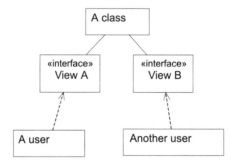

An interface provides a total or partial view of a set of services provided by one or more elements. The dependents of an interface use all or some of the services described in the interface.

Template Classes

Template classes are models of classes. They correspond to the generic classes of Eiffel, and to the templates of C++. A template class cannot be used as is. It is first necessary to instantiate it, in order to obtain a real class that must in turn be instantiated to produce objects. During instantiation, actual parameters customize the real class based on the template class. Template classes facilitate the construction of universal collections, typed by parameters.

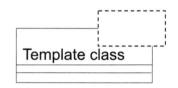

This type of class does not generally appear during analysis, except in the particular case of development environment modeling. Template classes are most often used in detailed design, to incorporate reusable components, for example. The following figure represents the instantiation of a generic table in order to implement a directory of people. Before instantiation, the formal parameter appears in the dotted rectangle of the template class, while afterwards the actual parameter is joined to the name of class obtained by instantiation. A dotted arrow is drawn from the instance to the template class.

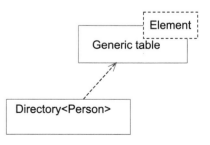

Utility Classes

It is sometimes useful to group elements (e.g. the functions of a mathematical library) within a module, without intending to build a complete class. The utility class makes it possible to represent such modules and to manipulate them graphically in much the same way as conventional classes.

Utility classes cannot be instantiated, as they are not data types. They must not, however, be confused with abstract classes, which cannot be instantiated because they are purely specifications (see the section that deals with generalization later in the chapter). In C++, a utility class corresponds to a class that contains only static members (functions and data).

The stereotype «utility» specializes classes as utility classes.

Associations

Associations represent structural relationships between classes of objects. An association symbolizes a piece of information with a lifecycle that is non-negligible in comparison to the general dynamics of object instances of the associated classes. Most associations are binary, i.e. they connect two classes. Associations are represented by drawing a line between the associated classes.

Associations may be represented by straight or diagonal lines, according to the preference of the user. Experience recommends staying limited as far as possible to a single presentation style for lines in order to simplify the reading of diagrams within a project.

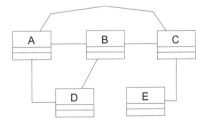

Association Naming

Associations may be named; in the diagram below, the name of the association appears in the middle of the line that symbolizes the association. In general it can be on, above or below the line.

Associations may be named in order to facilitate model understanding

Without making it a systematic rule, experience recommends naming associations using a verbal form — either active, like 'works for', or passive, like 'is employed by'.

In both cases, the direction in which the name should be read may be indicated using a small triangle pointing towards the class designated by the verbal construct, and positioned close to the name of the association. In order to simplify things, the small triangle may be replaced by the symbols < and >, which are available in any font.

Associations between classes mainly express the static structure, so naming them using verbal constructs that evoke a behavior is somewhat in conflict with the general spirit of class diagrams. Naming association ends (described below) makes it possible to clarify diagrams, just like naming associations, but in a more passive way that is more in agreement with the static tone of class diagrams.

Role Naming

The end of an association is called the **role**. Each binary association has two roles, one at each end. The role describes how a class sees another class via an association. A role is named using a noun. Visually, the name of a role can be distinguished from the name of an association as it is positioned near to one end of the association.

The person sees the company as their employer, and the company sees the person as its employee.

Either associations or roles may be named, but it is rare to name both on a single association. It is usual to start by labeling an association with a verb, and then to use that verb at a later stage to build a suitable noun to name the role.

When two classes are linked by a single association, the names of the classes are often sufficient to identify the role; role naming is most beneficial when many associations connect two classes. In this case, there is no default correlation between the objects that participate in the two relationships. Each association expresses a different concept. In the following example, there is no relationship between the passengers and the pilot.

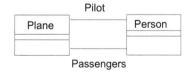

The presence of a large number of associations between two classes may be suspicious. Each association augments the coupling between the associated classes, and strong coupling may indicate a bad decomposition. It is also common for beginners to represent the same association more than once, by naming each association with the name of one of the recurring messages between object instances of the associated classes.

Person	Drive	Car
	Start	
	Wash	
	Stop	

*Example of confusion between associations and messages — a single 'owns' association
is sufficient to enable a person to drive, start, wash, and stop their car.*

Multiplicity of Associations

Each role of an association has a multiplicity value that indicates how many objects of the given class may be linked to an object of the other class. Multiplicity is a piece of information carried by the role, and it corresponds to a bounded integer expression.

1	One and only one
0..1	Zero or one
M..N	From M to N (natural integers)
*	From zero to any positive integer
0..*	From zero to any positive integer
1..*	From one to any positive integer

A multiplicity value greater than 1 implies an collection of objects. This collection is unbounded in the case of a value of *, meaning that simply that 'several' objects participate in the relationship, without restricting the total possible number of objects. The term 'collection', which is more general than 'list' or 'set', is used to avoid any assumptions concerning the data structure that contains the objects.

Multiplicity values express constraints linked to the application domain that are valid for the whole of the object's existence. The multiplicities must not be considered during transient states, such as the creation or the destruction of objects. A multiplicity of 1 indicates that during normal operation, an object has an obligatory link to another object; however, this should not result in an attempt to deduce the parameter lists of the constructors. Multiplicity values do not imply anything specific with respect to the object creation order. The following example shows two classes connected by an association where both roles have a multiplicity of 1, without assuming anything about the parameter profile of the object constructors. It is not necessary to have a car in order to build an engine, or vice-versa.

When determining the optimal multiplicity, is very important to find the proper balance between flexibility and extensibility on the one hand, and between complexity and efficiency on the other. As far as analysis is concerned, only the multiplicity is important, but at design time, it is necessary to choose data structures (stack, file, set...) in order to implement collections that correspond to multiplicities of type **1..*** or **0..***. Overestimating the multiplicity results in overpricing the storage size and limiting the search speed. Similarly, a multiplicity that starts with zero implies that the various operations must contain code to test the presence or the absence of links within the objects.

Multiplicity values are often used to describe associations in a generic fashion. The most common types are the 1 to 1, 1 to N, and N to N associations represented in the following figure.

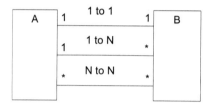

Constraints on Associations

Many kinds of constraints may be defined on an association or on a group of associations. The multiplicity introduced in the previous section is a constraint on the number of links that may exist between two objects. Constraints are represented in diagrams by expressions delimited with braces.

The constraint **{ordered}** may be placed on the role to specify an ordered relationship describing the objects that are part of the collection. In this case, the model does not specify *how* the elements are ordered, but only the fact that the order must be maintained during, for example, the addition or the removal of objects.

The constraint **{subset}** indicates that a collection is included in another collection. The following example illustrates how the representatives of schoolchildren's parents are also parents of schoolchildren.

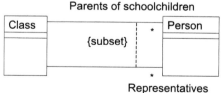

The constraint **{exclusive or}** indicates that, for a given object, only a single association among a group of associations is valid. This constraint prevents the introduction of artificial subclasses in order to represent exclusivity.

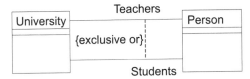

An association may also link a class to itself, as is the case in recursive structures. This type of association is called a **reflexive association**. Again, role naming becomes most important to distinguish the instances that take part in the relationship. The following example illustrates the `Person` class and the relationship that links parents to their children:

Every person has between zero and two parents, and between zero and several children. Role naming is key to the diagram's clarity.

Association classes

An association may be represented by a class to add attributes and operations to that association. A class of this type is a class like any other, and as such it can participate in other relationships within the model. The notation uses a dashed line to attach a class to an association. In the following example, the association between classes **A** and **B** is represented by the class **C**, which is itself associated to class **D**.

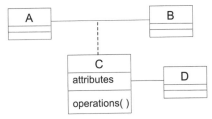

An association that contains attributes but does not participate in relationships with other classes is called an **attributed association**. In this case, the class attached to the association does not carry a specific name.

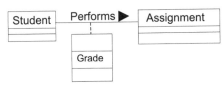

N-ary Associations

Most associations are referred to as 'binary', since they link two classes. A class may be linked to more than one other class, however, by means of an n-ary association. This is represented using a diamond, pointed to by the various components of the association.

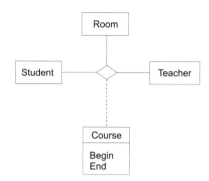

Example of a ternary relationship that represents a course

N-ary associations can generally be represented by promoting the association to the rank of a class, and by adding a constraint that expresses the fact that the various branches of the association are instantiated simultaneously, in a single link. In the following example, the constraint is expressed using a stereotype that indicates that the **Course** class implements a ternary association.

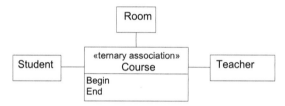

Just as for binary associations, the ends of an n-ary association are called roles and may have a name. If it is difficult to find a different name for each role of an n-ary association, it is often a sign that the association is between the wrong number of classes.

Location of Attributes According to Multiplicity Values

The process of giving attributes to associations is most beneficial in the case of N to N associations. For 1 to 1 associations, association attributes can always be moved into one of the classes that participate in the association. For 1 to N associations, the movement is generally possible into the class on the N side, although it is common to promote the association to the rank of a class, in order to increase its readability, or to accommodate the presence of associations with other classes. The following example illustrates the various cases:

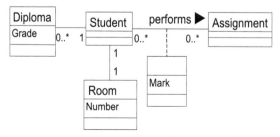

Examples of attribute placement according to multiplicity

The association between the **Student** and **Assignment** classes is of type N to N. The **Assignment** class describes the topic; the solution given by the student is not retained.

In the case of tests, each student works individually on a given assignment, and the mark obtained *cannot* be stored either in a particular student (as he performs many different assignments in his career), or in a given assignment (since there are as many marks as there are students). The mark is an attribute of the association between the student class and the assignment class.

At the end of the year, each student receives a diploma with a grade that depends on the individual student's performance. The relationship between the diploma and the student is unique, since a diploma only applies to a given student. The grade becomes an attribute of the diploma. The grade is not stored in the **Student** for two reasons: it does not specify a student, and a student may obtain several diplomas.

Each student has a room, and multiple students do not share a room. The association between students and rooms is of type 1 to 1. The number is an attribute of the **Room** class, since a number specifies a room.

Association Qualifiers

The qualification of an association consists of selecting a subset of objects from the set of objects that participate in an association. The restriction is implemented by means of a particular attribute or set of attributes (known as a **qualifier**) and used jointly with an object of the source class. The qualifier is represented at the end of the association, in a rectangular box. The qualifier belongs to the association and not to the associated classes.

Each instance of the class **A**, accompanied by the value of the qualifier, identifies a subset of the instances of **B** that participate in the association. The restriction reduces the association's multiplicity; very often, multiplicity is reduced to **1**.

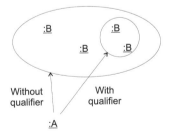

An association may be restricted by combining the values of the various attributes that make up the qualifier.

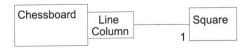

Combination of a line and a column to identify a square on the chessboard.

Aggregations

An aggregation represents an asymmetric association, in which one of the ends plays a more important role than the other end. The aggregation only applies to one of the roles of an association, regardless of the number of classes involved. Aggregation is represented by adding a small diamond next to the aggregate:

The following criteria imply an aggregation:

- A class is part of another class
- The attribute values of one class propagate to the attribute values of another class
- An action on one class implies an action on another class
- The objects of one class are subordinates of the objects of another class

The opposite is not always true — aggregation does not necessarily imply the criteria evoked above. If there is any doubt, associations are preferable. In general, it is always necessary to choose the solution that implies the weakest coupling.

Like associations, aggregations may be multiple. As long as no implementation has been chosen, there is no particular constraint on the multiplicity values that may be held by the roles of an aggregation. This means, in particular, that the multiplicity on the aggregate side may be greater than 1. This type of aggregation corresponds, for example, to the concept of co-owner. The following diagram illustrates that people may be co-owners of the same buildings:

The concept of aggregation does not assume a particular form of implementation. Physical containment is a particular case of aggregation referred to as **composition**.

Composition

Attributes are a particular case of aggregation implemented by value — they are physically contained in the aggregate. This type of aggregation is called composition, and is represented within diagrams by a black diamond.

Composition implies a constraint on the multiplicity of the aggregate side: it can only take the values 0 or 1. A value of 0 on the component side would correspond to an uninitialized attribute.

Composition and attributes are semantically equivalent; their graphical representations are interchangeable. The notation of composition is used in a class diagram, while an attribute participates in other relationships within the model. The diagram below illustrates the equivalence between the attribute notation and the composition notation:

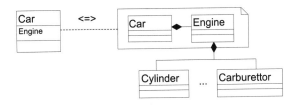

An aggregation by value is semantically equivalent to an attribute; it makes it possible to show how an attribute participates in other relationships within the model.

Classes implemented by composition are called **composite classes**. These classes supply an abstraction of their components.

Navigation

Associations describe the network of structural relationships that exist between classes, and give birth to links between the objects that are instances of these classes. Links may be viewed as inter-object navigation channels. These channels facilitate moving around within the model and implementing the types of collaboration that correspond to the various scenarios.

By default, associations can be navigated in both directions. In some cases though, only one navigation direction is usable; an arrow pointing in the direction that navigation is possible illustrates this. The absence of an arrow implies that the association may be navigated in both directions. In the following example, object instances of **A** see object instances of **B**, but the object instances of **B** cannot see the object instances of **A**.

An association that can only be navigated in one direction may be seen as a half-association. This distinction is often implemented at design time, but it can also appear during design, when study of the domain reveals an asymmetry in the communication requirements.

Navigation Expressions

UML defines a pseudo-language to represent paths within class diagrams. This very simple language defines expressions that are used, for example, to specify constraints. The left part of the expression specifies a set of objects. A class name identifies the set of all object instances of the class.

The syntax for the target of the navigation expression can be obtained using the four following rules:

```
set '.' selector
```

The **selector** corresponds either to the name of an attribute of the objects within the **set**, or to a role name attached to a link that relates to the objects of the **set**. The target is a set of values or objects, and their number depends on the multiplicity of the **set** and of the association.

In the case of an association, the expression returns a collection of objects that contains the number of elements specified by the multiplicity of the role. The expression **APerson.Children** refers to all the children of a given person.

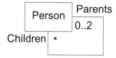

```
set '.' '~' selector
```

The **selector** corresponds to a rolename placed next to the **set**. The target is a set of objects obtained by navigation in the direction opposite to the rolename. In the above example, the parents of a child are identified by the expression **APerson.~Children**.

```
set '->' 'select' '(' boolean_expression ')'
```

The **boolean_expression** is built from objects contained within the **set**, and from links and values accessible by these objects. The target is a set of objects that satisfy the expression, and a subset of the initial set. In the above example, the **boolean_expression** **APerson.Children [age>=18 years]** refers to all the responsible children of a given person.

```
set '.' selector '[' qualifier ']'
```

The **selector** indicates an association that partitions the **set** based on the **qualifier**. The target is a subset of the **set** defined by the association.

In the following example, adding qualifiers to the association, which results in reducing the multiplicity, performs a restriction. The general expression **APerson.Child[AFirstName]** identifies a given child in an unambiguous way, since each child of the same family has a different first name.

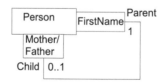

The above expressions are particularly well adapted to the formation of pre- and post-conditions attached to the operations' specifications. In the last example, the operations that create family links must correctly associate parents and their children. This can be expressed by the following constraint.

```
{APerson = APerson.Child[AFirstName].(Parent[Mother] or Parent[Father])}
```

Or else, by navigating in the opposite direction:

```
{APerson = APerson.Child[AFirstName].(~Child[Mother] or ~Child[Father])}
```

Or, finally, by setting:

```
{daddy = APerson.Parent[Father]}
```

And:

```
{granddad = APerson.(Parent[Father] or Parent[Mother]).Parent[Father]}
```

Then:

```
{granddad.Parent[Father] = daddy.Parent[Father].Parent[Father]}
```

Which is equivalent to saying, as everyone knows, that the daddy of the granddad is the granddad of the daddy!

Generalization

UML uses the term **generalization** to specify the classification relationship between a general element and a more specific element. In fact, the term 'generalization' specifies a viewpoint focused on a classification hierarchy. For example, an animal is a more general concept than a cat, a dog, or a raccoon. Conversely, a cat is a more specialized concept than an animal.

The more specific element may contain information that is particular to it, as long as it remains completely consistent with the description of the more general element. Generalization applies mainly to classes, packages and use cases.

In the case of classes, the generalization relationship expresses the fact that the elements of one class are also described by another class (in fact, by the *type* of another class). The generalization relationship signifies 'is a' or 'is a kind of'. A cat *is an* animal; that has to do with generalization. A cat *has* two ears; that does not have to do with generalization, but rather with composition.

The generalization relationship is represented by an arrow that points from the more specialized class to the more general class. The tip of the arrow is an empty triangle, which allows it to be distinguished from the open arrow that symbolizes the navigation property of associations. In the following example, the **Animal** class is an abstraction of the classes **Cat**, **Dog** and **Raccoon**.

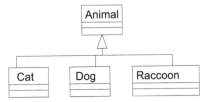

In the above example, the **Animal** class is called a superclass, and the classes **Cat**, **Dog** and **Raccoon** are referred to as subclasses of the **Animal** class.

In the case of multiple subclasses, the arrows may be aggregated in a single arrow, as before, or represented independently as shown below. These two different ways of symbolizing generalization do not carry any particular meaning.

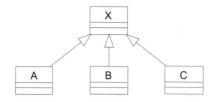

The attributes, operations, relationships and constraints defined in the superclasses are fully inherited in the subclasses. When programming, the generalization relationship is very often implemented using the inheritance relationship between classes, as supplied by object-oriented languages. Inheritance is one way to implement classification, but it is not the only one. The generalization relationship defined by UML is more abstract than the inheritance relationship as it exists in object-oriented programming languages like C++. Inheritance is a static relationship; it implies a very strong coupling between classes and is less well adapted to the concept of dynamic classification, or to the concept of metamorphosis. During analysis, it is better to talk about generalization or classification, and to worry about implementing generalization later, as part of the design stage.

Classes may have several superclasses. When this is the case, generalization is said to be 'multiple', and several arrows are drawn from the subclass to the various superclasses. Multiple generalization is the fusion of several classes into a single one. Superclasses do not necessarily have a common ancestor. In the example below, the **Flying carpet** class has two completely disjoint ancestors, the classes **Carpet** and **Vehicle**. The kind of generalization that groups the classes **Vehicle**, **Land vehicle**, **Air vehicle** and **Flying carpet** is called **diamond generalization**.

To convince yourself that carpets are indeed land vehicles, just look at my children...

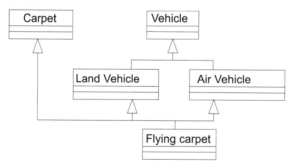

A class may be specialized according to several simultaneous criteria. Each generalization criterion is indicated in the diagram by associating a **discriminator** with the generalization relationship. When arrows are aggregated, the discriminator only appears once. The absence of a discriminator is considered a particular case of generalization.

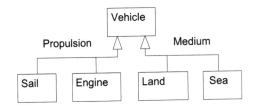

Example of generalization according to independent criteria.

Different constraints may be applied to generalization relationships in order, for example, to distinguish exclusive generalization variants from inclusive ones. Constraints on generalization relationships are represented using parenthesized expressions that are directly attached to the aggregated generalizations, or associated with a dotted line that links the generalization relationships concerned.

By default, generalization symbolizes an exclusive decomposition; that is, an object can only be an instance of *one* of the subclasses. The constraint **{disjoint}** indicates that a class descended from class **A** may only be the descendant of one of the subclasses of **A**.

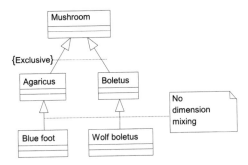

The constraint **{overlapping}** indicates that a class which is a descendant of class **A** belongs to the Cartesian product of the subclasses of class **A**. A concrete object is then built from a class obtained by mixing several superclasses.

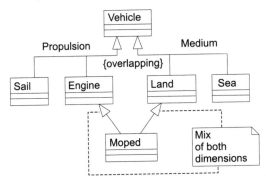

The constraint **{complete}** indicates that the generalization is finished, and that it is no longer possible to add subclasses. Conversely, the constraint **{incomplete}** specifies an extensible generalization.

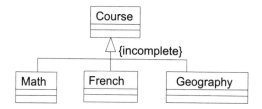

The constraint {incomplete} must not be confused with an incomplete view. A constraint carries semantic content that affects the model. An incomplete view does not mean that the model is incomplete. In general, a partial view is represented symbolically by an ellipsis that replaces model elements in various diagrams. The following example partially illustrates the generalization of the class **Course**.

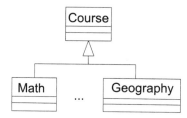

Abstract Classes

Abstract classes cannot be instantiated directly. They do not give birth to objects, but may be used as a more general specification — of type — in order to manipulate objects that are instances of one (or more) of their subclasses.

Abstract classes form a basis for extensible software applications. The set of general mechanisms is described according to the specifications of the abstract classes, without taking into account specific features gathered within concrete classes. New requirements, extensions and improvements are gathered into new subclasses, and the objects resulting from these subclasses may be manipulated transparently by mechanisms that are already in place.

A class is specified as abstract using the Boolean property **Abstract**, which is defined for all elements that may be generalized (types, packages and stereotypes). By convention, the names of abstract classes are italicized.

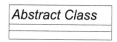

The **Abstract** property may also be applied to an operation to indicate that the body of the operation must be defined explicitly in subclasses.

Introduction to the Metamodel

Many model elements present an 'type/instance' dichotomy, in which a type represents the essence of an abstraction, and the instance forms a concrete sample. There is also a 'type/class' dichotomy, in which classes and primitive types implement types.

A **type** specifies a domain of values and a set of operations applicable to those values. A class implements a type: it provides the representation of attributes and the implementation of operations (methods). This distinction is propagated with subclasses, so that the specification given for a type is valid for all subclasses, and a subclass may implement several types.

90

The class diagram below represents both the type/instance dichotomy and the type/class dichotomy.

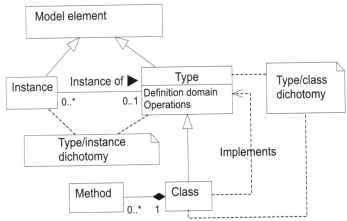

Simplified metamodel — an instance expresses a type; a class implements a type.

The **Type** class includes the following subclasses:

- The *primitive type*, corresponding to a type that is not implemented by a class, such as integers or string types
- The *class*, which provides the implementation of a type
- The *use case*, which corresponds to a sequence of actions performed by an actor and a system

The following diagram represents the different kinds of types proposed by UML:

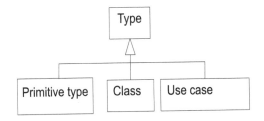

Simplified metamodel — representation of different kinds of types.

The **Class** class comprises the following subclasses:

- The *active class*, which substantiates one or more execution flows
- The *signal*, which corresponds to a named event
- The *component*, which corresponds to a reusable element that contains the physical constituents of the model elements
- The *node*, which is the physical device on which components may be deployed for execution

91

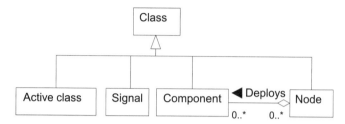

Simplified metamodel — representation of the various kinds of classes.

Relationships

UML defines five kinds of relationships. The most general is called a dependency relationship and applies uniformly to all the model elements. Association and generalization apply to all types, in particular classes and use cases. The last two relationships — transitions and links — apply to certain model elements pertaining to behavior.

This section is limited to the description of static relationships between classes, shown in the diagram below. Links and transitions are discussed later on in this chapter.

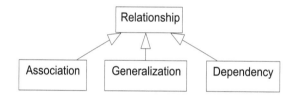

Simplified metamodel—representation of relationships between classes.

Association

An association specifies a bi-directional, semantic connection between types. An association has at least two roles, which describe the part played by the types that participate in the association.

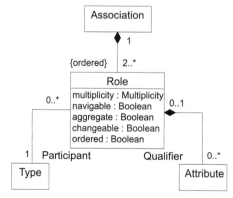

Simplified metamodel — representation of the main characteristics of associations.

Each role comprises the following attributes:

- **Multiplicity** — specifies the number of instances that participate in the relationship
- **Navigability** — specifies if links (association instances) may be navigated along in the direction of the role being considered.
- **Aggregation indicator** — specifies if the instances of the type associated to the role correspond to the whole in a (whole, part) relationship. Only one of the roles of an association may have an aggregation indicator set to **True**. If the multiplicity is larger than 1, several instances play the role of the whole and share the parts.
- **Changeability** — specifies if the semantics of the association are preserved when an instance of the type that participates in the role is replaced by another instance
- **Ordering** — applies when the multiplicity value is greater than 1, to mean that the instances are ordered

An association role may also include a set of attributes whose values implement a partition of the set of objects of the associated class.

Generalization

Generalization specifies a classification relationship in which an instance of a subtype may be substituted for an instance of a supertype. A supertype may have several subtypes, and a subtype may have several supertypes.

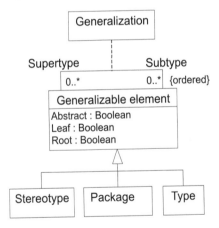

Simplified metamodel — representation of the generalization relationship and of elements prone to generalization.

Any element that may be generalized includes the following Boolean attributes:

- *Abstract* — the value **True** specifies that the element cannot be instantiated directly
- *Leaf* — the value **True** specifies that the element may not have subtypes
- *Root* — the value **True** specifies that the element may not have supertypes

UML defines three kinds of generalizable elements:

- *Stereotypes* allow the classification of a model element and, eventually, the definition of a particular graphical representation. A stereotype cannot have a subtype.

- *Packages* provide a general mechanism for grouping elements (both model and visual elements). A package cannot have supertypes.

- *Types* specify a definition domain and the operations applicable to that domain.

Dependency

Dependency is a unidirectional usage relationship between elements (both model and visual). The dependency relationship connects elements within the same model.

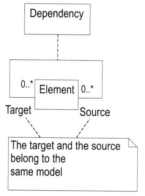

Simplified metamodel—representation of dependency relationships

UML also provides a 'trace' relationship between elements that belong to different models. Notably, the trace may be used to represent the history of current constructions in various models. This trace relationship is a stereotyped dependency relationship.

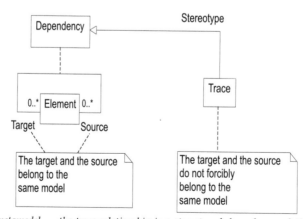

Simplified metamodel — the trace relationship is a stereotyped dependency relationship.

94

Use Case Diagrams

Use cases were invented by Ivar Jacobson*. They describe the behavior of a system from a user's standpoint by using actions and reactions. They allow the definition of the system's boundary, and the relationships between the system and the environment.

Use cases address a lack of support in the early object-oriented methods, such as OMT-1 and Booch'91, which did not supply any technique for determining requirements. In this sense, use cases associated with object-oriented techniques provide a complete approach for the whole project lifecycle, from specification to implementation.

A use case corresponds to a specific kind of system use. It is an image of a system's functionality, which is triggered in response to the stimulation of an external actor.

The Use Case Model

The use case model includes the actors, the system, and the use cases themselves. The set of functionality of a given system is determined through the study of the functional requirements of each actor, expressed in the use cases in the form of 'families' of interactions. Actors are represented by little stick people who trigger the use cases, which are represented as ellipses contained within the system.

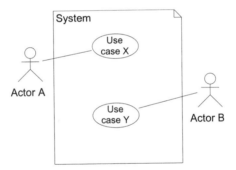

An actor represents a role played by a person or a thing that interacts with a system. Actors are determined by observing the direct users of a system — those who are responsible for its use or its maintenance — as well as the other systems that interact with the one under study. The same physical person may play the role of several actors (vendor, client). Additionally, several people may all play the same role and therefore act as the same actor (all the customers). The name of the actor describes the role played by the user.

In the following example, Mr Schmoldu, a garage worker, spends most of his time acting as a mechanic, but may sometimes act as a salesman. On Sundays, he plays the role of customer and services his own car.

*Jacobson I. 1992, *Object-Oriented Software Engineering, A Use Case Driven Approach*, Addison-Wesley.

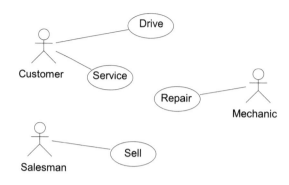

The same physical person may play the roles of several actors

Candidate actors are recruited from users, customers, partners, suppliers, salespeople, and other systems; in summary, the people and things that are outside a system and interact with it by exchanging information. Determining the actors facilitates the specification of the system's limits in an incremental way: while fuzzy in the beginning, they become more precise as the various use cases are implemented. This delineating activity is very important, as it serves as the contractual basis by which everything that must be done is specified — what is part of the system to be developed and what is not. It also specifies the inviolable elements that the team of developers may not modify.

There exist four main categories of actors:

- *Principal actors* — people who use the main system functions. In the case of a cash dispenser, they are the customers.

- *Secondary actors* — people that perform administration or maintenance tasks. In the case of a cash dispenser, it is the person in charge of reloading the money cassette contained within the dispenser.

- *External hardware* — the unavoidable hardware devices that are part of the application domain and must be used. It has nothing to do with the computer on which the application is executed, but pertains to the other hardware peripherals. In the case of a cash dispenser, this may correspond to the printer.

- *Other systems* — the other systems with which the system must interact. In the case of a cash dispenser, the bank network system that manages a set of dispensers plays the role of an actor.

Once identified, actors must be described clearly and precisely, in three or four lines at most. When there are many actors within a system, it is advisable to group them in categories to facilitate navigation within the use case model.

Use cases are determined by observing and specifying, actor by actor, the interaction sequences (**scenarios**) from the user's standpoint. They are described in terms of the information exchanged and the way the system is used. A use case groups a family of usage scenarios according to a functional criterion. Use cases are abstractions of dialog between the actors and the system: they describe potential interactions without going into the details of each scenario.

Use cases must be seen as classes whose instances are the scenarios. Each time an actor interacts with the system, the use case instantiates a scenario. This scenario corresponds to the message flows exchanged by objects during the particular interaction that corresponds to the scenario. Analysis of requirements by use cases is very well complemented by an iterative and incremental approach.

The scope of use cases goes far beyond solely defining of the requirements of the system. Indeed, use cases come into play throughout the lifecycle, from the specification stage to system testing, through the analysis, design, implementation, and documentation stages. From that standpoint, it is possible to navigate first towards the classes and objects that collaborate to satisfy a requirement, then towards the tests that verify the system performs its duties correctly.

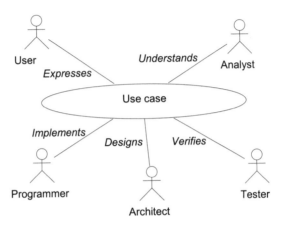

Relationships Between Use Cases

Use case diagrams represent use cases, actors, and relationships between use cases and actors. UML defines three types of links between actors and use cases:

The Communicates Relationship

The participation of the actor is signaled by a solid line between the actor and the use case. This is the only relationship between actors and use cases.

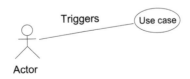

The Uses Relationship

A uses relationship between use cases means that an instance of the source use case also includes the behavior described by the target use case.

Representation of the uses relationship using a stereotyped generalization relationship

The Extends Relationship

An extends relationship between use cases means that the source use case extends the behavior of the destination use case.

Representation of the extends relationship using a stereotyped generalization relationship

The diagram below gives an implementation example of the various relationships between use cases. Money transfer by computer is an extension of the transfer operation performed at the bank lobby. In both cases, the customer must be identified.

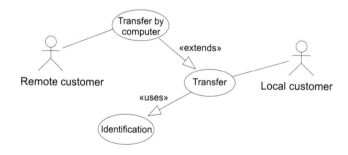

Issues regarding the benefits of use cases, and how to identity, construct and refine them, are covered in much greater depth in the next chapter.

Object Diagrams

Object diagrams, or instance diagrams, illustrate objects and links. As in the case of class diagrams, object diagrams represent the static structure. The notation used for object diagrams is derived from that of class diagrams; elements that are instances are underlined.

Object diagrams are primarily used to show a context — before or after an interaction, for example. However, they are also used to aid the understanding of complex data structures, such as recursive structures.

Representation of Objects

Each object is represented by a rectangle, which contains either the name of the object, the name and the class of the object (separated by a colon), or only the object's class (in which case the object is said to be anonymous). The name by itself corresponds to an incomplete model, in which the object's class has not yet been specified. The class on its own avoids the introduction of unnecessary names into diagrams, while allowing the expression of general mechanisms that are valid for many objects. The diagram below illustrates the three representation possibilities.

Object name	Object name : Class	: Class

The name of the class may contain the complete path built from the names of the various containing packages separated by double colons, as in this example:

ButtonOK : UI::Controls::PushButton

The stereotype of the class may reappear in the object compartment, either using its textual form (between guillemets («») above the name of the object), its graphical form (in the top right corner), or using a particular graphical representation that replaces the object symbol. There is no object stereotype; the stereotype that appears within an object is always the stereotype of the class.

| «Exception»
DivisionByZero |
|---|

Rectangles that symbolize objects may also include a second compartment that contains the attribute values. The attribute type is already specified in the class, so it is not necessary to display it in representations of objects. The following diagram represents an anonymous object of class **Car**, with a **Color** attribute that has the value **red**:

:Car
Color = red

Representation of Links

Objects are connected via links, which are instances of associations between the classes of the objects being considered. The concrete representation of a structure by objects is often more revealing than the abstract representation of a structure using classes, especially in the case of recursive structures. The object diagram below illustrates a portion of the general structure of cars. Each car has an engine and four wheels (excluding the spare wheel!).

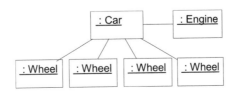

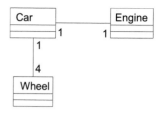

The preceding object diagram is an instance of this class diagram:

Links that are instances of reflexive associations may connect an object to itself. In this case, the link is represented by a loop attached to a single object. The following example illustrates two links that are instances of the same reflexive association. The first link shows that Etienne is Jean-Luc's boss, the second link shows that Denis is his own boss.

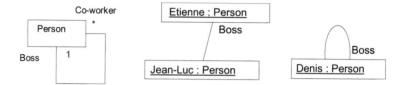

Most links are binary. However, there exist some links that may connect together more than two objects — those that correspond to ternary relationships, for instance. The representation of ternary relationships may be combined with the other notation elements: the diagram below represents a family of ternary links that are instances of a ternary association with multiplicity **N** on the **Student** class side. This notation has the advantage of removing any ambiguities inherent to the representation of multiplicity for non-binary associations.

Example of a combination of notation elements in order to represent multiple ternary relationships in a condensed way.

Composite Objects

Objects made of sub-objects may be represented using a composite object in order to reduce diagram complexity. Composite objects are represented like normal objects except for the fact that the attributes are replaced by objects, either using underlined text or a graphical representation. The following diagram illustrates the graphical representation of composite objects:

Composite objects are instances of composite classes — classes built from other classes using the strongest form of aggregation. The following diagram represents a composite **Window** class.

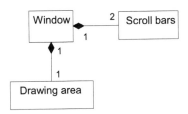

The following object diagram is an instance of the above composite class. It represents the most general form of composite **Window** objects, from the objects' point of view.

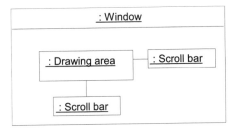

Similarities with Class Diagrams

The labels that figure in class diagrams can mostly be copied into object diagrams to facilitate understanding of the interaction. This applies to all the association characteristics (name, rolename, aggregation, composition, and navigation), with the exception of multiplicity, which is represented explicitly by links. The following object diagram can be distinguished graphically from a class diagram because the object names are underlined:

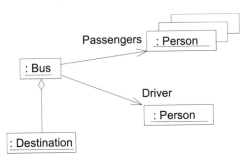

The values of association qualifiers may also be added to object diagrams. The diagram on the next page represents parental links between Lara, Jonathan, Roxane, Anne and Pierre-Alain.

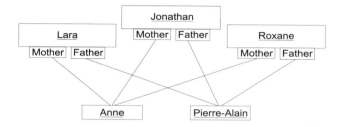

Collaboration Diagrams

Collaboration diagrams illustrate interactions between objects, using a static spatial structure that facilitates the illustration of the collaboration of a group of objects. Collaboration diagrams express both the context of a group of objects (through objects and links) and the interaction between these objects (by representing message broadcasts). These diagrams are an extension of object diagrams.

Representation of Interactions

The context of an interaction comprises the arguments, the local variables created during execution, and the links between the objects that participate in the interaction.

An interaction is implemented by a group of objects that collaborate by exchanging messages. These messages are represented along the links that connect the objects, using arrows pointed towards the recipient of the message. The diagram below represents an elevator cabin that asks the door to open itself.

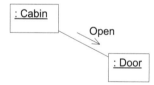

Unlike a sequence diagram, time is not represented explicitly in a collaboration diagram, and as a result the various messages are numbered to indicate the sending order.

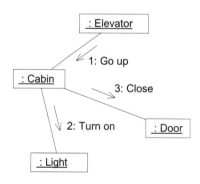

Collaboration diagrams show the interactions between objects and the structural relationships that facilitate these interactions simultaneously. The following diagram represents the context of a mechanism for canceling a deletion operation. Before triggering the deletion operation of object **B**, object **A** performs a local copy of **B**, so that if the deletion operation were to be canceled, object **B** could be retrieved just as it was before the beginning of the interaction.

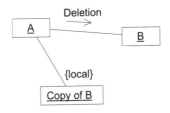

Objects and links created or deleted during an interaction may respectively be subject to the constraints **{new}** or **{deleted}**. Objects created and deleted within the same interaction are subject to the constraint **{transient}**.

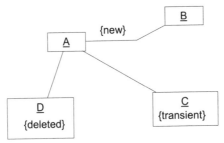

The notation allows the condensed representation of a family of links that are instances of the same association. This approach is particularly interesting when the group of objects under consideration is treated in a uniform way — being the target of the same message, for example. The following example illustrates a teacher who asks all his students to stand up; the iteration is indicated by the character * placed in front of the message.

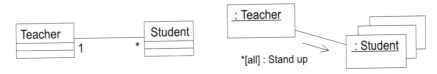

The Place of the User

The notation allows an actor to be displayed within a collaboration diagram, in order to represent the triggering of interactions by an element that is external to the system. Thanks to this representation, the interaction may be described in a more abstract way, without getting into the details of user interface objects. The first message of the interaction is sent by the actor, represented either by the graphical symbol of the actors of the use case model, or by an object with a stereotype that specifies its role as an actor. The following diagram illustrates an interaction fragment; it corresponds to a person calling an elevator.

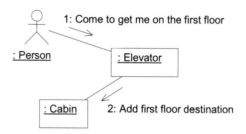

Active Objects

Objects that own a flow of control are called active. An **active object** may activate a passive object for the duration of an operation by sending a message to it. Once the message has been processed, the control flow is given back to the active object. In a multitasking environment, many objects may be active simultaneously. An active object is represented by a rectangle with a thicker frame than the one used for a passive object.

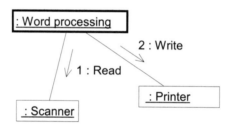

Representation of Messages

A message is represented by an arrow placed next to a link and pointing towards the object that is the destination of the message. A link is used as the transmission infrastructure for the message. A message triggers an action within the target object.

The syntax for a message label satisfies the general form:

```
synchronization sequence ':' result ':=' name arguments
```

The message, its arguments and return values, its rank within the interaction, and many other pieces of information, such as the nesting level or the synchronization, are specified at broadcast time.

Synchronization

The synchronization point of a message is expressed as a sequence of message broadcasts, terminated by the character /. All the messages referenced in this list must have been sent in order to validate the broadcasting of the current message.

The syntax of a synchronization point has the following form,

```
rank {',' synchronization} '/'
```

Where **rank** is given by:

```
[integer | name of flow of execution]{'.' rank}
```

The integer represents the rank of the message broadcast within the containing nesting level. The name identifies a parallel flow of execution within a nesting level. Therefore, the broadcast of message **3.1.3** immediately follows the broadcast of **3.1.2** within the nesting level **3.1**, while the broadcast of **3.1.a** is performed at the same time as that of **3.1.b**.

In the following example, the message **Message** is sent when broadcasts **A.1** and **B.3** have been satisfied:

Sequence

The sequence specifies the nesting level of the message broadcast within the interaction. The sequence consists of a sequence of terms separated by points. Each sequence has the following syntax:

```
rank [recurrence]
```

The **recurrence** represents iteration and conditional branching, and takes the form:

```
'*' '[' iteration clause ']' block
```

Or:

```
'[' condition clause ']' block
```

The iteration clause is optional; it is expressed in a free form:

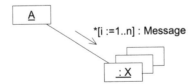

The notation of iteration infers the sequential broadcast of messages contained within the block. Parallel broadcast (also called diffusion) is represented by the sequence of characters ***||**.

The condition clause is used to validate or invalidate the sending of messages contained within the block. The condition clause is expressed in a free form:

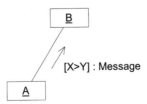

105

Result

Results consist of a list of values returned by the message. These values may be used as parameters for the other messages that are part of the interaction. This field does not exist in the absence of return values. The format of this field is also free:

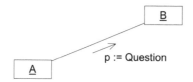

Name

The name of the message often corresponds to an operation defined in the class of the object that is the destination of the message.

Arguments

The arguments are the list of message parameters. The arguments and the message name uniquely identify the action that must be triggered in the target object. The arguments may contain return values from messages that were sent earlier, as well as navigation expressions constructed from the source object.

The following table of expressions gives some examples of the message broadcast syntax:

Label	Meaning
4 : Display (x, y)	Simple message
3.3.1 : Display (x, y)	Nested message
4.2 : age := Subtract (Today, BirthDate)	Nested message with return value
[Age >= 18 years] 6.2 : Vote ()	Conditional message
4.a, b.6 / c.1 : Turn on (Lamp)	Synchronization with other flows of execution
1 * : Wash ()	Iteration
3.a, 3.b / 4 *|| [i := 1..n] : Turn off ()	Parallel iteration

Message arguments are represented within diagrams using either pseudo-code, or directly in the programming language's syntax. The notation also proposes a graphical representation for arguments, using arrows ended with small circles. The following diagram gives an example of the graphical representation of the arguments of a message.

106

Collaborations

A collaboration is a mechanism composed of structural and behavioral elements. Collaborations provide an organization mechanism, but unlike packages they have an identity and a semantic scope. A given element may play a role in several collaborations.

A collaboration includes two types of construction: a context, which is composed of a description of the static structure of the objects being considered, and an interaction represented by a sequence of messages exchanged by these objects. The two viewpoints are necessary to document the behavior completely, but each viewpoint may be displayed independently.

Collaborations are used, depending on their level of detail, to describe specifications and express implementations. The table below summarizes the model elements that may be described by a collaboration:

Specification	Type	Operation	Use case
Implementation	Class	Method	Use case implementation

Collaborations also exist in a generic form (model), parameterized by classes, associations, attributes, and operations. A generic collaboration is called a **pattern**, or a scheme. Patterns always have a name, in contrast to collaborations that may remain anonymous.

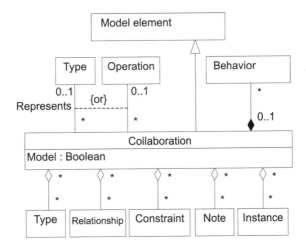

Simplified metamodel representation of collaborations

Interactions

An interaction expresses the behavior resulting from the collaboration of a group of instances. An interaction may be displayed with respect to the time perspective (by sequence diagrams), or with respect to the space perspective (by collaboration diagrams). Interactions comprise the following main elements:

- *Instances*, which are concrete examples of a type
- *Links*, which connect instances and are used to support message broadcasts
- *Messages*, which trigger the operations
- *Roles*, played by the ends of the links

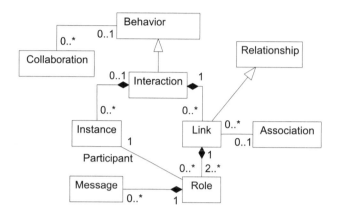

Simplified metamodel representation of interactions.

Sequence Diagrams

Sequence diagrams display interactions between objects from a temporal standpoint. Unlike collaboration diagrams, the context of the objects is not represented explicitly. The representation focuses on expressing interactions.

Representation of Interactions

A sequence diagram represents an interaction between objects that focuses on the message broadcast chronology. The notation is derived from the *Object Message Sequence Chart** of the *Siemens Pattern Group*. An object is represented by a rectangle and a vertical bar called the object's lifeline.

Objects communicate by exchanging messages, represented by horizontal arrows drawn from the message sender to the message recipient. The message sending order is indicated by the position of the message on the vertical axis. The vertical axis may be labeled to express the temporal constraints precisely — in the case of the modeling of a real time system, for example.

*Wiley 1996, Pattern-Oriented Software Architecture : A System of Patterns. ISBN 0471958697.

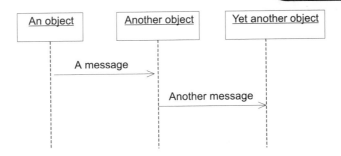

In object-oriented modeling, sequence diagrams are used in two very different ways, according to the phase of the lifecycle and the desired detail level.

The first use corresponds to the documentation of use cases — it focuses on the description of the interaction, often in terms that are close to the user, without getting into the details of synchronization. In this case, the information carried by the arrows corresponds to events that occur within the application domain. At this stage of modeling, the arrows do not yet correspond to 'message broadcasts' in the sense of programming languages, and the difference between control flows and data flows is not generally established. The diagram below represents the beginning of a phone conversation:

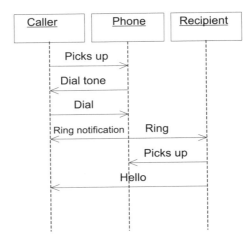

Example of the use of a sequence diagram to represent events that occur within a domain.

The second use is more software-oriented, and allows the precise representation of interactions between objects. The concept of a message unites all the types of communication between objects, in particular, procedure calls, discrete events, signals between flows of execution and hardware interrupts.

Sequence diagrams distinguish two main categories of message broadcasts:

 synchronous broadcasts for which the transmitter is blocked and waits until the called object has finished processing the message

 asynchronous broadcasts for which the sender is not blocked and can continue executing

109

A synchronous broadcast is represented by an arrow drawn from the message sender to its recipient. An asynchronous broadcast is represented by a half arrow:

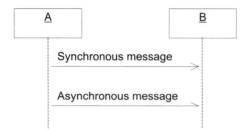

The arrow that symbolizes a message may be drawn diagonally to represent transmission delays that are non-negligible with respect to the overall dynamics of the application:

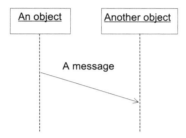

An object may also send itself a message. This situation is represented by an arrow that loops along the lifeline of the object:

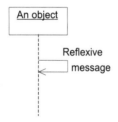

This construct does not always correspond to a real message — it may indicate an entry point into a lower level activity that is performed within the object. Internal interactions (between objects contained within a composite object) that are represented by a reflexive message may also be described in a sequence diagram.

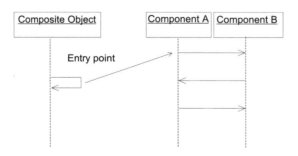

Use of a reflexive message as an entry point into an internal interaction.

110

Object creation is represented by having the creation message point to the rectangle that symbolizes the created object. Deletion is identified by a letter **X** at the end of the lifeline, either at the same height as the message that causes the deletion, or after the last message sent by an object committing suicide.

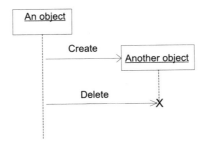

Sequence diagrams also allow the representation of **activations** for objects. An activation corresponds to the time during which an object performs an action, either directly or through another object that it uses as a sub-contractor. Activations are represented by rectangular stripes positioned along lifelines. The beginning and the end of a stripe correspond respectively to the beginning and the end of an activation.

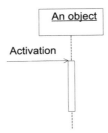

The following diagram illustrates the case of an object **A** that activates another object **B**. The activity period of **A** 'covers' the activity period of **B**. In the case of a procedure call, the flow of execution is passed by **A** to **B**. Object **A** is then blocked until **B** returns to it.

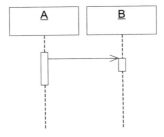

In the case of a procedure call, and more generally in the case of synchronous broadcasts, there is an implicit return at the end of the execution of the operation: it is not necessary to represent it in diagrams. Object **A** resumes execution when the action triggered in object **B** terminates. When messages represent procedure calls, solid arrowheads are used to signify this fact.

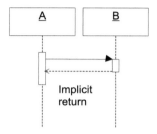

Implicit
return

Conversely, in the case of asynchronous broadcasts, the return must be shown when it exists. The following example shows an object **B**, initially activated by an object **A**, that returns a message to object **A** before ceasing its execution. It is necessary to be aware that the end of an object's activation does not correspond to the end of its life. A given object may be activated several times during its existence.

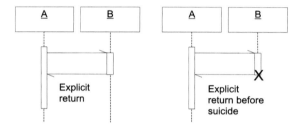

Explicit
return

Explicit
return before
suicide

The particular case of a recursive message broadcast is represented by a replication of the rectangular stripe. The object appears as if it were active multiple times.

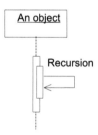

Recursion

Control Structures

The forms of the sequence diagrams indirectly reflect the choices of structure. The following two diagrams present a centralized and a decentralized control mode respectively.

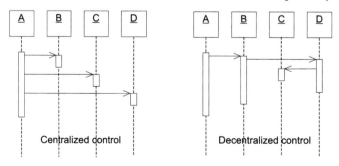

Centralized control

Decentralized control

Sequence diagrams may be completed by textual notes, expressed either as free text or pseudo-code. The moment of emission of a message, called **transition**, may be specified within the diagram close to the starting point of the arrow used to represent the message. This name is then used as a reference — to build temporal constraints, for example — as in the diagram below. When propagation of the message lasts a significant time compared to the system's dynamics, the emission and reception times are shown by a (name/name´) pair.

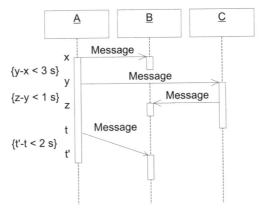

Examples of temporal constraints built from transition names

The addition of pseudo-code on the left side of the diagram enables the representation of loops and branches so that sequence diagrams may represent the general layout of an interaction beyond the sole consideration of a particular scenario.

The following diagram represents a **while** loop. Object **A** sends a message to **B** without stopping, as long as the condition **X** is true.

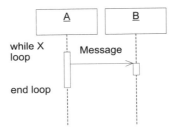

The **while** loop may also be represented using an iteration condition, positioned directly on the message. The iteration is symbolized by the character *****, placed in front of the condition between brackets.

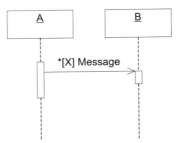

As with loops, conditional branches may be represented using pseudo-code, placed on the left of the diagram. The following diagram shows that object **A** sends a message to object **B** or object **C** according to a condition **X**.

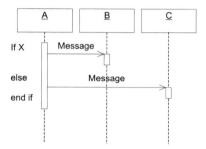

As before, conditions placed in front of messages may replace pseudo-code. The various branches are then represented by several arrows originating at the same moment, and can be distinguished by conditions placed in front of the messages. For each branch, conditions must be mutually exclusive and all cases must be dealt with.

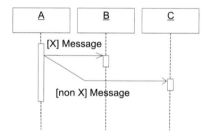

Conditional branches on the message destination side are represented by doubling the lifeline of the target object. The difference between branches is indicated by a condition placed after the message, close to the entry point on the lifeline of the target object.

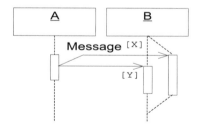

Pseudo-code also enables the putting into agreement of an initial interaction, as described by the user during the use case study, and an interaction between domain objects as built by the analyst.

Statechart Diagrams

Statechart diagrams represent state machines from the perspective of states and transitions.

State Machines

The behavior of objects of a class may be described formally in terms of states and events, using a **state machine** connected to the class under consideration.

A state machine may be associated with each class of the model

Objects that do not present a very pronounced reactive behavior may be considered always to stay in the same state. In this case, their classes do not possess a state machine.

The formalism selected by UML for representing state machines is inspired from **Statecharts***. Statecharts are hierarchical state machines that support the concepts of orthogonality, aggregation and generalization (notions that are defined later on in this chapter).

A state machine is an abstraction of all possible behaviors, similar to the way class diagrams are abstractions of the static structure. Each object follows the behavior described in the state machine associated to its class and is, at a given moment, in a state that characterizes its dynamic states.

State machines and scenarios are complementary. Scenarios are represented by an inter-object collaboration. The type of inter-object interaction occurring between objects that collaborate within a scenario is determined by the respective states of the various objects. State machines may be used to describe the behavior of groups of objects by associating a state machine to a composite, or even to a use case.

A traffic light goes successively from green to orange, then to red before going back to green, and so on, during its whole operational life:

In general, all traffic lights are either in the red, orange, or green state

It is obviously necessary to synchronize traffic lights that are positioned around the same intersection. This synchronization, which depends on the state of the intersection, may also be described in a state machine that is associated to the intersection class.

*Harel, D. 1987. Statecharts : A Visual Formalism for Complex Systems. Science of Computer Programming vol. 8.

States

Each object is in a particular state at a given point in time. States are represented as rounded rectangles; each state has an identifying name.

States are represented using rounded rectangles — each state has a name that must be unique within a given lexical scope.

States are characterized by the concepts of duration and stability. An object is not always in the same state at a given time, and an object cannot be in an unknown or undefined state. A state is the image of an instantaneous combination of the values contained in the object's attributes, and the presence or the absence of links from the given object to other objects.

The following class diagram represents people that work for companies:

People do not all have a job and are, at any given point in time, in one of the following states: employed, unemployed, or retired.

To understand the situation of a particular person, it is necessary to study the following combinations:

- Age of the person
- Presence of a link to a company

In the diagram on the next page, there are no links between Toto, who is 30 years old, and a company: Toto is therefore unemployed. Cedric, for his part, has a link to a company and is 40 years old: Cedric is therefore employed. Finally, Ernest does not have any link to a company and is 75 years old: Ernest is therefore retired.

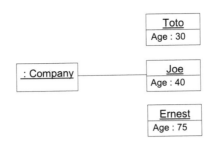

The state of the three people is different. Toto is unemployed, Cedric is employed, and Ernest is retired.

The state machines defined by UML are deterministic. Therefore, a statechart diagram must not leave any room for ambiguous constructs. This means, in particular, that it is always necessary to describe the system's initial state. For a given hierarchical level, there is always one and only one initial state. Conversely, it is always possible to have several final states that each correspond to a different end condition. It is also possible to not have any final state — in the case of a system that never stops, for example. The initial state is represented by a big black dot. A final state is represented by a big black dot surrounded by a circle.

Transitions

When dynamic conditions evolve, objects change state by following the rules described in the state machine associated to their classes. Statechart diagrams are directed graphs. States are linked via unidirectional connections called **transitions**. The passing from one state to another is performed when a transition is triggered by an event that occurs within the problem domain. The change from one state to another is instantaneous, since the system must always be in a known state.

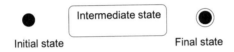

A transition enables going from one state to another; it is represented using an arrow drawn from the initial state to the final state

Transitions do not necessarily link distinct states. The following example describes a fragment of a lexical analyzer. The recognition of lexical units is performed in a 'reading' state. The state machine remains in that state as long as the characters read are not separators.

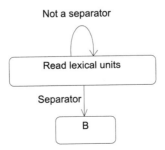

Events

An event corresponds to the occurrence of a given situation in the problem domain. In contrast to lasting states, an event is by nature an information snapshot that must be treated immediately. An event is used as a trigger to go from one state to another. Transitions specify paths in the statechart. Events determine which paths must be followed. Events, transitions, and states cannot be dissociated from the description of dynamic behavior. An object, when put in a given state, waits for the occurrence of an event to go to a different state. From that perspective, objects behave as passive elements that are controlled by events coming from the system.

An event triggers the transition associated with it.

The general syntax of an event looks like this:

```
Name_Of_The_Event (Parameter_Name : Type, ...)
```

The complete specification of an event includes:

- The name of the event
- The parameter list
- The sending object
- The target object
- The description and significance of the event

In the following example, each transition holds the event that triggers it:

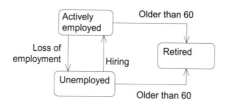

Communication by events is asynchronous, atomic, and unidirectional. An object may send an event to another object, which must always be able to interpret it.

An object may send an asynchronous event to another object

Requirements for communication by synchronous events or bi-directional exchanges can be represented using two asynchronous exchanges going in opposite directions:

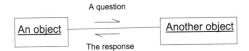

In this case, it is the role of the object sending the request to wait for the answer. This implies that the state machine describing it has a sequence of the following type:

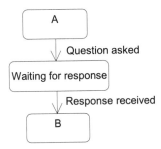

Guards

A **guard** is a Boolean condition that may or may not validate the triggering of an event occurrence.

Guards make it possible to maintain the determinism of a state machine, even when many transitions can be triggered by the same event. When the event takes place, guards — which must be mutually exclusive — are evaluated, and then a transition is validated and triggered. In the following example, when it is too warm, guards make it possible to start the air conditioning *or* simply to open the windows, according to the season.

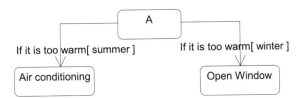

Operations, Actions, and Activities

The link between the operations defined in the class specification and the events that appear in statechart diagrams is performed using actions and activities.

Each transition may be labeled with the name of an action to execute when the transition is triggered by an event. To respect the general semantics of the transition, the action is considered as instantaneous and atomic.

When a transition is triggered, the action that is attached to it is executed instantly.

The action corresponds to one of the operations declared in the class of the object that is to receive the event. The action has access to the event's parameters, as well as the object's attributes. In reality, every operation takes some time to execute, so the concept of an instantaneous action must be interpreted as an operation with a negligible execution time compared to the system's dynamics.

States may also contain actions; these are executed upon entering or exiting a state, or when an event occurs while the object is the state.

State A
entry/
AnEvent/
exit/

An action may be executed upon entering or exiting the state, or upon occurrence of an event within the state.

The action on entry (which is symbolized by the keyword **entry /**) is executed in an instantaneous and atomic way upon entry into the state. Similarly, the action on exit (symbolized by **exit /**) is executed upon exiting the state. The action on an internal event (symbolized by the event name followed by **/**) is executed upon the occurrence of an event that does not lead to another state. An internal event does not trigger the execution of the input and output actions, unlike the triggering of a self-transition.

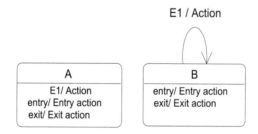

Actions correspond to operations with a negligible execution time. An operation that takes time corresponds to a state more than to an action. The keyword **do /** indicates an **activity** — an operation that takes a non-negligible time, and that is executed while the object is in a given state.

In contrast to actions, activities may be interrupted at any moment, immediately a state exit transition is triggered. Some activities are cyclic and *only* stop when an exit transition is triggered. Other activities are sequential and start when the state is entered (immediately after the execution of the entry actions). When a sequential activity reaches its end, it is possible to leave the state if one of the transitions can be traversed. This type of transition is not triggered by an event and is called **automatic transition**.

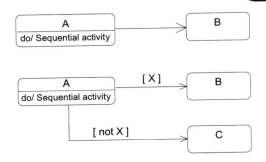

*When the activity ends, the automatic transitions — without events,
but possibly protected by guards — are triggered.*

States may also contain variables expressed as attributes. State variables belong to the class associated to the state machine, but may be shown in the statechart diagrams when they are manipulated by actions or activities.

Execution Points of Operations

To summarize, there are six places for specifying operations that must be executed. These places are, in their order of execution:

- Action associated to the state entry transition (**Op1**)
- State entry action (**Op2**)
- Activity within the state (**Op3**)
- Action associated to internal events (**Op4**)
- State exit action (**Op5**)
- Action associated to the state exit transition (**Op6**)

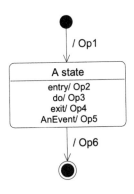

Generalization of States

Statechart diagrams may become rather difficult to read when, because of the combinatorial explosion, the number of connections between states becomes high and the resulting diagram can look like a plate of spaghetti!

The solution for this situation is to apply the principle of state generalization — the more general states are called superstates, and the more specific states are called substates. The approach to this abstraction proceeds along the same lines as class generalization or specialization. It facilitates representation and makes it possible to mask details.

A state may be decomposed into several disjoint substates, where the substates inherit characteristics from their superstate — in particular, state variables and external transitions. The decomposition into substates is also called disjunctive decomposition (decomposition of type 'exclusive-or'), since an object must be in one and only one substate at a given time.

The following two diagrams illustrate the simplification resulting from state generalization:

Internal transitions may be inherited, except in the case where the goal of the decomposition into substates is to define a particular state for the treatment of an internal transition. Entry transitions are not inherited by all the states — only one state (the superstate or one of its substates) may be the target of the transition. In the following example, state **B** is divided into two substates, **B1** and **B2**. The entry transition into state **B** must be deferred onto one of the substates, either directly (as in the case of the following diagram) or indirectly, using an initial nested state.

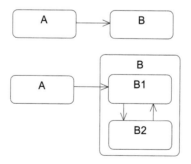

In the above example, state **A** is connected to substate **B1**. This situation compromises abstraction and is comparable to a mechanism written according to the specification of a superclass, but with a need to know the details of its subclasses. It is preferable to limit the links between the hierarchical levels of a state machine, by systematically defining an initial (pseudo)state for each level. The next diagram limits the knowledge between levels.

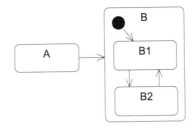

Displaying substates exhaustively puts a large information load on the diagrams. The detail of substates may be hidden to give a higher-level perspective. By using **stubs**, it is possible to show that the input transitions into a composite state refer to a particular substate, without getting into the details of the representation of this substate.

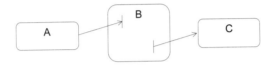

Stubs reduce the information load while showing the presence of substates of **B**

Aggregation of States

State aggregation is the composition of one state from several other independent states. The composition is of a conjunctive type (composition of type 'and'), which implies that the object must simultaneously be in all the states that constitute the aggregation. State aggregation corresponds to a kind of parallelism between state machines.

The following example illustrates different views of the concept of state aggregation. State **S** is an aggregation composed of two independent states **T** and **U**; **T** is composed of substates **X**, **Y** and **Z**, and **U** is composed of substates **A** and **B**. The domain of **S** is the Cartesian product of **T** and **U**.

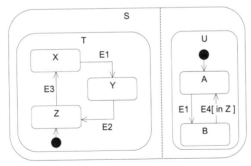

An input transition into state **S** implies the simultaneous activation of state machines **T** and **U**, i.e. the object is initially placed in the composite state **(Z,A)**. When event **E3** occurs, the **T** and **U** state machines can keep evolving independently, which brings the object to the composite state **(X,A)**. State machines **T** and **U** may also evolve simultaneously, which is the case when event **E1** moves the object from composite state **(X,A)** to **(Y,B)**. Adding conditions to the

123

transitions, such as the guard **[in Z]** placed on the transition from **B** to **A**, makes it possible to introduce dependency relationships between the components of the aggregate. When event **E4** occurs, the transition from **B** to **A** is only valid if the object is also in state **Z** at that time.

State aggregation, together with state generalization, simplifies the representation of state machines. Generalization simplifies by factorization, and aggregation simplifies by segmentation of the state space. Without state aggregation, the state machine equivalent to the above would look like this:

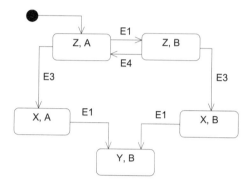

At worst, the number of states of such a 'flat' state machine is equal to the product of the number of states of each component state machine. In the case of an aggregation of three state machines with a few hundred states each (which is already a lot), the equivalent flat state machine could contain up to a million states!

History

By default, a state machine does not have any memory. The special notation **H** offers a mechanism to memorize the substate last visited, and to get back to it during a transition entering the encompassing superstate. The history indicator applies to the level in which the **H** symbol is declared. The **H** symbol may be placed anywhere within the state — the bottom left corner is the default location.

The following diagram represents a state **C** that memorizes the last active substate. The history is initialized when the transition issued from the initial state **A** is triggered.

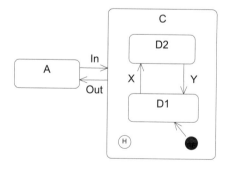

It is also possible to memorizing the last active substate, regardless of its depth; this is indicated by the **H*** symbol. The intermediate memory levels are obtained by placing a symbol **H** in each hierarchical level. In the following example, state **A** memorizes the last active substate, independent of the nesting of substates.

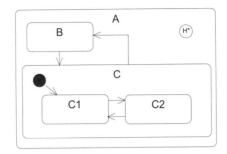

The next example shows the use of history to implement a dishwasher. The washing cycle is split into three main stages: washing, rinsing, and drying. The door may be opened at any time — to add a cup, for example. As soon as the door is closed, the washing cycle restarts at the same point as where it was stopped.

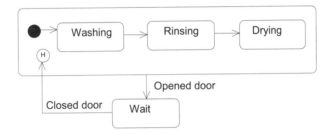

Object Intercommunication

Objects communicate by exchanging messages. When it receives a message, the target object triggers an operation to deal with it. The message is a very general concept that may represent a procedure call, an interrupt coming from the hardware, or a dynamic link.

Messages are the way to visualize the exchange within object interaction diagrams — both sequence and collaboration diagrams. These diagrams show particular behavior cases within a use case.

State machines represent behavioral abstractions from the point of view of a group of objects (most often, a class). The behavior described by scenarios is the specific result of the states of all the objects that collaborate within those scenarios.

Message broadcasts between two objects are represented within the statechart diagram formalism in an abstract way, by sending an event between the final state machines of the classes of the objects concerned. The display within statechart diagrams is more abstract because every event sent between two state machines corresponds to many message broadcasts between objects.

The syntax of an event broadcast towards a class takes the form:

```
^ Target.Message (Arguments)
```

Here, **Target** refers to the class of the objects that are targets of the event, and **Message** is the name of a message the target will understand.

The complete syntax of a transition is therefore:

```
Event (Arguments)[Condition] / Action ^ Target.Message (Arguments)
```

The following example shows state machine fragments of a TV set and its remote control. The TV set may be turned on or off by manipulating a flip switch, and the remote control has a pushbutton. The TV set may be controlled directly or using the remote control.

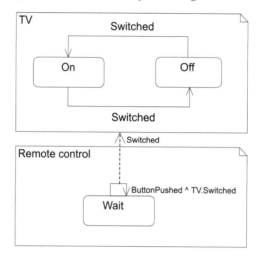

Broadcasting towards any set of objects is possible using generalization. (A class is a particular example of a set of objects.) The most usual kinds are the broadcast to all the objects (spreading) and the broadcast to a particular object (point to point). In the case of a state machine that describes a composite class, the actions may make direct reference to the operations that are declared in the various classes contained within the composite class.

Object Creation and Destruction

Object creation is represented by sending a creation event to the object's class. The event parameters make it possible to initialize the new object, which then starts to exist with the initial state described within the class state machine. The following example shows a creation transition that registers a plane. In the case of a crash, the plane stops existing.

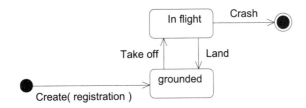

The creation transition brings the object from its initial state to its first operating state.
Reaching the final state implies that the object disappears.

Object deletion is effected when the control flow of the state machine reaches a non-nested final state. Ending up in a nested final state implies going back up to the encompassing state, instead of ending the lifecycle of the object.

Timed Transitions

By definition, delays are activities that last a certain time. A delay is therefore naturally attached to a state, rather than to a transition — it is represented using a delay activity. The delay activity is interrupted when the expected event takes place. In fact, this event triggers a transition, which allows the state encompassing the delay activity to be exited. The control flow is then transferred to a different state.

The following example illustrates a delay sequence in an automated teller machine. When the flap that accepts deposits is open, the system tells users that they have three minutes to make their deposit. If the deposit is performed within three minutes, the delay activity is interrupted by the triggering of the transition towards state **B**. Conversely, if the deposit is not performed within the given time, the automatic transition towards the cancellation state is triggered at the end of the delay activity. In both cases, the flap is closed by the exit action of the delay state.

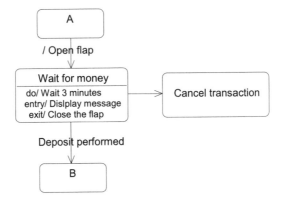

Representation of a timer by combination of a wait activity and an automatic transition

Timers may be represented using a more compact notation, which is directly tied to the transition triggered after the delay. The triggering event has the generic name **after**, and the parameter specifies the timer duration.

The syntax of a timer event takes the form:

```
after (timer_duration)
```

The previous diagram is then transformed in the following way:

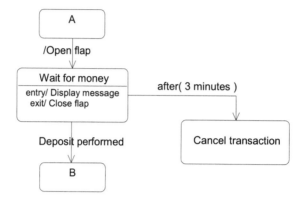

State machines provide a formalism that is well adapted to the representation of complex behaviors. In analysis, statechart diagrams capture the expected behavior. During implementation, state machines may be written easily, using tables containing the states and actions to execute at the time of the transitions.

Metamodel Introduction

A state machine represents a behavior resulting from operations executed after a sequence of state changes. A state machine may be displayed according to the point of view of the state (by statechart diagrams) or the action (by activity diagrams). A state machine specifies the behavior of a collaboration.

The execution of a state machine instance cannot be interrupted. At any time, a state machine may react to a particular event that moves it from a stable state to another stable state. The execution of a state machine starts with the initial pseudo-state and continues, event by event, until a final, non-nested pseudo-state is reached.

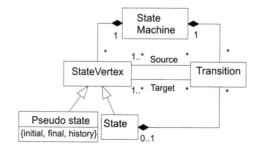

Simplified metamodel — a state machine is a graph composed of states and transitions.

Events trigger transitions. The triggering of a transition brings the state machine from the source state to the destination state. Along the way, one or more actions may be triggered on one or more objects.

UML defines three different kinds of events:

signal event, caused by a signal

call event, caused by an operation

time event, caused by the expiry of a timer delay

The following diagram represents transitions, their actions, and the various events that trigger them:

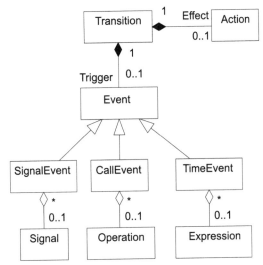

Simplified metamodel representation of the various kinds of events.

Activity Diagrams

An activity diagram is a variant of statechart diagrams organized according to actions, and mainly targeted towards representing the internal behavior of a method (the implementation of an operation) or a use case.

Representation of Activities

An activity diagram represents the execution state of a mechanism as a sequence of steps grouped sequentially as parallel control flow branches.

A statechart diagram may also represent this sequencing of steps. However, given the procedural nature of the implementation of the operations — in which most events simply correspond to the end of the preceding activity — it is not necessary to distinguish states, activities, and events systematically. It is therefore beneficial to have a simplified representation for directly displaying activities. In this context, an activity is displayed as a stereotype of a state. An activity is represented by a rounded rectangle, in the same way as states, but more oval in appearance.

129

The diagram below displays the graphical representations of activities and states, and highlights the simplification resulting from the direct representation of activities.

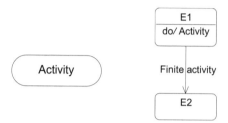

Each activity represents a particular state within the execution of the encompassing method. Activities are linked by automatic transitions, represented by arrows, in the same way as transitions within statechart diagrams. When an activity terminates, the transition is triggered and the next activity starts. Activities do not have internal transitions or transitions triggered by events.

The following figure represents two activities linked by an automatic transition. It is not necessary to place an event name on the transition.

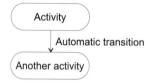

Transitions between activities may be guarded by mutually exclusive Boolean conditions. Guards are shown next to the transitions whose triggering they validate.

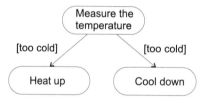

UML defines an optional stereotype for displaying **decisions**. A decision is represented by a diamond with many transitions coming out of it. The diagram below is equivalent to the last one, except for the fact that the decision is shown explicitly.

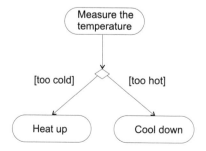

Activity diagrams show synchronizations between control flows by using synchronization bars. A synchronization bar makes it possible to open and close parallel branches within the flow of execution of a method or a use case. The transitions pertaining to the start of a synchronization bar are triggered simultaneously.

The following example shows that, in order to cool down a room, it is necessary simultaneously to switch off the heating and open the windows.

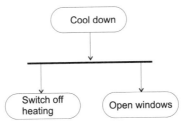

Conversely, a synchronization bar may only be crossed when all the input transitions on the bar have been triggered. The following figure extends the previous example and shows that the measurement of temperature is performed again once the heating has stopped and the room has been ventilated.

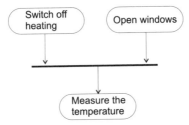

In order to show the various responsibilities within a mechanism or an organization, activity diagrams may be split into **swimlanes** (in much the same way as a swimming pool). Each responsibility is assumed by one or more objects, and each activity is allocated to a given lane. The relative position of the lanes is not important; transitions may freely cross lanes.

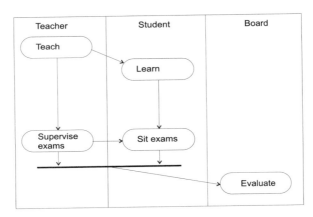

It is possible to show objects clearly within an activity diagram, either within swimlanes, or independently of them. Objects are represented by vertical lines, as in sequence diagrams, and activities appear, object by object, along their lifelines.

Often, several activities manipulate the same object, which changes state according to the progress of the mechanism. To increase readability, this object may appear in many places within the diagrams; its state is then specified with a bracketed expression at each occurrence.

Object flows are represented by dotted arrows. In this way, arrows relate an object to the activity that created it, and to the activities that involve it. When an object produced by an activity is used immediately by another activity, the object flow also represents the control flow. It is then unnecessary to represent this control flow explicitly.

The diagram below shows the various cases referred to in this discussion. In particular, the example shows an **Order** object manipulated by various activities.

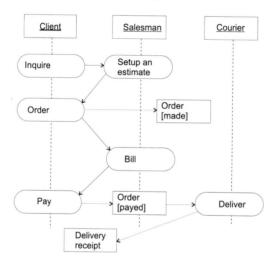

Activity diagrams may also contain states and events represented in the same way as in state transition diagrams. The following diagram gives an example of the simultaneous use of both notations:

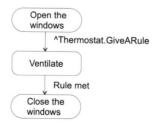

UML also defines stereotypes for representing transition information explicitly. A signal broadcast is symbolized by a convex pentagon, linked by a dotted arrow to the object that is to receive the signal. Signal receipt is represented by a concave pentagon, linked by a dotted arrow to the object broadcasting the signal.

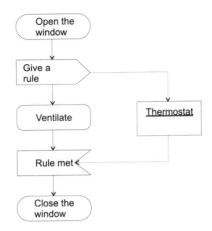

Component Diagrams

Component diagrams describe software components and their relationships within the implementation environment; they indicate the choices made at implementation time.

Components

Components represent all kinds of elements that pertain to the piecing together of software applications. Among other things, they may be simple files, or libraries loaded dynamically.

By default, each class in the logical model has a specification and a body. The specification contains the class interface, shown here with UML's lollipop notation, while the body contains the implementation of that same class, represented by the component symbol itself.

In C++, a specification corresponds to a file with a `.h` suffix, and a body corresponds to a file with the suffix `.cpp`.

Dependencies Between Components

Dependency relationships are used within component diagrams to indicate that a component refers to services offered by other components. This type of dependency reflects implementation choices. A dependency relationship is represented by a dashed arrow drawn from the client to the supplier.

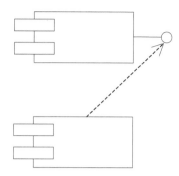

In a component diagram, dependency relationships generally represent compilation dependencies. The compilation order is given by the dependency relationship graph.

Processes

Processes are objects that have their own control flow (or *thread*), and as such are special kinds of active objects. Processes may be contained within components, and just as for all model elements, the addition of stereotypes makes it possible to specify the semantics of a dynamic component. The stereotypes «process» and «thread» are predefined by UML.

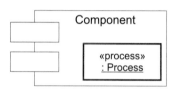

Subsystems

To speed up the implementation of applications, various components may be grouped within packages according to logical criteria. They are often stereotyped as subsystems to add the concepts of compilation libraries and configuration management to the partitioning semantics already included within packages.

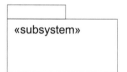

Subsystems organize the implementation view of a system; each subsystem may contain components and other subsystems. By convention, any model component is positioned either at the root level, or within a subsystem. Subsystems should be seen as big bricks for building systems.

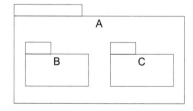

Decomposition into subsystems is *not* a functional decomposition. From the user's standpoint, system functions are expressed within the use case view. Use cases are translated into interactions between objects whose classes are themselves encapsulated in categories. Objects that implement the interactions are distributed into the various categories — the corresponding code is stored in modules and subsystems.

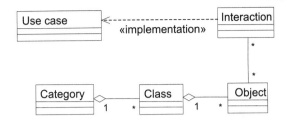

The subsystem in the physical view is the equivalent of the category in the logical view. The following figure shows the correspondence between these two views.

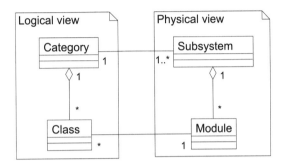

A subsystem provides a means of managing complexity by encapsulating details. Subsystems have a public and a private part. Unless explicitly indicated otherwise, any module positioned within a subsystem is visible from the outside. Subsystems may depend on other subsystems and components, and similarly, a component may depend on a subsystem.

Integration with Development Environments

Subsystems do not exist, *per se*, in all software development environments. It is therefore the role of the user to establish a structure based on directories and files in order to implement them physically.

```
                    Subsystem
        ┌──────┬────────┬───────┬──────┐
    Interfaces  Sources   Tests   Docs
```

In this scheme, it is particularly judicious to use the subsystem concept as a means of integration, along with software analysis and design tools, compilation systems, and version and configuration management systems. Each subsystem is embodied by a directory that contains files. These files correspond to the different components included within the subsystem. The subsystem also contains the various files necessary for component compilation, documentation, and testing. The integration with compilation systems makes it possible to link the concept of the program library with that of the subsystem. The integration with a configuration management tool leads to building systems by combining compilation libraries. Integration may be still further enriched by a version manager, ideally with two levels of granularity. It then becomes possible to build a system by combining versions of subsystems (expressed as program libraries), that are themselves composed of component versions.

Deployment Diagrams

Deployment diagrams show the physical layout of the various hardware components (nodes) that compose a system, as well as the distribution of executable programs on this hardware.

Representation of Nodes

Each hardware resource is represented by a cube, evoking the physical presence of the equipment within the system. Any system can be described by a small number of deployment diagrams, and a single diagram is often sufficient.

The nature of the equipment may be specified using a stereotype. The following example proposes three stereotypes to distinguish devices, processors, and memory. If necessary, the user has the possibility of defining other stereotypes.

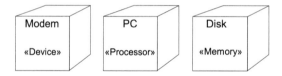

The difference between a device and a processor depends strongly on the viewpoint. A terminal **X** will be seen as a device by the terminal user, while it will correspond to a processor for the developer of a server **X** that executes on the embedded processor contained in **X**.

The various nodes that appear in the deployment diagram are connected to each other by lines representing a communication infrastructure, which is *a priori* bidirectional. The nature of that infrastructure may be specified using a stereotype.

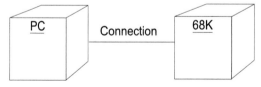

Deployment diagrams may show node classes or node instances. As with other types of diagram, the graphical difference between classes and objects is implemented by underlining the object name. The example on the next page shows the deployment diagram of a building access management system.

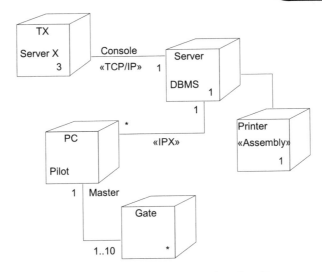

The presence of multiplicity and role information shows that the diagram represents classes of nodes. The diagram shows a system composed of a server with surrounding PCs that drive the opening and closing of gates. The number of PCs has not been established. Conversely, it appears that every PC may control at most 10 gates. Three X-terminals play the role of console to access the system. A printer is connected to the server.

The diagram describes the nature of the communication links between the various nodes. The server and the PCs are connected via an IPX link; the X-terminals and the server communicate via TCP/IP. The nature of the connections between other nodes is not specified.

Nodes corresponding to processors from the application's standpoint — the «processor» stereotype does not forcibly appear in the deployment diagrams — also hold the name of the processes they contain. The server executes a database management system, and the PC houses the driver software that drives and controls the gates. The names of these processes facilitate the linking between the deployment diagram and the component diagram. Each process named in the deployment diagram executes a main program with the same name as the one described within the component diagram.

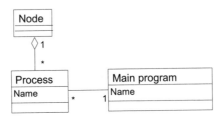

Deployment diagrams may also exhibit node instances (identified by underlined names). The diagram overleaf gives us precise information concerning the situation with respect to the system site deployment. It appears that gates 6, 7, 8 and 9 are driven by PC4.

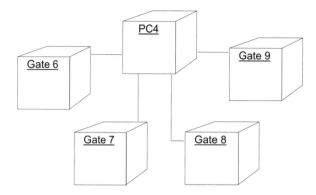

Summary

It is difficult to summarize a chapter whose goal is to introduce the complete UML syntax — in a sense the material forms its own summary. However, the nine major diagram categories are worth reiterating and remembering. They are:

- Activity diagrams, which represent the behavior of operations using sets of actions
- Class diagrams, which express the static structure of a system in terms of classes and their relationships
- Collaboration diagrams, which illustrate the interactions between objects using a spatial structure that represents their physical layout
- Component diagrams, which describe the software components of an application in the implementation environment
- Deployment diagrams, which show the locations of components on particular pieces of hardware
- Object diagrams, which express the static structure of a system in terms of objects and their relationships
- Sequence diagrams, which illustrate the interactions between objects using a temporal structure that represents the order of communication
- Statechart diagrams, which represent the behavior of classes using state machines
- Use case diagrams, which are representations of the functionality of a system, from the point of view of its users

In the next chapter, the notation described here will be used to assist in the discussion of using object-oriented techniques to perform the analysis, design and implementation of a software project using UML, use cases, and an iterative development cycle.

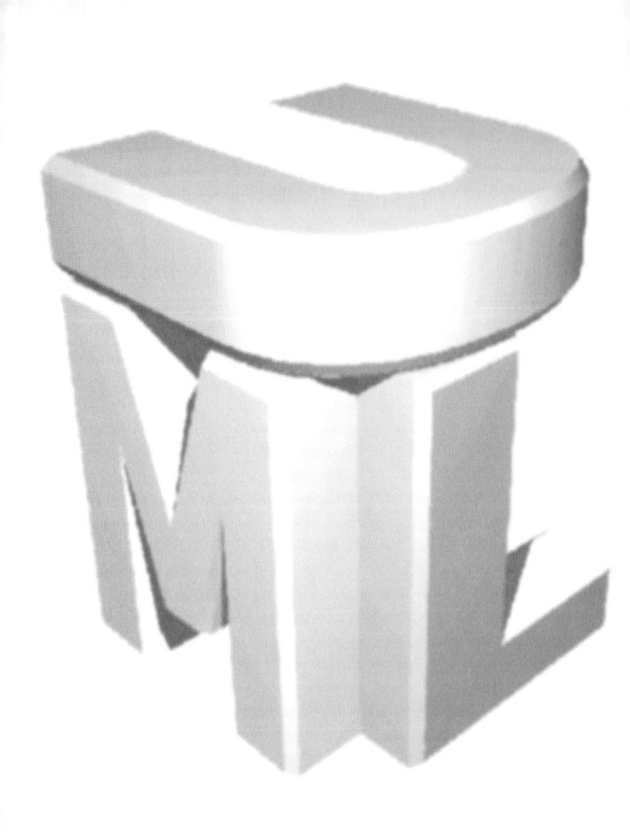

Chapter

Object-Oriented Project Support

The existence of a formal development process, well defined and well managed, is the key to the success of a project. A process is stable if its future performance can be statistically[1] predicted. UML is a modeling language and does not define a particular development process. Nevertheless, it can be used as a notation for various object-based methodologies.

The goal of this chapter is to introduce the overall area of project support through a generic, methodic framework, close to the one described by Objectory 4.0[2]. It is the role of each project or organization to refine this framework depending on its needs.

Software Characterization

The goal of this chapter is to specify the software development process, to identify the origin of the difficulties bound to its development, and to outline the procedures necessary to master them.

The Software Crisis

Thirty years ago, the formula for describing the limits of available technologies and the difficulty in mastering the resulting software was born[3]. Of course, during the past thirty years, much progress has been made, but software is always in crisis. It is probable, as suggested by Grady Booch, that it is not really a crisis at all, but rather a permanent state.

Object-oriented methods have replaced traditional structured techniques — object-oriented programs are more extensible, closer to the users' needs and easier to maintain, but they still remain difficult to implement.

Needless to say, one of the reasons behind the software crisis is the increasing complexity of modern applications. The inherent complexity of each new generation of system is even greater than the last, so technical solutions that were adapted for the previous generation reach their limits for the next generation. The software crisis has no end.

[1]*Deming W. E. 1982, Quality, Productivity, and Competitive Position. Massachusetts Institute of Technology Center for Advanced Engineering Study, Cambridge, MA.*
[2]*Rational Software Corporation 1996, Rational Objectory Process – Introduction.*
[3]*Buxton J. N. & Randell B. (eds) 27-31 October 1969, Software Engineering Techniques. Report on a Conference Sponsored by the NATO Science Committee, Rome, Italy.*

There exist many kinds of software programs, and each one may be characterized by the constraints they impose on the development process.

Software Categories

Amateur software makes up the first category. The term 'amateur' should not be taken as derogatory — it just designates any software that does not have any significant economical ramifications. This type of software is generally developed by individuals within groups sharing common interests, such as radio hams or astronomy enthusiasts. Software developed by students also falls into this category.

The second category groups disposable software, also called consumable software, like word processors or spreadsheets. This type of software is not very expensive to purchase (a few thousand dollars at the most) and its replacement by an equivalent piece of software does not compromise the financial position of the business that acquired it. The perspective of a manufacturer of this type of software is rather different, mostly due to its broad distribution. Once software is being used by thousands of customers worldwide, it is not easy to make corrections to errors, especially since there is little income to be derived from maintenance contracts. It is therefore difficult to maintain a balance between product quality, development cost, and distribution. The objective of quality at reduced cost is difficult to maintain, but imperative for products with a small margin and broad distribution. The Internet and the shareware principle greatly simplify the distribution of this type of software, but they do not get rid of the quality imperative.

The third category comprises programs that are necessary to operate a business and may not be exchanged easily. They were built for a given task and are the fruit of sizable investment. These types of software demand reliable, safe and predictable behavior — their failure may cause the failure of the businesses that use them. They exist in the industrial and financial sectors — to control a switchboard or to manage a dealing room, for example. The great complexity of this software — or more precisely, of these software systems — comes partly from the inherent complexity of the application domain, and partly from the complexity of the execution environments, which are often heterogeneous and distributed. Their continuing maintenance becomes more and more difficult, as the software becomes increasingly intricate with each modification. Software engineers are then subject to the weight of history, often up to a breaking point that must be anticipated. The sad reality is that software entropy reflects universal entropy — it does not stop increasing. From that perspective, a development process must limit the software chaos.

The last software category includes safety critical systems — those on which human lives depend. These systems can be found in transportation, defense and medical fields. The usage constraints on such software have nothing in common with the previous categories. A defective operation is not quantified in terms of money, but rather in terms of human lives.

Software Complexity

In general, software engineers have a serious fault: they do not know how to make things simple. On the other hand, making things simple is extremely difficult. Making things simple means learning to encapsulate complexity; it also means resisting the pleasure that comes from manipulating arcane features of programming languages. Making things simple is about learning to make them *appear* simple, creating the illusion of simplicity.

The software engineer must learn to mimic nature, which in all its creations, from the most elementary to the most complex, always searches for a stable balance and minimal energy consumption; nothing is superfluous.

Too often, software implementation remains an area of specific and independent activity. If the software engineer were to build furniture, he would start by planting trees for the wood, then look in the ground for iron ore to make nails, and finally he would assemble everything to make up a piece of furniture. This method of construction engenders a massive effort and requires mastery of too wide a range of skills. During the past centuries, our ancestors have learnt to specialize human activities, and this is why some specialists know how to plant trees, while others know the secrets of nail manufacturing. The immediate advantage of this approach is that the people involved may focus on their own knowledge domain — furniture manufacturing in this case. A development method that rests on the shoulders of programming heroes, gurus and other software magicians does not constitute a lasting and reproducible industrial practice.

The formalizing of the development process proceeds from this observation. The activities performed during software implementation must be described, explained, and justified. Software knowledge and know-how must be propagated other than from the druid's mouth to the druid's ear*. A process describes the chain of activities within the development team — it directs the tasks of each individual, as well as of the group. The process defines reference points and criteria to control and measure products and project activities.

Unfortunately, the formalization of the development process only partially applies to the software domain. In contrast to woodworking, software engineering is a very young knowledge domain, and poor in terms of transferable know-how. Moreover, the level of formalization of software know-how is very weak. Before being able to propagate the experience, it is first necessary to describe it, represent it, and model it.

This is equivalent to saying that software engineering is a trade that can be learned like any other trade. It is not possible to improvise a software engineer. A company looking for a software specialist must therefore look for a software engineer rather than a specialist in chemistry or textiles.

Origins of Software Complexity

It is not enough to put the blame on software engineers. More and more, the problems that they have to deal with are complex, due to the very nature of the application domains. No matter how willing they are, software engineers cannot reduce this complexity. However, it can be funneled and confined within weakly coupled closed areas. By judicious segmentation of the state space, the characterization of the behavior of discrete systems — the programs — is made easier.

In the same way, the complexity bound to the software environment — methods, languages, operating systems — can, and should, be minimized as much as possible. Solutions that are less costly but more complex must be avoided.

*Goscinny, Uderzo 1961, Asterix the Gaul, Dargaud.

Over and above these problems of complexity, it is necessary to stress the infinite flexibility of software, which is at the same time its greatest advantage and its greatest drawback. It is extremely easy to write a line of code, but it is more difficult to debug it. It is easy to modify one line in a program, but it is infinitely more difficult to guarantee that the program will continue operating correctly.

Consequences of Complexity

Due to the complexity tied to software implementation, it is unlikely that a piece of software is free from defects. Conversely, the likelihood of important deficiencies is high. Software defects, or bugs, are like false notes in music*. The best musicians are not guaranteed against a false note — what they do is difficult, and ensuring constant quality over a long period of time is difficult as well. The software engineer is confronted with the same problem. He is not guaranteed against a false note, regardless of his skills. Software is written by human beings, and human beings are prone to making mistakes.

Debugging a software program is a slow and chaotic process, and the maintenance cost is disproportionate. Test and validation techniques make it possible to identify secure execution paths. If they are followed to the letter, they guarantee a reasonable level of confidence in the software.

Defects do not all have the same consequences. Analysis defects result in software programs that do not satisfy all their users. Design defects generate software programs that are awkward to manipulate, too slow, or inefficient. Implementation defects result in unforeseen behavior. All defects are undesirable; those introduced in the earlier activities, however, are more difficult to correct.

The software crisis is the fruit of our inability to master software defects. The result of this crisis is the astronomical cost of complex applications.

The Scope of the Object-Oriented Approach

The development of an application may be divided into several major areas. They are chained sequentially within a waterfall lifecycle, or they are distributed among the various iterations of an iterative lifecycle.

In general, regardless of the approach, linear or iterative, structured or object-oriented, the development of an application answers four questions:

Application = What to do + In what domain + How + With what skills

These questions correspond to different viewpoints and are relevant to different players. They may be studied according to various techniques, but they must always be considered in order to develop an application:

 What to do? The answer is expressed by the user, who describes what he expects from the system, how he expects to interact with it, and who the different actors are. It is a functional description that does not get into the details of the implementation: the *what to do* is purely descriptive.

*Adda J.-L., private communication.

- *In what domain?* The response must describe the domain (the environment) within which the application is to exist, and point out which are the important elements in that domain for the application. The domain study is the fruit of an analysis that is completely disconnected from any consideration of implementation. The analysis of the domain must be understandable by a user.

- *How?* This must be determined during design. The *how* is the fruit of the designer's experience and know-how. Design is the art of making possible the users' desires — expressed within the *what to do* — considering the application domain and bearing in mind the implementation constraints.

- *With what skills?* It is necessary to determine all that is necessary to build the application. This point rests on technical skills for developing classes, objects and mechanisms, on inter-personal skills for team support, and on organizational skills to maintain the overall logistics.

The object-oriented approach answers these questions, according to three different perspectives: object-oriented analysis, object-oriented design, and object-oriented programming.

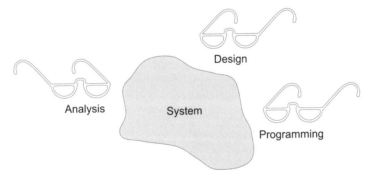

Object-Oriented Analysis

Analysis tries to understand, explain, and represent the underlying nature of the system it describes. Analysis is not preoccupied with solutions but with questions; it identifies the *what to do* and the environment of a system, without describing the *how*, which belongs to the design.

Analysis starts by determining the *what to do*, the user's needs. Very often, the user is not capable of clearly expressing his expectations, so the list of requirements is only an approximate representation of his real needs. The presence of a large requirements list is not always a good sign. Its quality depends strongly on the technique used for its development. Too often, requirements lists are dense, confused, contain contradictory items, and do not reflect the true requirements of the user. Experience shows that the use case technique is well adapted to the determination of user requirements.

Analysis continues with the modeling of the application domain — in other words, the identification of the objects and classes that fundamentally belong to the application environment, and the representation of interactions between these objects. Analysis expresses the static structure using relationships between classes and interactions between objects using messages. There is not a preferred order in the development of the different types of diagrams — they are often built simultaneously. Among the numerous diagrams defined by UML, those that show the elements from the logical view may be used in analysis, in particular the list overleaf.

145

- Use cases
- Specifications of classes and objects
- Collaboration diagrams
- Sequence diagrams
- Class diagrams
- Statechart diagrams

This list is not exclusive, and every project is free to use other techniques to perfect the analysis of its own problem. In particular, cognitive and systemic approaches often bring an interesting and complementary outlook to object-oriented modeling.

Starting with elements of the real world makes taking the first step easier, as it focuses the thinking on concrete elements. This absolutely must be followed, though, by an abstraction process whose goal is to help forget real world contingencies and determine the basic concepts from which they originate. If the thinking focuses too much on what exists, the risks of reproducing a solution instead of identifying the problem become great (see the later section on the role of software engineering or the cultural clash).

Analysis is the antithesis of conformity. Analysis is often surprising, as it requires changing perspective and forgetting what is already known. This is the necessary first step to finding the essence, the hidden nature of things. The role of analysis is to find a description that nobody has thought about so far, but that once it has been determined, imposes itself to the point of becoming obvious.

To take an example, analyzing is like looking at a point, a circle, an ellipse, a line, two intersecting lines, a hyperbola and a parabola, and recognizing that all these shapes may be obtained from the intersection of a plane and a cone. In this case, the generating principle may be expressed by an equation of the form $ax^2 + by^2 + 2cx + 2dy + e = 0$. This representation is economical because it describes the essentials. Analysis pertains to the essentials, and looks for a generic and more abstract model.

The immediate consequence of well-driven analysis is always a large saving in the following implementation, because of the essence/manifestation dichotomy underlying the object-oriented approach. The identification of the generating principle allows the implementation, in one go, of what generally manifests itself in many forms, and then to instantiate it to obtain the different forms desired, which are often not yet present in the domain.

Parallel to analysis of the environment, an analysis of what exists and of the implementation constraints also takes place. The goal of this analysis is to understand perfectly the characteristics and constraints of the implementation environment, in order to make justified and considered decisions at design time. This analysis is the only means of taking into account, in a realistic way, the implementation choices that may be imposed on a project, even before design. Unfortunately, this situation is all too common in software engineering. Software engineers must re-assemble a problem from a fragment of a solution!

When moving to design, one must be careful not to lose sight of analysis. The loss of this perspective is the result of the enriching of models during design. As mentioned earlier, design brings complementary information that enriches the *descriptions* performed during analysis. It is very tempting to start from diagrams obtained during analysis and to add design information to these diagrams. Analysis is then progressively merged with design, and the diagrams do not show the domain objects anymore, but the *how*. The situation is often even more complex, as the models undergo transformations that are more than just simple enrichments. Filtering is not sufficient to retrieve the analysis view.

There is no simple solution to the problem of model transformation, and in particular, to the bi-directional transformations that occur when clarifications to the design can bring about analysis modifications by retroactive effect. UML defines the concept of 'trace' between model elements, and between one model and another, so that it is possible to record the story of these elements.

Object-Oriented Design

Like analysis and design, design and implementation partially overlap. It is very rare to know how to do everything, and for this reason, it is necessary to try alternate techniques, to compare results, and then to choose by making compromises. Design and implementation are complementary. Design requires experimentation, implementation requires driving principles.

To maintain the benefits of abstraction for as long as possible, design is generally subdivided into two steps: a logical step that is independent from the implementation environment, and a physical step that focuses on the ordering of resources and details pertaining to programming languages or to the execution environment.

Design is often wrongly considered as a simple enrichment of results obtained during analysis. In this case, it is a highly reducing view, which simply ignores that design is the time when the know-how is put together. This know-how may be internal to the project, or acquired from the outside in the form of tools, reusable components or, more widely, development **frameworks**. The emergence of **patterns** (patterns and frameworks are described later) marks an advance in the formalization of object-oriented know-how, independently of programming languages and their detailed features.

Design starts with the determination of the software architecture — by the development of static and dynamic data structures that will be used as a skeleton for the whole development process. The **architecture** defines the general structure of the application, and the development and software evolution depend on its quality. The architecture is a consequence of the strategic decisions made during design and the tactical decisions made during implementation.

To have a software engineering strategy is to consider software as a key element in the enterprise development. It is also to look at securing a technological advance via choices of architecture that go beyond the scope of the immediate needs tied to a particular application.

Committing to a software engineering strategy involves choosing:

 *Internationalization* — to design the software in such a way as to enable communication with users in all languages

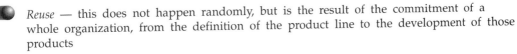 *Reuse* — this does not happen randomly, but is the result of the commitment of a whole organization, from the definition of the product line to the development of those products

- *Language standardization* for the whole set of development projects (Ada, for example, in the case of the American Department of Defense)

- *Display device independence* — the decoupling of the information to be displayed and the way to display it

- *Portability* of source code (and possibly executable programs), considerably reducing the development and especially the maintenance costs in the case of multitarget development

- *Generalization of the communication mechanisms* between objects, making the location of objects transparent, and thereby facilitating the distribution of applications and their components

Design is the domain of compromise. There is no solution that is all black or all white — the truth is always somewhere in the gray. Tactical decisions affect all the activities that will guide the search for that truth in the day to day development effort. They include the following choices:

- *Generalization of abstractions and mechanisms for ancillary tasks* — in other words, all the components that are largely reusable within programs, such as dates, character strings, basic data structures, sorting algorithms, etc.

- *Error processing* may be performed by exceptions or by statuses expressed as integer values. Exceptions may not be ignored, but processing them complicates the normal code. The error status is simple to implement but could be ignored, in which case error processing is not guaranteed.

- *Dynamic memory management* could be handled by the programmer or automated by the execution environment.

- *Inter-process communication* may rely on point-to-point, multi-point, or broadcast-based connections. It may be ensured by ad hoc mechanisms or written in a general application integration scheme, such as CORBA or COM.

- *Choice of communication modes* including the form and nature of messages and the various synchronization modes: synchronous, semi-synchronous, rendez-vous, timed, asynchronous, etc.

- *Presentation of user messages* to make all interactions with the user as homogenous as possible.

- *Programming languages* — compiled and interpreted languages have good points and bad points. Compiled languages make it possible to write more reliable programs, whereas interpreted languages add more flexibility during development. In some cases, it may be beneficial to mix various languages within the same application.

- *Choice of data structures and algorithms* that are encapsulated within objects in order to decouple the specification and the implementation of classes.

- *Optimization of the network of relationships* that reflect the user's communication needs. The designer may be lead to modifying this network for various reasons: to optimize access speed, or to take into account particular implementation constraints, such as the absence of bi-directional links in third generation programming languages.

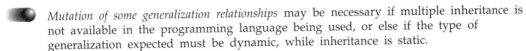 *Mutation of some generalization relationships* may be necessary if multiple inheritance is not available in the programming language being used, or else if the type of generalization expected must be dynamic, while inheritance is static.

Implementation of reusable components can mean two different things: programming with reuse and programming for reuse. The first type of reuse consists of incorporating an existing component, thereby accelerating the development in progress. The second form is more like an investment: the cost is immediate, but the profits are only received later.

The importance of the design phase depends on the nature of the application and the richness of the implementation environment. It is increasingly possible to perform a complexity transfer from applications to environments, thanks to a factoring of common elements and mechanisms. This is the case in families of applications that are well targeted in a given domain, such as client software that interacts with database servers. Conversely, the more technical an application, the more it interacts with particular hardware and the more the design effort is important.

RAD (rapid application development) tools propose a well-traced path. As with frameworks, it is necessary to follow the rules of the game, which are fixed in advance — offering the benefit of simplicity, but at the expense of originality. All the applications end up looking alike, which may or may not be a good thing. The real drawback of RAD tools is that they encourage a 'quick and dirty' approach, rather than one that is quick and well done.

Curiously, RAD is a mix of software engineering in its design, and software nightmare in its use. This is the consequence of the short-term vision of users for whom only the speed factor is important. As RAD specifically does not encourage modularity and layer abstractions, very quickly — and no mistake about it — the user interface code and the application code find themselves tightly intertwined. Software built in this way is difficult to maintain and almost impossible to reuse in another application.

The role of design is finding a balance between implementation speed and possibilities of reuse, between openness and ready-made solutions, and between short-term (tactical) and long-term (strategic) visions.

Object-Oriented Programming

Object-oriented programming is the last link of the object-oriented chain, after analysis and design. Programming in an object-oriented language is the easiest way to translate an object-oriented design into an executable program for a given machine. It is also possible to use a language that is not object-oriented, but this imposes an additional workload for the programmer who has to simulate object-oriented constructs.

In parallel with true object-oriented languages, such as Smalltalk, Java or C++, it is possible to find object-*like* languages or environments, such as Visual Basic from Microsoft or Powerbuilder from Powersoft. In some ways, these environments make it possible to write object-oriented programs easily, almost without noticing it.

Object-oriented programming languages are mostly algorithmic and structured languages. They provide, at least, the concepts of classes, objects, inheritance, dynamic linking and encapsulation. Bertrand Meyer insists, in particular, on the automatic management* of memory. Eiffel, Smalltalk

*Meyer B. 1988, *Object-Oriented Software Construction*, Prentice Hall, New York, NY.

and Java have a garbage collection system that frees the programmer from the difficult, hard-to-overcome problem of releasing dynamic memory. The main feature of object-oriented languages is that of reducing the gap between the way programmers think and the limited language understood by the computer. However, there are wide syntactical variations between the various object-oriented languages, according to whether they are a conservative extension like C++, or a complete innovation like Smalltalk.

The choice of an object-oriented programming language is often dictated by the software culture of the enterprise. To date, technical software has favored C++, while the world of management has shown a growing interest in Smalltalk, or the semi-object-oriented solutions mentioned earlier. 1996 was marked by the release of the Java language developed by Sun, which has created a lot of interest in the whole software community.

There are many object-oriented programming languages, and the main ones are described briefly below:

- Ada is a high-level programming language, designed to reduce high development costs incurred by the American defense department in the 70s. Ada was standardized by ANSI for the first time in 1983. After having been used for ten years, the Ada language was improved by adding object-oriented constructs, and its second version, standardized in 1995, makes it a fully object-oriented language. Ada 83 is a software engineering language; Ada 95 is an object-oriented software engineering language.

- C++ is a hybrid object-oriented language designed by Bjarne Stroustrup in the 80s: it is an extension of the C language. C++ extends C by adding strong typing, classes, overloading and dynamic linking. Its syntax remains dense like that of C, and makes C++ difficult to deploy.

- Eiffel is an object-oriented language deliberately made simple, with a very clean syntax. It was designed in the 80s by Bertrand Meyer and can be distinguished from other object-oriented languages by the importance it gives to the concept of programming by contract. Hence, it is the only language that takes into account the principle of substitution in its syntax.

- Java is the new kid on the block in the realm of object-oriented languages. It takes inspiration from C++ for its syntax and from Smalltalk for its virtual machine, while remaining voluntarily simple in much the same way as Eiffel. Initially designed for programming personal digital assistants, the Java language was sent to the forefront by its strong association with the Internet.

- Smalltalk is the object-oriented language par excellence. In Smalltalk, everything is an object, including the classes themselves. Smalltalk was designed in the 70s at the PARC (the Xerox research center in Palo Alto). Since 1980, Smalltalk has come with a sophisticated development environment and a large collection of predefined classes. Today, there is renewed interest in Smalltalk to build information systems, due to its flexibility of use and simplicity.

The following table summarizes the characteristics of the main object-oriented languages. Smalltalk is a special case, as intervening at the metaclass level makes it possible to extend the language characteristics.

	Ada 95	C++	Eiffel	Java	Smalltalk
Package	Yes	No	No	Yes	No
Inheritance	Single	Multiple	Multiple	Single	Single
Generic?	Yes	Yes	Yes	No	No
Typing	Strong	Strong	Strong	Strong	Untyped
Linking	Dynamic	Dynamic	Dynamic	Dynamic	Dynamic
Parallelism	Yes	No	No	Yes	No
Garbage Collection	No	No	Yes	Yes	Yes
Assertions	No	No	Yes	No	No
Persistence	No	No	No	No	No

The Transition to Object-Oriented Technology

The transition of an organization to object-oriented technology requires a significant time. For hardened developers, it takes on average:

- One month to master the constructs of an object-oriented language
- Six to nine months to acquire an object-oriented mode of thinking
- One month to master a class library
- Six to nine months to master a framework

However, it is important to realize that a small minority of reactionaries will never be able to bridge that gap (between 10 and 15 % of the developers). There are no simple criteria to aid their identification.

To facilitate the transition, it is strongly advisable to:

- Make use of external skills
- Start a pilot project
- Put in place a training plan that combines theory and practice
- Use technology transfer specialists who will go along with the project
- Train everybody, developers as well as the testing, quality assurance and support teams

The transition to object-oriented technology is costly. It is wise to anticipate an additional cost of 10 to 20% for the first object-oriented project, due to the learning curves of the different techniques for the development team, and the experiment of managing the iterative cycle by the support team. The benefits of the transition will only be obtained after the second or third project, which should require 20 to 30% fewer resources.

Towards a Development Method

The goal of a software development process is to formalize activities related to the development of software systems. The formalization of a development process aims at providing companies with a set of mechanisms which, when applied systematically, make it easier to obtain software systems of consistently high quality, in a predictable and reliable way. By its nature, the description of the process remains general, as it is not possible to define authoritatively a single standard that is adaptable to all people, applications and cultures. It is better instead to talk about a configurable scope, eventually refined by consensus through practice and the deployment of products that are widely adopted by the user community.

A development method comprises:

- Model elements that correspond to the basic conceptual building blocks
- A notation whose objective is to insure the visual rendering of model elements
- A process that describes the steps to follow during development of the system
- Know-how that is more or less formalized

Watts S. Humphrey has proposed five levels of maturity* for software development processes:

- *Initial*: the development is not formalized — the team reacts on a day by day basis and chooses solutions on a case by case basis, so that the success depends strongly on the people involved in the project

- *Reproducible*: the organization is capable of establishing reasonable plans in terms of budget and to verify the progress of the project with respect to these plans

- *Defined*: the development process is well defined, known and understood by all the parties involved in the project

- *Framed*: the performances of the development process are measurable objectively

- *Optimized*: the control data from performances of the process allows the improvement of the process

From this model, the SEI (Software Engineering Institute) of Carnegie Mellon University has developed an evaluation procedure for development processes known by the acronym CMM (Capability Maturity Model).

The following diagram represents the five levels of maturity of processes:

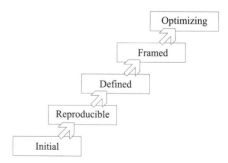

*Humphrey W. S. 1989, *Managing the Software Process*, Addison-Wesley.

152

Segmentation of the modeling process facilitates the management of complexity by reducing the scope of the study to one portion, one subset, or one point of view. This way, when the whole is too complex to be understood at one time, global understanding may surface by the parallel perception of many disjoint yet concurrent views. The choice of viewpoints — of what is being modeled — strongly influences the way the problem should be approached, and therefore the form of the solutions obtained. There is no universal model, and levels of detail, precision, or fidelity may vary. The best models are in tune with reality.

UML is a language for representing object-oriented models, but the process for the creation of these models is not described by UML. However, the authors of UML emphasize the following characteristics, which seem to them essential for a development process:

- *Driven by use cases*: all the activities, from the specification of what must be done, right up to the maintenance, are guided by use cases.

- *Centered on the architecture*: From the beginning, the project considers the determination of the overall architecture as a focal point. The architecture is designed to satisfy the requirements expressed in the use cases, but also to take into account evolutions and implementation constraints. The architecture must be simple and intuitively understandable. It is designed with and for reuse.

- *Iterative and incremental*: the whole task is divided into smaller iterations, whose definition is based on the level of importance of the use cases and the study of risks. The development proceeds with iterations that lead to incremental system deliveries. Iterations may be conducted in parallel.

The following diagram represents the general form of the development process recommended by the authors of UML.

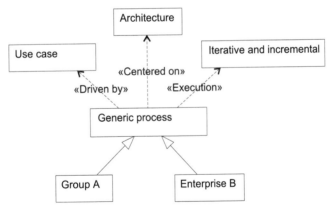

The development process suggested by the authors of UML is driven by use cases, centered on the architecture, and deployed iteratively and incrementally

Use Cases

Use cases complement the object-oriented approach and form the basis of the development process. In this context, use cases must be seen as a boundary delimiting the various activities pertaining to the expression of users' requirements. In this way, they facilitate the implementation of software that satisfies these requirements.

153

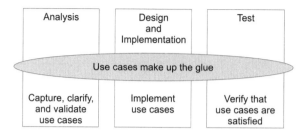

Benefits of Use Cases

The determination and understanding of requirements is often difficult, since the participants in such a study are swamped by large amounts of information. Requirements are often expressed in an unstructured way without much coherence, so requirements documents become long litanies that contain pieces of information of the following types:

- The system will have to do the following...
- The system should do the following...
- The system will end up doing the following...
- It is of the utmost importance that...
- It would be interesting to...

Frequently, requirements contradict each other, things are forgotten, inaccuracies remain, and system analysis sets off on the wrong foot. As a result, initial requirements are fuzzy and evolve constantly. When requirements change — and they invariably do — it becomes very difficult to appreciate the impact and cost of a modification.

Use cases refocus the expression of requirements on users, starting from the very simple viewpoint that a system is built first and foremost for its users. The organization of the approach is performed with respect to the interactions of a single category of users at a time; this partitioning of the set of requirements considerably reduces the complexity of requirements determination.

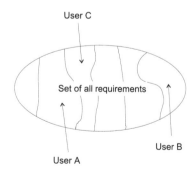

The formalism of use cases — based on natural language — is accessible without any particular user training. Users can express their requirements and expectations easily by communicating with domain experts and computer scientists. The terminology used to write up use cases is the same as the one employed by users in their everyday life, so as to facilitate the resulting expression of requirements. Through use cases, computer scientists are constantly pulled back to the main user concerns, and in this way they avoid being sidetracked by the appealing technical niceties that are not strictly necessary. Use cases focus the development effort on the true requirements.

Use cases help users structure and articulate their wishes. They oblige them to define the way in which they would like to interact with the system, to specify what information they expect to exchange, and to describe what they must do to obtain the expected result. Use cases make the future system concrete according to a formalization which is close to the user; they favor the definition of a set of specifications that really reflects requirements, even in the absence of a system to review.

Construction of Use Cases

A use case must be simple, intelligible, and described in a clear and concise way. The number of users that interact with the use case is very limited. As a general rule, there is only one actor per use case.

During the construction of use cases, it is necessary to think about the following:

- What are the tasks of the actor?
- What information must be created, saved, modified, deleted, or simply read by the actor?
- Will the actor have to notify the system of any external modifications?
- Will the system have to notify the actor of internal conditions?

Use cases may be presented through multiple views: an actor with all his use cases, a use case with all its actors, etc. Use cases may also be grouped according to their typical triggering sequences, that is, as a function of their links, or as a function of the various points of view, which are often related to the main categories of actors (customer, supplier, maintenance...).

The next step consists of classifying use cases according to their focus with respect to the activity of the company, their benefit to the customers, the nature of the risks, their ease of implementation, or their impact on the processes that are already in place.

Rules for Setting up Use Cases

A use case is not only a description of functionality or motivation, but also an interaction between an actor and a system in the form of a flow of events. The description of the interaction focuses on what must be done in the use case, not on how it is done.

A use case must remain simple. One should not hesitate to fragment a use case if the interactions become too complex, too intertwined, or if the various parts appear to be independent. It is also necessary to be careful to not mix use cases; actors and interactions of another use case must not be specified in the description. Finally, use cases must avoid the use of fuzzy and imprecise expressions built from words such as 'many', 'rather', 'sufficiently', 'enough', etc.

155

A use case description includes the following elements:

- *The beginning of the use case* — the event that triggers the use case. This must be clearly specified in the following way: "The use case starts when **x** occurs."

- *The end of the use case* — the event that stops the use case. This must be clearly identified and documented with the phrase, "When **Y** occurs, the use case terminates."

- *The interaction between the use case and the actors* — clearly describes what is inside the system and what is outside the system.

- *The exchanges of information* — corresponding to the parameters of the interactions between the system and the actors. A non-software formulation is recommended, for example, "The user connects to the system and gives his name and password."

- *The chronology and the origin of information* — describing when the system requires internal or external information, and when it records it internally or externally.

- *Repetitions of behavior* — may be described using pseudo-code

- *Optional situations* — must be represented in a uniform way in all the use cases; the various options must appear clearly, according to the following formulation:

    "The actor chooses one of the following elements, possibly several times in a row:
    a) option **X**
    b) option **Y**
    c) option **Z**
    Then the actor continues to..."

These points are not sufficient to obtain a good use case. It is also of the utmost importance to find the correct level of abstraction — the amount of detail that must appear — and to distinguish between a use case and a scenario. There is unfortunately no ready-made answer, so appreciation of the abstraction level rests mostly on experience. The answers to the following two questions may, however, be used as a guideline:

- Is it possible to execute a given activity independently from the others, or is it always necessary to link it with another activity? Two activities that are always linked are probably part of the same use case.

- Is it a good idea to group certain activities in order to document, test, or modify them? If so, these activities are surely part of the same use case.

When a use case becomes too complex (more than ten pages long, for example), it is possible to split it in smaller use cases. However, this operation should only be executed when the use cases have been described in detail, after examining the main scenarios.

Elaboration Process for Use Cases

Use cases allow teamwork as long as a writing style guide has been defined. This guide should include a description of the use case layout, the level of detail, and also a model use case that will be followed by all the participants.

The team begins by identifying the use cases roughly. The main steps of each use case are described in a couple of sentences by differentiating the normal case from the alternative and exceptional cases. Once this first task has been performed, groups selected from within the team focus on refining the understanding and the description of a particular use case. To do so, each group identifies the scenarios, and also the conditions that differentiate the scenarios based on knowledge of the problem domain and meetings with users.

A scenario is a particular path through the abstract and general description supplied by the use case. Scenarios go through the use case, following the normal path as well as any alternative and exceptional paths. Combinatorial explosion means that it is very often impossible to lay out all the scenarios.

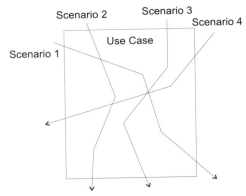

Once the content of the use case has been validated by the execution of the scenarios, the steps that have been stabilized must be described in a more detailed fashion. Each step is associated with a paragraph that describes what happens within the step, while taking into account all the scenarios that cross that step. At this stage, all the requirements identified within scenarios should be taken into account by a use case.

It is strongly advisable to synchronize the evolution of use cases through regular meetings between the various groups within the team. This presents the dual advantage of harmonizing the detail level of use cases, and allowing the re-allocation of orphan scenarios without use cases. These meetings also facilitate the validation of the use cases put together by one group, by the other groups. Simple criteria derived from experience help distinguish a good use case from a questionable one. For example, it is necessary to ask the following questions:

- Is there a brief description that gives a true image of the use case?
- Are the starting and ending conditions of the use case well tackled?
- Are the users satisfied by the sequence of interactions between the actor and the use case?
- Are there any steps that are common with other use cases?
- Do the same terms employed in different use cases have the same meaning?
- Does the use case take into account all the alternatives?

Last Pitfalls to Avoid

Use cases are not the only way to document the requirements of a system. Traditional techniques based on informal textual descriptions can complement use cases very well. It can be a good idea to establish cross references between the two types of documentation, and to study the following points:

- Have all the requirements identified in an informal way been allocated to a use case?
- Has the same requirement been allocated to several use cases?
- Are there use cases that are not referenced by informal requirements?

Moreover, prototyping based on user interface constructors is very often the best way to help an end-user articulate his wishes. Studying the interactions between the user and the prototype provides an important source of scenarios and, therefore, ways to validate the use case model.

The main difficulty associated with use cases has more to do with the determination of the detail level, than with the formulation of use cases. It is important to remember that use cases are an abstraction of a set of behaviors that are functionally linked within a use case. For example, the presence of a large amount of detail identifies a scenario more than a use case.

By the same token, a large number of use cases is a sign of a lack of abstraction. In any system, irrespective of its complexity and size, there are relatively few use cases but many scenarios. Typically, an average system includes between ten and twenty use cases — a large number of use cases means that the essence of the system has not been understood. A use case describes what the user fundamentally wants to do with the system. The name of a use case may be a good indicator; object/operations or function/data associations are very suspicious.

Another difficulty is that of resisting the temptation to over-describe the internal behavior of a system while neglecting the interaction between the actor and the system. It is true that a use case must describe what the user exchanges with the system, and the main steps pertaining to the implementation of these exchanges; but this does not extend to explaining how the system implements these exchanges. The use case is an analysis tool used to determine what the user expects from the system — the *what* and the *what it does* of the system. As soon as the description uses *how*, it is part of the design rather than the analysis.

The Transition to Object-Oriented Technology

Use cases refocus the development on user requirements, and therefore they help to *build the right system*. However, use cases do not strictly define how to *build the system right*, or specify the overall software architecture. They indicate what a system must do, not how it must do it. The use case view is a functional description of requirements, structured with respect to an actor. The transition to the object-oriented approach is performed by associating a collaboration with each use case. A collaboration describes domain objects, the connections between these objects, and the messages exchanged between the objects. Each scenario, which is an instance of the use case implemented by the collaboration, is represented by an interaction between the objects described within the context of the collaboration.

158

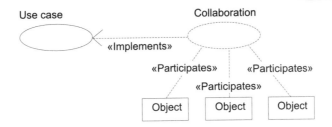

The implementation of a use case by using a collaboration is a crucial modeling step. It identifies the moment of the transition to object-oriented technology. A decomposition that follows directly from the use case study leads to a classical structured approach, with all the deficiencies associated with structures that are modeled from functions.

An object-oriented approach implements a use case based on the collaboration between objects. Scenarios, which are instances of that use case, are represented by interaction diagrams (collaboration and sequence diagrams). The diagram below illustrates the decomposition choices after studying use cases.

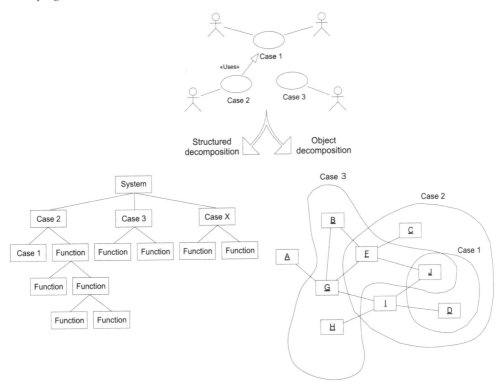

Representation of the transition towards object-oriented technology after studying use cases

The transition from analysis to design is indicated by the introduction of implementation considerations within the models. Analysis describes the *what* of a system, while design focuses on the *how*. Use cases continue to delimit the design, since they specify what these mechanisms must do. Use cases also describe the tests of functionality.

159

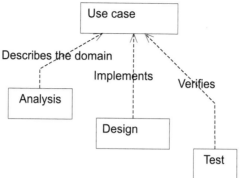

Use cases coordinate and delimit various models

Use cases do not, however, create the shape of a system. In an object-oriented approach, the form (architecture) of the software does not reflect the form of the use cases.

Software Architecture

The development of a piece of software may be seen like the crossing of an ocean in a boat. The departure date is known, the arrival date is less well known, and during the trip it may be necessary to confront storms and repair mechanical breakdowns. The goal of designing the architecture of a piece of software is to give to a development effort the means to arrive at a friendly port.

Software architecture is about the global form of an application. This form results from the design beyond data structures or algorithms[1]. The software architecture is concerned with integrity, uniformity, simplicity, and aesthetics. It is to the detriment of software development that nothing is predisposed to these virtues, mainly due to the intangible nature of software and the absence of physical constraints.

Putting a well-adapted architecture in place is the key to successful development. It is important to stabilize it as soon as possible. There is no universal architecture adaptable to all types of applications. However, there are reusable architectures within the limits of a particular domain.

Perry and Wolf[2] define software architecture using the following formula:

> **Software Architecture = Elements + Patterns + Motivations**

Within the context of the object-oriented approach, the elements are the objects and classes, patterns are groups of objects and classes, and motivations explain why a particular grouping is better adapted than another in a given context.

The architecture offers a global vision of the application. It describes the strategic choices that determine software quality, such as reliability, adaptability, or the guarantee of performance, while making room for tactical decisions made during development.

---

[1]*Garland D., Shaw M. 1993, An Introduction to Software Architecture. Advances in Software Engineering and Knowledge Engineering, Vol. 1, Singapore, World Scientific Publishing Co., pp. 1-39*
[2]*Perry D. E.and Wolf A. L. Oct. 1992, Foundations for the Study of Software Architecture. ACM Software Eng. Notes, pp. 40-52.*

To make a gastronomic analogy, development consists of transforming a piece of Gruyere cheese into a piece of Comté cheese by filling the holes!

Architecture

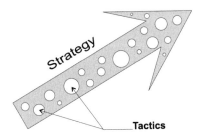

The architecture reflects the general strategic choices and makes room for timely tactical decisions

Good architectures are characterized by:

- Simplicity
- Elegance
- Intelligibility
- Well defined levels of abstraction
- A clear separation between the interface and the implementation of each level

The Architect's Vision

There is more than one way to consider a system. Multiple perspectives are required. Moreover, in order to satisfy many parties, each diagram type only gives a partial image of a system. All successful object-oriented projects are characterized by the presence of a strong architectural vision. The description of this vision may be based on multiple complementary views, inspired from the ones described by Philippe Kruchten* in his **4 + 1 view model**:

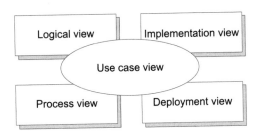

This architectural model is well adapted to the representation of various constraints that the architect must take into account.

Kruchten P. Nov. 95, The 4+1 View Model of Architecture. IEEE Software.

The Logical View

The logical view describes the static and dynamic aspects of a system in terms of classes and objects, and focuses on abstraction, encapsulation, and uniformity. The system is decomposed into a set of key abstractions, originally coming from the problem domain. Beyond satisfying the users' functional requirements, the logical view makes it possible to identify and generalize the elements and mechanisms that make up the various parts of the system.

The logical view brings the following model elements into play:

- Objects
- Classes
- Collaborations
- Interactions
- Categories (stereotyped packages)

The Implementation View

The implementation view is concerned with the organization of modules within the development environment. It shows the allocation of classes within modules, and the allocation of modules within subsystems. Subsystems are themselves organized in hierarchical levels with well-defined interfaces.

The implementation view deals with the following model elements:

- Modules
- Subroutines
- Tasks (in terms of program units, as in Ada)
- Subsystems (stereotyped packages)

The Process View

The process view represents the decomposition, in terms of execution flows (processes, threads, tasks ...), the synchronization between flows, and the allocation of objects and classes within the various flows. The process view also focuses on the availability of the system, the reliability of applications, and performance. It is most important in multitasking environments.

The process view manipulates the following model elements:

- Tasks, threads, processes
- Interactions

The Deployment View

The deployment view describes the various hardware resources and deployment of software within these resources. It deals with the items at the top of the next page.

162

- Response times and system performance
- Bandwidth and capacities of communication paths
- Geographical constraints (physical distribution of processors)
- The power requirements of distributed computing
- Overloading and load balancing in a distributed system
- Resistance to failures and breakdowns

The deployment view becomes most important when the system is distributed. The deployment view concentrates on the following model elements:

- Nodes
- Modules
- Main programs

The Use Case View

Use cases constitute the glue that unifies the four previous views. Use cases motivate and justify the architectural choices. They facilitate the identification of critical interfaces, they force designers to focus on the concrete problems, and they demonstrate and validate the other architectural views.

The use case view accounts for the following model elements:

- Actors
- Use cases
- Classes
- Collaborations

Organization of Models

The five views described above, and the associated concept of packages, allow the hierarchical structuring of a model. A model described by UML resembles the hierarchy represented in the following class diagram:

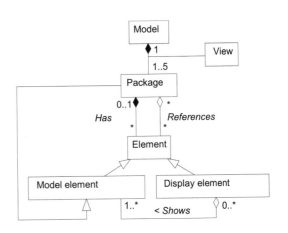

*Simplified metamodel — hierarchical organization of
models according to several views.*

Packages are both model elements and model structuring elements. The hierarchy of packages organizes models in the same way as directories organize file systems.

The following object diagram gives an example of the organization of a model, structured according to the five architectural views introduced earlier.

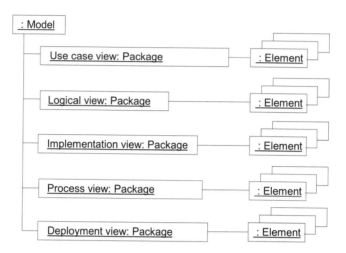

Documentation of Architecture

The architecture described in an architecture document comprises:

- A textual description of the features of the architecture (the views) and the key system requirements
- The compromises reached and the alternatives explored
- A high-level representation of the logical view (between 5 and 50 key-classes)
- Scenarios specific to the architecture
- Description of key mechanisms

Articulation of the Different Diagrams

Model elements are accessible to the user via graphical projections (visual elements) represented in the nine types of UML diagram introduced in the last chapter:

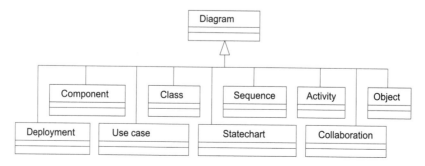

These diagrams form the basis of the architectural views described above. It is important to capture properly the concepts behind the links between the various model elements and their associated representations in order to document a system clearly and efficiently.

A model is a semantic construct, organized in the form of a network. This network may be traversed by following the general rules described in the UML metamodel. The various diagrams may be seen as graphical paths traversing the models. The following paragraphs give an example of a path, going from the expression of the requirements to the deployment on the hardware.

Expression of Requirements

The expression of the requirements of a category of users is described functionally in use cases. Use cases are expressed in a natural language, in the terms of the user.

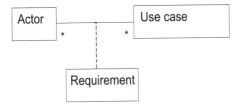

Transition to Object-Orientation

The analyst performs the transition towards object-orientation. He implements the behavior described in the use case by means of a collaboration between objects, initially from the application domain. The context of a collaboration is represented in an object diagram.

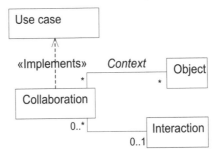

Expressing Behavior

The behavior of a collaboration or a class may be represented as an interaction or a state machine. Interactions are displayed from a temporal perspective using sequence diagrams, and from a spatial perspective using collaboration diagrams. State machines are displayed as statechart diagrams from the perspective of states and transitions, and as activity diagrams from the point of view of activities.

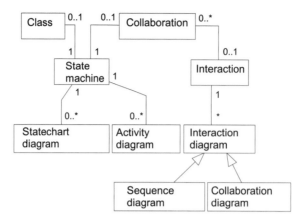

Representing the Structure

Each object is an instance of a class. Domain classes describe objects in a general way. Objects are represented in object diagrams, collaboration diagrams and sequence diagrams. Classes are represented in class diagrams.

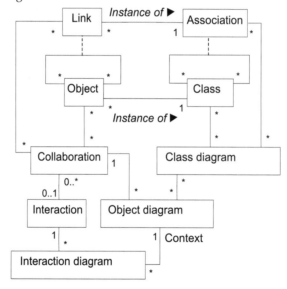

Implementing Objects and Classes

The code that implements classes, objects and the interactions between these objects is stored in components that constitute the building blocks of the physical structure of system. The term 'components' groups modules, subroutines, tasks (in the sense of Ada program units) and main programs.

Modules contain the code that corresponds to classes and objects, and main programs contain the code that corresponds to entry points in the implementation of interactions. A module may contain several classes and several objects, but, by default, there is only one class per module, and the class name is used to construct the module name in the development space.

A component diagram shows the compilation dependencies between the various components of an application.

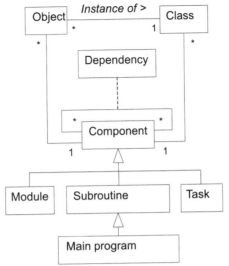

The code that corresponds to objects and classes is stored within modules

Deployment of executable code

A main program is a kind of component that contains the executable code corresponding to one or more interactions. Very often, a main program only corresponds to a single interaction. A main program is deployed on nodes, within the process that executes it. Deployment diagrams show the different kinds of processors and devices that make up the system execution environment. They also show the configuration of components, processes and objects that are executed in this environment. If necessary, object and process migration is represented using a stereotyped dependency relationship.

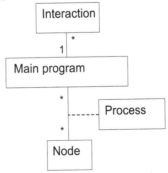

A main program is a kind of component that contains executable code corresponding to one or more interactions.

Organization of Models and Views

Packages organize views and models by encapsulating the model elements in a hierarchical decomposition, analogous to the structuring of a file system using directories:

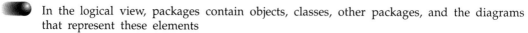

- In the logical view, packages contain objects, classes, other packages, and the diagrams that represent these elements

- In the implementation view, packages contain components and other packages, and their corresponding diagrams

Packages may be specialized as categories and subsystems in order to distinguish between the logical view packages and the implementation view packages respectively.

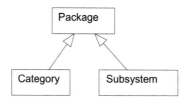

As a general rule, there is a direct correspondence between a category and a subsystem. Hierarchies of categories and subsystems may differ in order to, among other things:

- Group the objects that interact strongly

- Implement low-level functionality that is not represented as part of analysis

- Spread the workload across the development team

Granularity of Model Elements

UML model elements follow a dichotomy such that, for a given concept, there always exists a model element with a fine granularity and a model element with coarser granularity. The diagram below illustrates the relationships between coarse granularity elements:

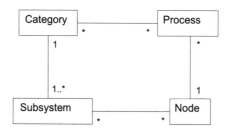

Fine granularity elements are also in correspondence, as you can see on the next page.

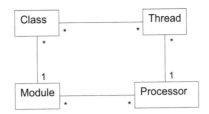

View by view, the coarse granularity elements are aggregates of elements with finer granularity. UML allows the construction of models compatible with this hierarchical decomposition, and therefore aids navigation between the various viewpoints, and between the detail levels of these viewpoints.

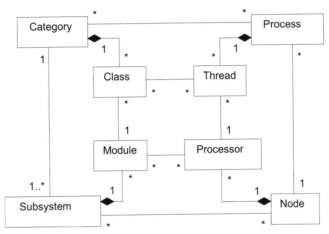

Correspondence between model elements within a hierarchical representation created by aggregations

This dichotomy between elements may be represented as a pyramidal stacking of the UML model elements. It shows that all the elements are simultaneously visible if necessary, but that the vision may also remain limited to a given abstraction level.

Pyramidal representation of UML model elements

The diagram above gives a view of this stack representation from the top, looking down. The elements that are at the same hierarchical level within the pyramid are in correspondence view by view. The base of the pyramid groups the coarse granularity elements, the intermediate layer contains fine granularity elements, and the top contains use cases. These latter elements are implemented by collaborations built using the elements in the lower levels.

Thanks to these correspondences between model elements, UML facilitates navigation between general viewpoints and more detailed viewpoints, as described by Grady Booch, for whom the general form influences the detailed forms, and vice versa. He qualifies his approach as being *Round Trip Gestalt**.

Summary of Elements and Views

The following table summarizes the standard use of elements within the different diagrams, in order to represent the various viewpoints. This representation is non-limiting — the user is free to represent the elements he finds useful in the diagrams of his choice.

	Use case view	Logical view	Implementation view	Process view	Deployment view
Use case diagram	Actors Use cases				
Class diagram		Classes Relationships			
Object diagram	Objects Links	Classes Objects Links			
Sequence diagram	Actors Objects Messages	Actors Objects Messages		Objects Messages	
Collaboration diagram	Actors Objects Links Message	Actors Objects Links Messages		Objects Links Messages	
Statechart diagram	States Transitions	States Transitions		States Transitions	
Activity diagram	Activities Transitions Actors	Activities Transitions		Activities Transitions	
Component diagram			Components	Components	Components
Deployment diagram					Nodes Links

*Booch G. 1994, Object-Oriented Analysis and Design, with Applications. Benjamin Cummings.

Patterns

The term **pattern** refers to recurring combinations of objects and classes. They are often found in object-oriented designs and could be called 'object know-how'. The main benefit of patterns is to allow the manipulation of architectural concepts that are more advanced than objects and classes. They augment the expressive power of modeling languages. This approach also avoids spending too much time on objects that are specific to the application domain, and in this way seeks out higher-level designs that may not do as much, but which are more flexible and extensible. It could be said that a pattern is to objects what sub-programs are to instructions, or integrated circuits are to transistors. The pattern is the object-oriented design unit of reuse.

The concept of pattern[1] was described by Christopher Alexander[2]. This architect wanted to formalize the main architectural characteristics in order to facilitate the construction of buildings. This idea of formalization of architectural elements, or architectural shapes (hence the term pattern), may be transposed to the software domain in order to define software 'shapes' that are reusable from application to application.

UML represents patterns by collaborations. A collaboration groups an object context and an interaction between these objects. A collaboration is therefore useful to represent structural patterns as well as behavioral patterns. Collaborations are represented by dotted ellipses connected to the participating objects.

The diagram below represents a 'chain of responsibility' pattern.

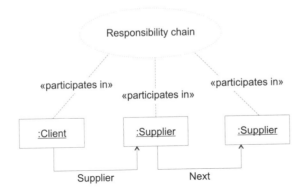

There are also analysis patterns, which are built from business objects and dedicated specifically to software programs deployed in a given domain.

---

[1]*Alexander C., Ishikawa S., Silverstein M., Jacobson M., Fiskdahl-King I., Angel S. 1977, A Pattern Language. Oxford University Press, New York.*
[2]*"Each pattern describes a problem which occurs over and over again in our environment, and then describes the core of the solution to that problem, in such a way that you can use this solution a million times over, without ever doing it the same way twice." Christopher Alexander*

Description of Patterns

The precise description of patterns is essential for their use. At the very least, a pattern is described by:

- A name to augment the abstraction level of the modeling language
- A problem, with its context and some pre- and post-conditions
- An abstract solution independent of programming languages
- Consequences, in terms of flexibility, extensibility and portability

Idioms

Patterns are specialized constructs that are completely independent of implementation languages. Patterns formalize architectural choices that may be deployed in a uniform way regardless of the implementation environment. In parallel to these independent forms, there are recurrent constructions that *are* specific to a given programming language. These particular forms, called idioms, group existing syntactic constructs. Idioms make it possible to build new constructs that, as such, are generally not transposable from one language to another.

Idioms belong to the wide variety of features and tricks that accompany a style of programming that is considered elegant in a given language. Based on the expressive power of languages, a given technique may be an idiom in one language and a syntactic construct in another.

Copying a string of characters in C++ may be implemented as follows:

```
While (*destination++ = *source++);
```

In Ada, names may be prefixed:

```
Standard.Mailbox.Open;
```

In C++, many programming techniques — such as memory management, input-output or initialization — are idioms. These idioms are described in books that present themselves as advanced programming manuals. As it spread, C++ proved to be a rather difficult language to use, due to the need to master a large number of idioms in order to program effectively.

Frameworks

The representation of large systems calls for many classes. Due to the complexity of models, whose content can quickly go beyond the limits* of human understanding, it is impossible to distinguish architectural features within tightly intertwined classes and relationships. The general architecture of an application cannot be represented using fine granularity elements — it is necessary to introduce larger structuring concepts to bring out the macrostructure and facilitate model understanding.

---

*Miller G. March 1956, The Magical Number Seven, Plus or Minus Two: Some Limits on Our Capacity for Processing Information. The Psychological Review V. 63 (2).

Patterns describe small, recurring entities, reusable on a day to day basis, in order to resolve specific problems. These patterns do not express the general form of an application. This is why larger representations group patterns within frameworks, which are truly reusable infrastructures, dedicated to the implementation of targeted applications. These frameworks may be represented using the three structuring concepts proposed by UML: use cases, packages and collaborations. These concepts express the behavior as seen from the outside, the static structure, and the patterns respectively.

The macro-architecture is represented using categories (packages that are stereotyped) to focus on their architectural function. Categories encapsulate classes and objects that are logically coupled within larger elements. In this way, they make it possible to build hierarchical layers which segment an application into levels of increasing abstraction. Each level has well defined interfaces. A level with a given rank only depends on levels of lower rank. Category diagrams represent the general form of an application — in fact, they are class diagrams that only contain categories. The various categories are connected to each other by stereotyped dependency relationships used to represent imports between categories.

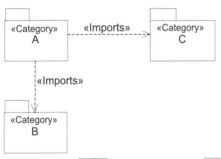

The following category diagram represents an example of macrostructure. The stereotype «framework» has been defined to specify sets of stable classes that are reusable across applications. The application is composed of four abstraction levels. The lowest level encapsulates the operating system's specifics. The second level offers communication and persistence services. The third level includes a control-command framework and two categories of business objects: the machine tools and the manufacturing instructions. The last level contains a framework of reusable graphical objects and a user interface category that contains proxy objects and business objects. The three lowest-level categories could most certainly be turned into a framework.

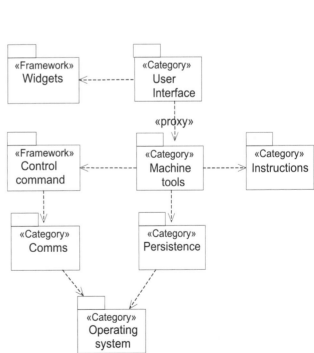

Example of a category diagram which represents the general structure of an application

173

The Role of Software, or the Cultural Clash

Based on the specific portion of hardware built by a corporation, a distinction may be made between the system architect and the software architect. The system architect is responsible for the overall system — the hardware, the software, and its use. The software architect only focuses on the software portion. This distinction is logical, but may be unfortunate when the system architect does not know the software well enough. A good architect must know both the application domain and the various techniques used in its implementation, including the software.

During the last fifteen years, many corporations have been confronted with a massive change in their activity, due to the introduction of computing into their products. Often, the architect's choice depends more on his knowledge of the domain than his knowledge of computing. This issue is particularly sensitive in companies that have built an electromechanical culture, and have then migrated towards electronics. They often perceive computing as an additional accessory, and not as the integrating link it should be.

The following diagrams describe the situation. At first, the hardware portion was predominant, and the business of the corporation was essentially expressed through that hardware.

Little by little, software elements were added to control, command, or regulate. These first programs were initially developed in assembly language and remained very close to the hardware.

This application topology is the result of a lack of a global vision. It translates into a total absence of integration between software components and by a duplication of effort that can sometimes go all the way up to hardware redundancy. In the automotive world, distinct traction control and anti-locking systems illustrate this phenomenon fairly well.

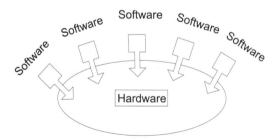

The cultural clash occurs when this tendency is reversed in favor of the software, sometimes due to economic necessity. It is acceptable to talk about software architecture from the moment that a reasoned, unifying, and integrating approach groups the software and the hardware under a co-operating umbrella.

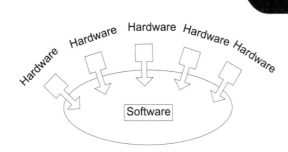

When the mutation is complete, the corporation know-how is transferred completely into the software. The specific hardware either no longer exists, or else it is integrated in the overall software architecture. Medical imaging companies have already lived through this mutation.

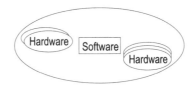

Software engineering is a catalyst. Software engineering has coiled up so tightly with hardware that it has stopped being secondary and has become primary. This is not always a painless transition, due to the profound cultural clash resulting from the mutation of the business. Corporate folks who traditionally had the business know-how are feeling dispossessed — they react unconsciously by stepping on the brakes with both feet, and trying to confine software to accessory tasks. This problem is difficult to manage, as it is often the case that the people who are slamming on the brakes are the ones with the decision-making power to impose their vision.

This conservative attitude results in an architectural imbalance in favor of hardware — software is then underused. An architect who does not have a software 'vision' builds systems in which the software is not well integrated with the hardware, instead of designing systems where the hardware is well integrated with the software. Besides habits, the problem is usually due to defective analysis. Solutions proposed are not sufficiently innovative, and are often restricted to adding software capabilities to existing systems.

This situation is not restricted to technical computing, and it also occurs in the world of information systems for corporations. Processes that are already in place within corporations are equivalent to the specific hardware elements described earlier; the corporation know-how is translated into these processes. The conservative approach waits — eagerly — for software to automate certain tasks, but only within processes that are already in place.

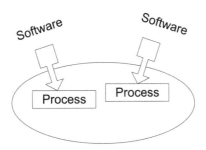

Limited software migration within the scope of processes already in place within the corporation

175

The break is accomplished when software engineering goes beyond the scope of one process and looks for integration between several processes — to exchange information, for example. This generally translates to the detection of inconsistencies, time wasting, and pointless activities. The resulting cultural clash is often more intense than in the technical world. The consequences of flattening processes within a company affect people and their jobs much more directly.

Iterative and Incremental Lifecycle

The iterative lifecycle relies on a very simple idea: when a system is too complex to be understood, designed or implemented in one shot (or all three of the above), it is better to implement it iteratively, by evolution. In nature, functionally complex systems are always evolutions of simpler* systems.

The implementation of this idea is not always as simple at it sounds in the world of software engineering: software does not spontaneously lend itself to evolution. On the contrary, software is often found to be very fragile when facing a change or a modification. This is directly tied to the internal form of programs and to the coupling that exists between the various constituents. The effect of a local modification may propagate throughout the application and, in the worst case, the flipping of a single bit is sufficient to completely trash an application that operated correctly beforehand.

Before discussing development based on evolution, it is important to focus on making software more stable and less prone to collapsing when facing evolution. Software engineering teaches us that in order to make a program more robust, it is necessary to segment the space of possible states, to reduce coupling using abstraction levels, and separate specification from implementation.

The object-oriented approach is built around concepts such as encapsulation and modularity that encourage a defensive programming style. By nature, object-oriented programs have a greater resilience in the face of change and surprise. From this perspective, the object-oriented approach favors the development of programs using an iterative approach. It should be clear that the object-oriented approach is not *necessary* to deploy an iterative development cycle: it does not result in or require any iterative developments, but simply facilitates them.

In summary, the object-oriented approach gives us a comfortable framework to develop in an evolutionary fashion, using an iterative approach.

Linear Lifecycle

The expression *linear lifecycle* refers to a software development approach that is based on a succession of steps, from the requirements list to the implementation.

---

*Gall, J. 1986, *Systematics: How Systems Really Work and How They Fail. 2nd ed. Ann Arbor, MI: The General*

176

The Tunnel Model

The tunnel[1] development model is an illustrative way to specify the absence of a development model. In projects that follow the tunnel approach, it is impossible to know what is going on. The development is in progress, the people are working — often very hard — but no reliable information is available either on the state of progress of the software, or on the quality of the elements already developed. This type of development model is only adapted to small efforts, with a very limited number of participants.

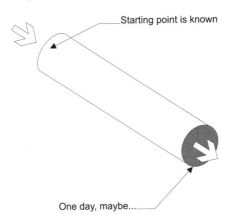

Starting point is known

One day, maybe...

The Waterfall Model

The waterfall[2] lifecycle, described by Royce in 1970 and widely used since, supports the general description of activities bound to the development of software. The waterfall lifecycle introduces software development as a series of phases that are linked into a linear execution, from requirements analysis to product delivery. Each phase corresponds to an activity. The waterfall development is carried out in time with the delivery of documents that are used as tangible support for the reviews that validate going from one phase to another.

In contrast to the tunnel model, the waterfall model has the huge advantage of providing concrete measurement points, in the form of documents. Hence, it increases the visibility of the progress status of the system being developed. The diagram below illustrates the increased visibility obtained by using the waterfall model.

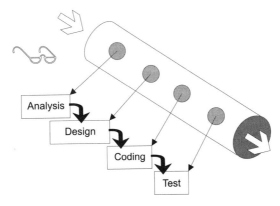

Analysis

Design

Coding

Test

[1] *Pierre D., private communication.*
[2] *Royce, W. W. August 1970, Managing the development of large software systems. Proceedings of IEEE WESCON.*

The waterfall cycle is often represented in the form of a letter V, signifying that the development of tests is performed synchronously with the development of software. This approach makes it possible to test what should be done as well as what has been done. The following diagram illustrates an example of a V model in which functional tests are specified during analysis, integration tests during design, and unit tests during the coding phase.

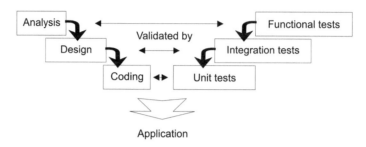

Example of a V development model — tests are developed in parallel with the software

Limits of the Waterfall Model

The waterfall model relies on a well-scoped sequence of phases. The project produces documents that are evaluated during reviews intended to validate the transition from one phase to another. However, the proof of the good (or bad) operation of the system is not available until later in the cycle — during the integration phase — when it is possible to evaluate the software in a concrete fashion. Before the integration phase, only documents have been produced.

However, simply because a document successfully goes through a stage of paper validation, this does not necessarily mean that the software it describes will give convincing results. In fact, the waterfall approach only gives satisfactory results when it is possible to link phases effectively without too many problems. It is necessary for the full set of requirements to be completely known and for the problem to be completely understood by the analysts. It is also necessary for the solution to be easily determined by the designers, and the coding should ideally reduce to automatic code generation, based on the design documents.

Alas, projects do not always present themselves under these ideal conditions. The reality is that the unknowns, and therefore the risks, can be significant within some development projects. These are frequently due to:

- Lack of knowledge of the requirements by the customer
- Misunderstanding of the requirements by the supplier
- Instability of requirements resulting from the above two items
- Technology choices
- Personnel moves

For all these reasons, information feedback between phases is necessary to incorporate upstream corrections, based on the discoveries found downstream. This feedback between phases affects the linear vision given by the waterfall lifecycle, as illustrated in the diagram on the next page.

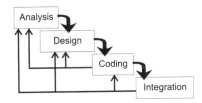

In fact, the feedback between phases only reflects reality. As long as these returns remain marginal and limited between adjacent phases, the waterfall model remains meaningful. If this is not the case, however, then the waterfall model is no longer applicable. It becomes more and more artificial to consider development as a linear chain. When a model no longer represents reality, it should be replaced, rather than trying to glue reality to the model*.

Characteristics of the Iterative Lifecycle

The iterative lifecycle is based on the evolution of measurable and executable prototypes, and therefore on the evaluation of concrete elements. This is in contrast to the waterfall lifecycle, which relies on the development of documents. Deliveries force the team to give concrete results on a regular basis, which avoids the syndrome of, "90% done, 90% still to do." The regular execution of iterations allows problems to be taken into account and changes to be incorporated in future iterations, rather than disturbing and interrupting the effort in progress.

During development, some prototypes are shown to the users and customers. The demonstration of a prototype presents numerous advantages:

- The user is confronted with concrete usage situations that allow him to better structure his requirements and to communicate them to the development team

- The user becomes a partner in the project — he takes part of the responsibilities in the new system and, therefore, accepts it more easily

- The development team is more strongly motivated, due to the proximity of the objective

- The integration of various software components is implemented progressively, during construction, without the *big bang* effect close to the delivery date

- Progress is measured by demonstrable programs, rather than by documents or estimates as in the case of the waterfall lifecycle — managers can therefore use objective elements and may evaluate progress and the state of advancement in a more reliable way

The iterative lifecycle requires more attention and involvement from the whole set of project actors. It must be presented and understood by everyone: clients, users, developers, support, quality assurance, testers, and documentation writers. Consequently, all must organize their work.

*Kuhn T. S. 1970, *The Structure of Scientific Revolutions*, 2nd edition. *The University of Chicago Press, Chicago.*

A Mini-Waterfall

In the iterative lifecycle, every iteration reproduces the waterfall lifecycle on a smaller scale. The objectives of an iteration are established based on the evaluation of previous iterations. Activities are linked thereafter in a mini-waterfall whose scope is defined by the iteration objectives.

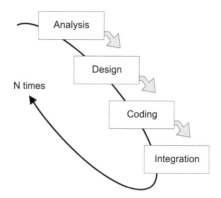

The iterative lifecycle revisits the various phases of the waterfall lifecycle several times.

Traditional phases are covered gradually, iteration after iteration. The nature of the activities conducted within phases does not vary according to whether the type of development is iterative or waterfall. The difference is to do with the distribution of these activities with respect to the phases.

Each iteration comprises the following activities:

- *Planning* the iteration based on the results of the risk study.

- *Analysis* studies the use cases and the scenarios to implement within the iteration. It updates the analysis model to take into account the new classes and associations discovered during the iteration analysis.

- *Design* focuses on the tactical choices necessary to implement the mechanisms allocated to the iteration. If necessary, modifications are applied to the architecture and the design model is updated. Test procedures are defined in parallel to the design of new mechanisms.

- *Coding and tests* whose code skeleton is automatically generated from the design model. The detail of the operations is implemented manually. The integration of the new code with existing code, issued from previous iterations, is implemented gradually during the construction. Unit and integration testing procedures are applied to the prototype.

- *Evaluation of the executable for delivery* — the examination of the test results is used as the basis for evaluating the prototype. Results are evaluated with respect to the criteria defined before launching the iteration.

- *Preparation of the delivery* — the prototype is frozen and the full set of elements that entered into its development is placed into controlled libraries. The various documents pertaining to the description and installation of the prototype are finalized.

In the following diagram, the internal activities overlap to show that, within an iteration, they do not need to end sharply and that the transition between two activities may be progressive. The iterative cycle hereby distinguishes itself from the waterfall cycle, which performs an amalgam between phases and activities.

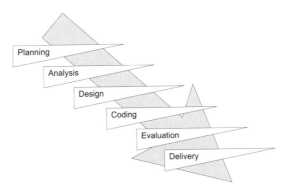

Misconceptions About the Iterative Lifecycle

The world is full of prejudices and false ideas. Software does not escape that tendency, and the iterative lifecycle in particular carries a fair number of myths, some of which are listed below.

The iterative lifecycle encourages tinkering.
The iterative lifecycle mostly encourages creativity, by allowing freedom to think, without rules that are over strict.

The iterative lifecycle causes problems.
The iterative lifecycle does not cause problems: it identifies problems early on that could have been detected too late with the waterfall lifecycle. The waterfall lifecycle seems predictable: analysis and design reviews follow each other within the expected time limits. Everything goes well until the integration phase, when a thousand contortions are performed to deliver something to the customer. The iterative lifecycle starts badly and ends well, in contrast to the waterfall lifecycle that starts well and ends badly.

The iterative and incremental lifecycle requires restarting n times before obtaining a good result.
The iterative lifecycle does not require the same program to be restarted over and over again, but rather enriches an existing program by adding new functionality. Confusion comes from the fact that certain parts must be refined, but that is because they had defects that were detected by an iteration. The sooner problems are detected within the development cycle, the less costly they are to correct.

The iterative lifecycle is an excuse to not plan and manage a project.
On the contrary, the iterative lifecycle requires more planning and sustained attention. Planning is not performed only at the beginning; it is spread out over the full development effort. It is easy to make plans, but harder to correct or change them.

The iterative lifecycle only applies to developers.
The iterative lifecycle supports the whole development effort. It provides more measuring points than the waterfall cycle, and these measurements are more reliable. They are connected to the reality of prototype evaluation, rather than to the abstract reading of documentation.

The iterative lifecycle encourages the endless addition of new requirements.
This is a false idea that is very important to get rid of. Iterative analysis is not about continually adding new requirements. It allows the major requirements to be focussed on first, and incorporates secondary requirements later. The iterative lifecycle avoids analysis paralysis.

Lifecycle and the Stability of Requirements

The iterative lifecycle is often criticized by software engineers who have suffered with projects in which the user requirements were not stable. These software engineers become more and more virulent as the iterative lifecycle appears to them as a perpetual invitation to overbid. They contrast it, in that sense, to the waterfall cycle, in which phases theoretically have a well-defined limit.

This fear of the iterative lifecycle is not justified. Regardless of the form of the lifecycle, the requirements explosion is always the consequence of a bad starting point. There are not so many new requirements; rather, there are mostly underestimated or ill-identified requirements. The diagram below represents the requirements explosion phenomenon. On one hand, requirements are not stable, and on the other hand, users always add new ones.

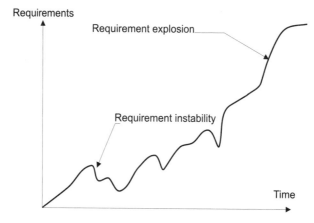

To address the issue of requirements explosion, it is imperative to help (or rather to force) the users to articulate their requirements in a stable and structured way. Use cases provide a very good technique to do so; their elaboration forces users to imagine how they expect to use the future system. This remains difficult in the absence of concrete elements to criticize, as is the case with the waterfall cycle, which only produces documents in its initial phases. The iterative lifecycle comes to the rescue of its users by providing them with prototypes to evaluate. Software engineers may, for their part, experiment with their implementation choices at full scale.

From the beginning of the development, an iterative cycle produces documented prototypes that may be evaluated objectively. It contrasts with the waterfall cycle that only provides documents. First of all, the software is brought forward, and then the sub-products are brought forward. For an equivalent quality of support, an iterative model produces more stable results than a linear model.

The waterfall cycle does not do enough to shake up its users. The documents it produces provide an illusion of progress, but there is nothing to show that their content really satisfies requirements. Design reviews go well, and the project follows the development plan until the integration phase. There, nothing works anymore — numerous repairs are performed quickly and without sufficient planning. This translates into delays and a product that is fragile and difficult to maintain.

The following graph represents the 'knowledge of requirements' curve in an iterative approach. All requirements are not necessarily known from the beginning; the knowledge of requirements may progress with the iterations.

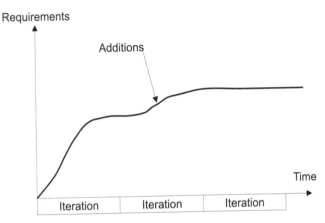

Adopting the iterative approach does not make all the problems magically disappear. The iterative approach is only a tool for better management of problems.

Documentation

Prototypes are the main tangible products issued from the iterative lifecycle. It is not necessary to provide documents used in support of end of phase validation reviews, as in the waterfall cycle. Nevertheless, it is possible to build a conventional documentation when it is required by contract. This documentation is composed of analysis and design documents — in the standardized format DoD 2167a, for example.

The documentation is not built in a single pass, but gradually, during each iteration. At the end of development, documents obtained in an iterative fashion cannot be distinguished in their appearance from those obtained conventionally. They give back a true image of the final state of the project with which they have evolved in a synchronous fashion.

The diagram below shows that the documentation obtained gradually during iterative development may very well be presented as if it was issued from conventional development. As far as the readers are concerned, the iterative aspect of the development is hidden once the project is complete.

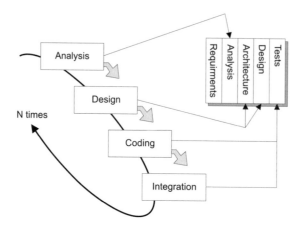

Iterative Lifecycle Variants

There are many variants of the iterative lifecycle, based on the project size, domain complexity, and the architectural choices. In its most simple variant, the form of the iterative lifecycle is like the letter b. The 'b' shape was identified by Birrel and Ould*, who used iteration solely for the maintenance phase.

The b shape is well adapted to applications of a modest size or to those that are defined and implemented within the realm of a proven architecture that will not generate surprises. The cycles are quick and the integration is continuous, so that the main advantage of the iterative form, in comparison to a waterfall cycle, is the suppression of the big bang effect associated with the integration phase at the end of the cycle.

The diagram below represents the way the activities are linked within an iterative, b-shaped lifecycle. The iterations are centered on the construction.

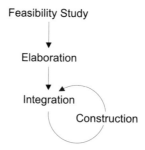

The b-shaped cycle focuses on iterations pertaining to construction. In the case where the requirements are not all known from the beginning, or in order to take into account architectural modifications, it is usual to add recovery loops on the feasibility study or on the elaboration. The main iteration flow stays focused on the construction by increments, while secondary flows focus on refining the analysis or the architecture, rather than questioning them.

*Birrel N. D. and Ould M. A. 1985, A Practical Handbook for Software Development. Cambridge University Press, Cambridge, U. K.

The diagram below illustrates how the b-shaped cycle has the tendency to open itself up when design or analysis modifications must be performed as a result of information obtained during construction.

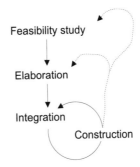

The b-shaped cycle is very well adapted to highly focused developments. Secondary branches become more common in situations where there are greater uncertainties concerning the requirements, where the architecture is only partially defined, or where the project is lead by multiple teams in parallel. In these cases, the cycle shape is closer to that of the letter O. The O-cycle is derived from the spiral cycle of Boehm[1]. It has been described by Philippe Kruchten[2] and is inspired from an open letter from Mike Devlin[3].

The diagram below represents an O-shaped lifecycle. The iteration comprises analysis and design.

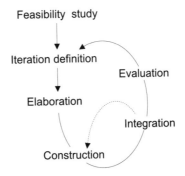

The iterative O-shaped lifecycle is well adapted to large projects

Regardless of the shape of the iterative lifecycle used, it is important to drive the analysis as far as possible without being paralyzed by the search for 'perfect' analysis. The iterative cycle, with its demand for regular deliveries of executable programs, encourages projects to get started and produce concrete results.

[1]*Boehm B. W. May 1988, A Spiral Model of Software Development and Enhancement. IEEE Computer.*
[2]*Kruchten P. December 1991, Un processus de développement de logiciel itératif et centré sur l'architecture. Proceedings of the 4th International Conference on Software Engineering, Toulouse, EC2, Paris.*
[3]*Mike Devlin is co-founder and chairman of the board at Rational Software Corporation.*

185

Iteration Evaluation

The evaluation criteria of an iteration must be defined before it is started. Each iteration is described by a detailed plan, which is itself included in a general development plan. An iteration is labeled with intermediate steps, such as critical code review meetings. They make it possible to measure progress and to sustain the morale of the team, which focuses on short-term objectives.

The following diagram represents an iteration of a small project bounded by two reviews: the first to start the iteration formally, after verifying the allocation of resources, and the second to validate the iteration and authorize the delivery of the corresponding prototype.

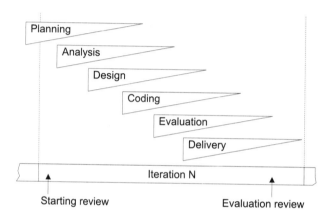

The number of reviews depends on the length of the iteration. For small iterations — between one and three months — there are two reviews:

- The initial review that fixes the iteration objectives, the evaluation criteria and the list of scenarios to implement

- The evaluation review that validates the iteration results with respect to the criteria defined before executing the iteration

For longer iterations, it is necessary to plan more intermediate reviews to approve the test plans, deploy quality assurance, etc.

The results of the iteration are evaluated with respect to criteria defined during iteration planning. They are a function of the performance and capacity, and measurements of quality. It is also necessary to take into account possible external changes, such as the emergence of new requirements or the discovery of competitors' plans, and to determine whether it is necessary to revive certain parts of the system and assign them to later iterations.

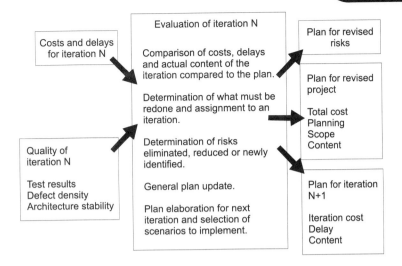

Evaluation is an essential step for gaining the full benefit from the iterative approach. It is necessary to keep in mind that it is sometimes better to revise criteria, than to modify the system. An iteration may reveal that a particular requirement is not as important as expected, that it is too difficult to implement or too expensive to satisfy. In this case, a comparative analysis between cost and benefit must be conducted.

Planning Iterations

There is no ready-made answer to the question of iteration planning. For a project that takes about 18 months, there will be between three and six iterations. Iterations all have approximately the same duration. The following diagram represents examples of the allocation of effort in an iterative development:

- Curve B corresponds to a first iteration that is too ambitious. Project B confronts the drawbacks of the waterfall cycle — integration fails, the development enters an unstable period and ends up going beyond the deadlines without reaching its objectives or satisfying its quality imperatives.

- Curve A corresponds to a project that has spent its first two iterations on setting up a stable architecture at the expense of small modifications, and has an iterative evolution with no surprises. The slight achievement overflow represents the fact that evolving requirements have been taken into account.

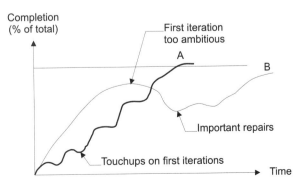

The first iteration is the most difficult to conduct, as it requires setting up the whole development environment, as well as the team. The project generally encounters numerous problems with tools, integration between tools, and relationships within the team.

Teams that apply an iterative approach are generally too optimistic. It is necessary to remain modest and not expect too much from the first iteration. If this does not happen, deadlines will not be satisfied, the number of iterations will eventually be reduced, and the benefits of the iterative approach will be limited.

The team usually loses a lot of time working with a new compiler, putting in place version and configuration management, non-regression tests, and the million other things that must be taken care of during the first iteration. For the second iteration, everything falls into place, everybody knows how to proceed with the tools, and the team can focus on the functionality.

Driving Object-Oriented Projects

Why talk about driving object-oriented projects? Do object-oriented projects require a particular form of support, and, conversely, isn't it possible to drive object-oriented projects just like classical projects? The answer is in fact both yes and no. The adoption of object-oriented technologies does not strictly imply reviewing the development procedures already in place. Nevertheless, it should be clear that the only way to take real advantage of the object-oriented approach is to establish a completely object-oriented solution.

This evolution of a corporation's practices requires the complete adherence of all the parties involved. There is no single development process that is adapted to all projects, application domains, and corporation cultures. The development process described in this chapter is defined in a general way. Each project must adapt it to match its own constraints.

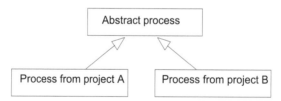

A software program development process may be observed according to two complementary views:

- The support view, focusing on the financial, strategic, commercial, and human aspects
- The technical view, focusing on engineering, quality control, and the modeling method

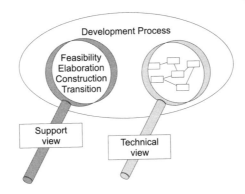

The Support View

The support view represents the software development as a progression of four phases:

- **Feasibility study** — comprises the market study, the specification of the final product, and the definition of the scope of the project
- **Elaboration** — corresponds to the specification of the product features, the planning of activities, the determination of resources, and the design and validation of the software architecture
- **Construction** — groups the product implementation, and the adaptation of the vision, architecture, and plans until product delivery
- **Transition** — gathers the large-scale manufacture, training, deployment in the user community, and technical support and maintenance

A development cycle corresponds to a complete pass across all four phases, and supplies a new generation of the software:

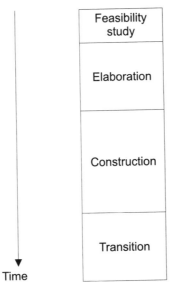

Progress is measured in terms of advancement within the phases. Some software requires many cycles to take into account improvements, new functionality requests, etc. The transition phase of one generation will often overlap with the feasibility study phase of the next generation. In the case of large projects, cycles may be conducted in parallel, and several subsystems developed independently.

The Technical View

The technical view focuses on the deployment and the organization of all the technical activities that lead to the delivery of a generation of the software.

The development cycle is perceived as a sequence of iterations through which the software evolves incrementally. Each iteration results in the delivery of an executable program. The content of an iteration must be useful for the development or for the user. It is determined by choosing a subset of the application's functionality within the use cases. Some deliveries are purely internal, others are used to demonstrate the state of advancement, and others still are sent to the user's site. From iteration to iteration, the program grows in functionality and in quality, until a particular iteration produces the first generation of the software.

Traditional activities are not performed sequentially as they are in a waterfall lifecycle. They are distributed — interspersed — among the various iterations. Every iteration includes planning, analysis, design, implementation, and test and integration activities, of which the numbers vary based on the location of the iteration within the cycle.

The executable program resulting from an iteration is called a prototype. A prototype is a concrete step in the construction of a piece of software. It is a tangible — measurable — proof of the progress made. A prototype is a subset of the application, useful to formulate requirements or validate technology choices. Prototypes enrich themselves during each iteration.

The first prototype often has the single goal of proving the concept of an application. It is developed as quickly as possible without taking into account the usual quality criteria. This type of prototype, usually disposable, is called a mockup. The penultimate iterations produce beta versions that are generally sent for testing to a selected set of participating users.

The version delivered to the user is a prototype like any other, issued from the series of prototypes. It can be seen as the last prototype of the current generation, and the first prototype of the next generation of the system.

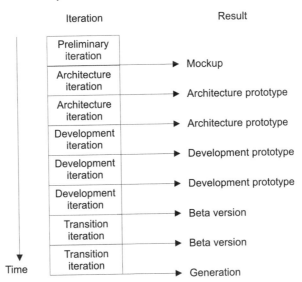

Integration of the two Views

The support and technical views are synchronized at the end of each phase, on the tangible result of an iteration. The feasibility study may invoke a prototype to determine the viability of a project or its technical feasibility. The evaluation of the executable prototype, delivered by the development team, plays a role in the decision of whether or not to continue a project, which is made at the end of the feasibility study.

The elaboration phase has the main objective of defining an architecture that allows the development and evolution of the application. It is difficult to find a good architecture the first time, hence the interest in implementing a certain number of architectural prototypes. Elaboration ends with the definition of an architectural basis, validated by an architectural prototype.

The construction phase progresses in time with the development of prototypes, whose main objective is to measure the progress and guarantee a stable design. The design phase ends with the delivery of preliminary versions (beta versions), which are deployed at user sites, to be tested as if they are fully active within the deployment environment.

The transition phase *starts* with the installation of beta versions on site. It progresses in time with the delivery of new versions to correct defects detected by users. Depending on the organizations involved, the transition phase stops either when the software has reached its production version, or as soon as the next generation is delivered to the users.

It is necessary in each project to determine the number of iterations that exist in each phase. The following diagram illustrates a typical example.

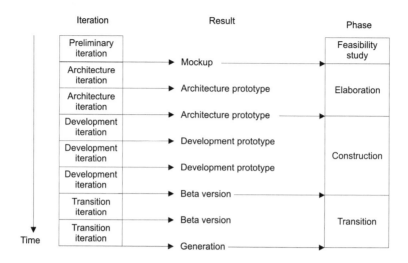

Risk Management in Iterative Development

Any human activity has its share of risks, and software development is no exception to this rule. Software projects must manage risks to minimize their consequences.

Risk analysis consists of evaluating the project, technology, and resources, in order to determine and understand the nature and the origin of the risks. Each risk is briefly described, and the relationships between risks are underlined. The evaluation of risks determines the extent to which the consequences of a risk are acceptable.

Risks must be described in writing, although not necessarily in a very formal way. All the project members must know them. The risks must be quantified, otherwise it is impossible to know whether or not they have been eliminated. Ambiguous expressions like, "The system should be fast," or, "Its memory capacity will be sufficient," should never be left anywhere in the documentation.

There are four main categories of risks:

- *Commercial risks*: Can the competition capture the market before this product is ready? Is it better to come out with a minimal delivery to cover the ground?

- *Financial risks*: Does the corporation have sufficient financial capacity to take the project to completion?

- *Technical risks*: Is the technology foundation solid and proven?

- *Development risks*: Is the team sufficiently experienced? Has it mastered the technologies being deployed?

But, first and foremost, it is important to understand that the biggest risk is not knowing where the risks are. It is also necessary to be careful about having too many teams, and to look out for project leaders who measure their prestige based on the number of developers reporting to them. There is no use in having too many developers — it is important to have good ones, and to know how to get them working in teams. Risk management groups all the activities required to build a risk reduction plan, and then takes this plan to completion.

For each identified risk, the risk reduction plan describes:

- The importance with respect to the client
- The importance with respect to the development
- The action undertaken and its economic implications
- The means of verifying that the risk has been suppressed or reduced, and in what proportion
- The scenarios affected by the risk
- The allocation to a prototype

Risk reduction drives the iterations within the iterative lifecycle. The goal of each iteration is to eliminate part of the overall risk associated with the development of an application. The following diagram illustrates the risk reduction mechanism through iterations. Each iteration is built as a small project that has the objective of reducing some of the risks identified during the project definition.

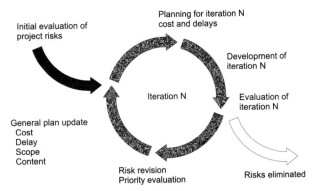

When following the waterfall approach, the risk reduction is insignificant until the beginning of the integration phase. The biggest technical risks are tied to the architecture: performance (speed, capacity, precision), integrity of system interfaces, and system quality (adaptability, portability). These elements cannot be evaluated before the development and integration of a significant amount of code. The diagram below represents the way the curve of decreasing risk appears in a waterfall development. The risk remains high during most of the lifecycle.

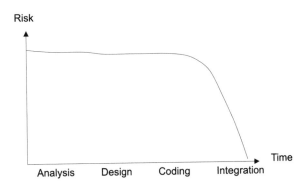

The iterative approach identifies and treats risks sooner in the lifecycle, so that risks may be significantly reduced as early as the elaboration phase. From iteration to iteration, executable prototypes validate the project choices in a concrete and measurable way, and the level of confidence in the application increases. The following diagram shows the fast decrease of risk in an iterative development.

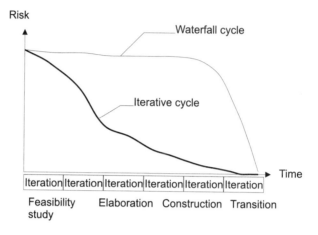

Each iteration is based on the construction of a reduced number of scenarios, which begin with the most important risks and determine the classes and categories to build within the iteration. The categories form a workspace that is well adapted to the developers.

The testers use the same scenarios to build the test plan and the test procedures for the iteration. At the end of the iteration, the evaluation determines the risks that have been eliminated or reduced. The prototyping plan is revised as a result.

The diagram below shows an example of allocating risks between two consecutive prototypes. It illustrates the effect of one iteration in terms of risk reduction.

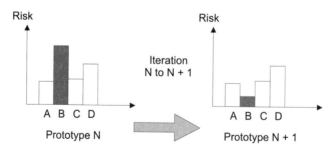

The objective of iteration is to reduce the risk associated with a part of the application. The partitioning of application functionality is implemented according to the use cases.

Each prototype explores a portion of the application in order to reduce a portion of the risks. The next diagram represents different kinds of prototypes:

- A UI prototype, limited to the user interface, is often a mockup built to help the user articulate the expression of his needs

- A middleware prototype (an intermediate software layer) tests and validates a reusable software layer which was most probably purchased rather than programmed

- A technology prototype verifies, for example, the quality of the encapsulations of the hardware, or the features of the operating systems

- A functional prototype traverses the whole architecture — it guarantees that the full set of strategic choices is meaningful

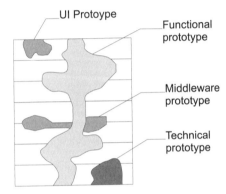

Prototypes are bound once the architecture has been validated. Each one of these prototypes corresponds to one or more use cases. The coverage of requirements increases with each iteration.

The diagram below shows how four prototypes have been deployed to develop an application. The first two prototypes had to be modified to correct the architecture or to take into account new requirements.

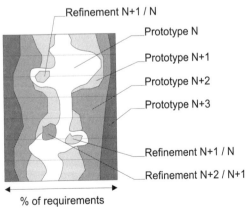

Representation of requirement coverage, prototype by prototype

Iterative development is not about redoing the same work. Although it is normal to redo certain parts*, the general tendency is to preserve the result of the previous iterations. The first prototype is disposable, so the upper limit for modifications is positioned at 100%. If the system reuses existing code, the quantity of modifications must be lower. Once the architecture is established and stabilized, modifications remain small and well localized. The sum of the modifications for the following iterations should remain below 25%. The percentages indicated in the following figure pertain to the whole system, not only to the most recent iteration.

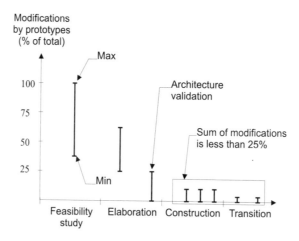

Example of evolution of modifications with the execution of prototypes

Each phase of the development contributes to reducing risks, but from different angles:

- *The feasibility study* tries to delimit the project risks by building a prototype to validate the concepts.

- *The elaboration* starts by reducing the risks of misunderstanding between users and developers. It develops a shared vision of the project scope and explores scenarios with the users and domain experts. Secondly, it validates architectural choices. The architecture is then refined by the following iterations, as required.

- *The construction* is the phase where the incremental construction of the application takes place. The gradual integration of the various components removes the risk of 'misfits' encountered in the phases dedicated specifically to integration at the end of waterfall development.

- *The transition*: the risks associated with the transfer of software ownership are reduced by the incremental deployment of the application during the transition phase, and the risks are reduced even further when the users have been involved in earlier phases.

- *The post-deployment*: corrective or evolutionary maintenance is performed in the same scope of development as construction, through iteration and implementation of new prototypes. Maintenance is a normal evolution of the product, similar to the construction. The risks of degradation of the architecture and the design are found to be greatly reduced.

Brooks, F. P. 1975, The Mythical Man-Month. Addison-Wesley, New York.

Examples of Risks

All projects encounter risks, which vary in number according to the size and complexity of a project, how novel the project is, and the qualifications of the development team. Some risks are common, such as those that come from naïve participants, awkward relationships between client and supplier, instability of requirements, etc.

The main causes of project failure are often related to...

- The geopolitical situation far more than to technical aspects, particularly in the case of very large projects
- Absence of a real vision of the architecture, so that the software cannot be integrated
- Bad relationships within the development team
- Absence of motivation resulting from delivery dates that are too distant or ill defined
- Lack of vision on the project, resulting both from developers that do not understand the full picture, and from the support team lacking precise information and navigating in the fog
- A lack of qualified personnel, sufficiently skilled in the various technologies involved
- An excess of people on the project, mainly in large organizations, where the prestige of the project leader is proportional to the number of developers who report to him
- Lack of involvement on the part of the user during the development process
- Lack of support of the whole organization, caused by the lack of belief of a given group, such as quality assurance or intermediate support
- Underestimation of the training and teaching budgets necessary for any project that requires new technologies
- Underestimation of delays, often resulting in the bypassing of intermediate iterations, and as a result, returning to the waterfall cycle
- Underestimation of the project size, resulting from, among other factors, unstable requirements
- The technology selected, sometimes simply according to fashion
- The dependency with respect to other developments performed in parallel

The table below summarizes the ten main recurring risks, and the actions that should be undertaken to reduce them.

Risk	Impact	Resolution
Integration too complex	Quality	Focus on the architecture
Absence of convergence	Cost Deadline	Middleware Iterative development
Demotivation	Quality Cost Deadline	Iterative development Short-term objectives Planing of requirements
Poorly adapted development environment	Cost Deadline	Investment in integrated tools
Users not favorable	Cost Deadline	Early user involvement Prototype demonstration
Technology too complex	Cost Deadline	Focus on the architecture Purchase of external skills
Manual activities too heavy	Cost	Automation using integrated tools
Inadequate reusable components purchased	Deadline	Prototypes
Insufficient performance	Quality	Independence with respect to the hardware
Excessive bureaucracy	Deadline	Focus on the prototypes, not the documentation
Poorly adapted functions	Quality	Prototypes

Each organization or project should define a list of criteria to determine what functionality must be developed in a given iteration. The table below gives examples of criteria that are sufficiently general to be applicable to all projects.

Criterion	Description
Interest	Degree of importance of the elements for the users
Cost of manufacture	Estimate of the difficulty of development of the element by the developers
Novelty	Is the element completely new?
Necessary interfaces	What does the element need?
Politics	How will the presence or the absence of the element be perceived?
Technology	Have the developers mastered the necessary technologies?
Planning	Does the element affect the delivery of prototypes?
Springboard	Does the element facilitate the development of other elements?

Assembling the Development Team

There are some very gifted software engineers, but regardless of the quality of the individuals, there is a time when the size of the task to perform is such that individual effort is no longer sufficient. It is then important to work as a team to coordinate efforts, and to look for collective performance based on the average capability of each person.

The choice of the people that make up a development team strongly determines the execution of the project. Beyond the technical aspects, the success of a project depends largely on human factors. A good development process makes it possible to extract the best out of a development team in a predictable and controlled way. The members of an efficient team must complement one another, but also be very conscious of their individual roles in the development process. It is up to the project leader to put together this team of people and to maintain the morale of the troops throughout the development.

In general, a software development process may be decomposed into three sub-processes:

- The software development itself
- The logistics that address the requirements of software development
- The interface with the rest of the world that isolates the development team from external perturbations

Ivar Jacobson has shown how corporate processes may be modeled with use cases. The diagram below uses this formalism to illustrate the three development sub-processes:

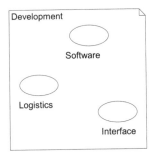

The development team is organized with respect to the use cases described earlier. The different people involved are represented by actors who interact with the three identified use cases.

Software Development

Software development is driven by the following three actors:

- *Architect* — defines the general form of the software and is responsible for the definition and organization of the iterations
- *Abstractionists* — identify the objects and mechanisms that will make it possible to satisfy the user's requirements
- *Developers* — master technologies and implement the abstractions identified by the abstractionists

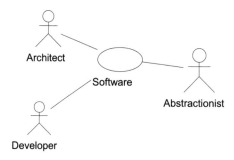

Logistics

The logistics interact with the following actors:

- *Project leader* — puts the team together, manages the budget and the people, and coordinates the various activities

- *Analyst* — a domain expert in charge of understanding the user requirements

- *Integrator* — assembles elements produced by the developers, and does so during the development in the case of an object-oriented project

- *Quality assurance expert* — evaluates all the elements produced by the development and drives the system tests

- *Documentation writer* — puts together the documentation targeted at the user

- *System administrator* — manages and maintains the hardware used by the project

- *Tool builder* — builds and adapts the software tools that make up the development environment

- *Library manager* — ensures the archiving and saving of all the development artifacts and their rules of production

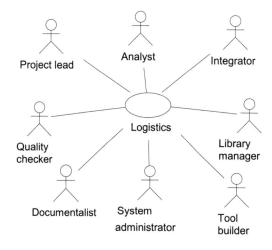

Interface

The interface interacts with the following actors:

- *Project leader* — ensures the interface between the development team and the rest of the world

- *Product manager* — oversees a product line; he coordinates the marketing, training, and technical support activities

- *Accountant* — controls the budget allocation and its sensible usage

- *User/client* — participates in prototype reviews

- *Technical support* — resolves or works around problems encountered by the users

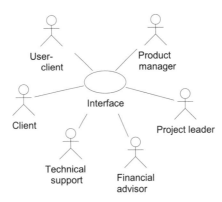

The same person may play all the roles described above. In small organizations, it is not unusual for the project leader also to play the roles of architect and analyst. Similarly, developers and abstractionists are often the same people.

Detailed Description of Phases

This section describes the various phases of the development cycle, based on the general viewpoint adopted by project supervisors. The phases bring a vision that is structured across time, and which is well adapted to the management of the contractual and financial aspects.

Feasibility Study

The feasibility study is not generally conducted by software engineers, but rather by market study and competition analysis specialists. They try to determine whether or not the construction of a new system or a major improvement of an existing system is justified economically and presents an advantage to the corporation.

The first operation consists of getting a general picture of a product in order better to identify and extract elements for evaluation. This picture may be summarized by the following formula*:

> **Picture = What + For whom + How much**

Morel E., private communication.

The various constituents are defined as follows:

 *What* expresses the overall features of the product

 *For whom* determines the target population

 *How much* estimates the price that the product buyers will agree to pay

The general project vision is expressed in a preliminary list of requirements, in a list of 'non-objectives' specifying what the project is not, and in a financial leaflet that provides the first economic elements — in terms of estimating the return on investments, for example.

These different elements may be difficult to appreciate in the absence of tangible measurements. This is why the feasibility study is often based on a preliminary domain analysis (10 to 20% of the classes). When there are a large number of unknowns concerning the feasibility of a project, it is usual to implement a conceptual prototype. Its main goal is to extract concrete elements in order to evaluate the risks tied to the expected functionality, the performance required, the size or the complexity of the topic, or the adoption of new technologies. From there, the decision is made as to whether or not to validate the concept of the product.

This type of prototype does not respect the usual rules of development. It looks above all for a rapid result, without insisting on reliability or speed of execution. It is first and foremost a disposable mockup, whose code will not play any role in the final application. There is benefit in implementing this mockup, in a rapid prototyping environment, such as Smalltalk. Some applications are developed completely, based on the first prototype; to do this, rapid application development (RAD) tools are used. This approach works well for projects with a modest size, but is not well adapted to larger systems.

By this stage, the team is composed of a small number of people gathered around the system or software architect. They will continue to participate in the project development. Later, once the product vision is defined and the risks that are inherent to the project have been generally identified, the feasibility study tries to estimate the project cost and the return on investments.

Estimate of Costs and Return on Investment

Determining the return on investment is rather difficult to do in the case of software, due to the essentially intangible character of software programs and the lack of objective elements that make it possible to appreciate their cost.

It is important to search for a balance between the reliability of a cost estimate and the time necessary to produce that estimate. The first estimate will never be right, and the exact cost is known only at the end of the development, so it is judicious to decompose the estimate into several steps in order to refine it incrementally.

The diagram on the next page represents qualitatively the accuracy of the cost estimate of a software development effort.

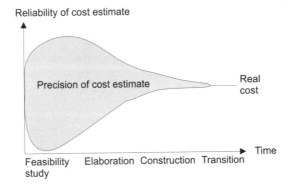

Reliability of cost estimate

Precision of cost estimate

Real cost

Time

Feasibility study   Elaboration   Construction   Transition

Because of the low visibility level with respect to real requirements and the nature of the risks during the feasibility study, it is not very realistic to attempt to estimate the resources necessary for the project precisely.

Nevertheless, the client frequently requests that estimation. It is then necessary to explain to him that the only way to have a good idea of the cost is to finance the first slice until the end of the elaboration phase. Based on the information obtained, the client will be able to decide whether the development effort should be continued before absorbing the increasing costs of the construction phase.

The object-oriented approach itself is not sufficient to evaluate the final cost any faster than traditional approaches. However, when associated with an iterative approach, it makes it possible to guarantee a more precise determination of that cost based on the elaboration phase.

For a small project, the feasibility study is often limited to a requirements list. For a medium sized project, of about a year, the feasibility study — including prototype building — takes approximately a month. For large projects, the prototype becomes a small project in its own right (often referred to as a demonstrator) that also goes through the different phases listed above.

Elaboration Phase

The elaboration phase starts with requirements analysis and domain modeling. It has the objective of defining the architecture choices, reducing the project risks, and finally, defining a complete plan that quantifies the means to put in place the tasks necessary to complete the development.

A restricted team driven by the software architect conducts the elaboration phase. This team is composed of a small group of developers and one or two domain experts or users. It is often useful to add a representative of the test and quality assurance team, a tool builder (responsible for putting together the development environment) and a documentation writer.

Activities Conducted during the Elaboration Phase

Requirements analysis is based mainly on the study of use cases, but without excluding all the other techniques that could help users articulate and formulate their desires.

Use cases are expressed according to the user's terminology, and in a textual form that is far from the formalism of software engineering. The transition to a more 'computerized' representation is effected by analysts. They transform use cases into collaborations between objects within the application domain. A collaboration remains understandable by the users, although it is necessary to explain to them that these objects represent an entity from their world, and that they collaborate to build the functions represented by the use cases.

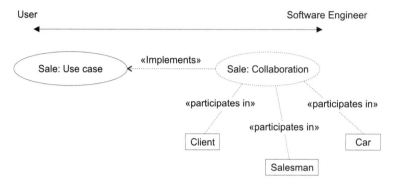

Example of implementation of a use case using a collaboration between three objects

As the detailed study of use cases progresses, the domain model is updated to take into account the new classes identified in the collaborations that support the various interactions. A second analysis pass, after the domain analysis, searches for abstractions and more general scenarios. It extracts the abstract classes that will be used as specifications to write generic mechanisms.

The elaboration phase gives birth to the following products:

- Description of the system's behavior (expressed as use cases), the system's context, the actors, the scenarios, and a model of the domain classes (80% of the classes)
- A plausible architecture, a document describing the architecture, and a revision of the product vision and the risk description
- A complete development plan for the whole project
- A detailed plan for the iterations, the evaluation criteria, the requirements list for each iteration, and the results of quality assurance
- Perhaps a preliminary user manual

For medium sized projects, there are typically:

- A few tens of use cases
- About a hundred main scenarios
- A few hundred secondary scenarios
- Between 50 and 100 classes in the domain

Pratical Tips about the Elaboration Phase

Any application should be able to obtain a sufficient number of reusable components to form between 10 and 30% of its implementation. Frameworks and ready-made solutions make it possible to predict a reuse level of about 60% for a given type of application in a given domain.

The duration of the elaboration phase can be very variable. It depends a lot on the types of applications and the infrastructure choices. For a one-year project, the phase will last for between two and four months.

In all cases, it is absolutely necessary to avoid analysis paralysis — to waste too much time looking for a perfect analysis. It is better to jump in the water (to go from design to architecture) when approximately 80% of the main scenarios have been examined.

During the study of scenarios, one should not go too far into the details, at the risk of sinking too soon into design and consequently lacking abstraction in the solutions that are put in place.

Construction Phase

This phase has the objective of developing a software product ready for transition into the user community. In b-shaped iterative cycles, the construction phase corresponds to the effective deployment of iterations. Some iterations are purely internal, while others are visible from outside the project. Each iteration results in the delivery of an executable prototype.

A prototype forces the end of an iteration and obliges the development team to produce a concrete, measurable result. A prototype is stable and self-sufficient. It is an executable version of the system, driven as a small project and paired with all the products necessary to make use of it.

The implementation of an iteration groups the following activities:

- Identification of the scenarios to complete or reuse in the iteration based on the study of the risks and the result of the previous iteration
- Assignment of precise tasks to the development team to complete the iteration
- Definition of the evaluation criteria for each iteration, control points, and deadlines
- Compilation of user and deployment documentation (delivery and installation notes)

The delivery flow is characterized by:

- A steady increase in the functionality, measured by the number of new scenarios taken into account by each iteration
- A greater depth, measured by the degree of implementation of the domain model and the mechanisms
- A greater stability, measured by the reduction of changes made to models
- The continuous adjustment of the project plan
- The evaluation of each iteration, with the results of tests and quality assurance

205

With the transition to the construction phase, the team is complete. In large projects, several increments may be developed in parallel. In general, 80% of the team works on developing a delivery, while the remaining 20% explore the new risks and prepare the development of the subsequent deliveries.

For a modest project, the construction phase lasts for between 2 and 3 months; for a typical project, it takes between 6 and 9 months on average. These days, the total duration of a typical object-oriented project is one year, with a small team of 5 or 6 developers. In the case of very large projects, every subsystem behaves like a project and then has its own iterations within an O-shaped iterative lifecycle.

Managing Change

In an iterative lifecycle, development artifacts mature with the iterations. The project is therefore confronted with the difficult problem of managing consistency, due to the numerous versions of each element. This consistency management may be assured successfully and at a reasonable cost, only if version and configuration management tools are completely integrated in the development process.

In modest projects, managing change pertains mainly to the software and the documentation. In more ambitious projects, it is necessary to become preoccupied with the management of change within the full development environment, from the software versions, such as compilers or operating systems, to the hardware itself. In extreme cases — some military or aerospace projects, for example — the whole development environment (software and hardware) is preserved without any modification during the full system lifecycle!

The main types of changes made to software are the following:

- The adjustment of a class or a collaboration with a class
- The changing of the implementation or the operations of a class
- The changing of the representation of a class
- The reorganization of the structure of classes
- The changing of the interface of a class

The first three are frequent in the construction phase. In the final iterations, changes in the latter two areas indicate that the design is not stable. With time, changes must be more and more localized (due to encapsulation). Changes made to the architecture are the most costly in terms of modifications.

Practical Tips about the Construction Phase

Each delivery gives the developer a certain satisfaction, associated with the concept of work well done. Deliveries constitute 'sub-objectives', which are relatively easy to reach within a reasonable time limit, based on the total duration of the project. This keeps the morale of the team positive, even if the prototyping approach forces the tackling of problems from the beginning. Each delivery also provides an aspect of objective control concerning the state of advancement of the project. Each prototype is a step forward in the satisfaction of requirements.

Finally, every delivery gives confidence back to the users who receive, through the prototype examination, a tangible result from which they can benefit directly in their everyday jobs. This supposes that no delivery is imposed on the users without having the scope of the prototype defined with them first. It is absolutely necessary for the users to understand that a prototype is a step and not a complete system, otherwise frustration can grow.

In case of urgency, it is better to postpone certain functionality than to miss a rendez-vous with the users. Any demonstrable prototype, even an incomplete one, increases the users' level of confidence, and consequently that of the client. It is, however, important to pay attention to the **snowdrift effect**, which is characterized by an accumulation of unsatisfied functionality that is always postponed to the next delivery. It is important to try to satisfy the delivery plan, as the natural tendency is to delay deliveries due to delays in implementation of functionality. By delaying the ends of the iterations, and consequently the prototype delivery, there is a danger of returning to the waterfall model and losing the benefits of the iterative approach.

Categories make it possible to allocate responsibilities within the team. Small changes are taken into account inside a class or a category. Important changes require the coordination of the people responsible for each category, and shifting the decision up to the level of the architect. It is not unusual to have to throw away code during the construction phase, although if changes within the construction deliveries accumulate to more than 25%, the architecture should be considered unstable. The architecture's instability is generally a sign of an elaboration phase that has not been given enough room for experimentation.

Transition Phase

The transition phase consists of the transfer of the software to its user community. This phase has variable complexity, based on the type of application. It includes manufacturing, shipping, installation, training, technical support and maintenance. The development team is reduced to a small group of developers and testers, who are supported part-time by the architect, who safeguards the overall consistency, and by someone responsible for updating the documentation. The control is passed to the technical support personnel, as well as to the marketing and sales people.

During the transition phase, the initial development is almost complete. All the artifacts have reached a sufficient maturity to be distributed widely to the two categories of recipients: users and project managers.

The main products targeted to users include:

- Executable programs, in beta and then final versions
- User manuals
- Deployment and installation documentation

The main products targeted to the project managers include:

- Revised models
- Evaluation criteria for each iteration
- Description of deliveries

Results of quality assurance

The results of the post-mortem analysis of project performance

The duration of the transition phase is very variable, and depends on the size and complexity of the project, and on the end of phase criteria.

Practical Tips about the Transition Phase

The difficulty of the transition phase is inversely proportional to the quality of the product and to the degree of user preparation. All the products require training. The product installation phase should not be neglected; a difficult installation may discourage users and reduce their confidence in the product.

For a replacement system, a lot of effort is necessary to put the new system into place in parallel with the existing system.

In some organizations, the maintenance team and the development teams are clearly dissociated. This situation is not optimal, as it results in too sharp a break in the development cycle. It induces a period of uncertainty in the division of responsibilities between the initial developers and the maintenance developers. It is more judicious to ensure overlap between the two teams by including people from technical support and maintenance right from the beginning of the project, and by assigning several part-time initial developers to the maintenance team.

Post-Deployment Development Cycles

For most software products, deployment indicates the beginning of a maintenance and improvement period. This period is characterized by the repetition of the development cycle, going from the feasibility study to the transition. The relative importance of each of these activities may change. As a result, there is normally no impact on the architecture within a simple maintenance cycle, as long as the modifications remain well encapsulated.

Each iteration starts by establishing a repair priority list and by designating development teams. It ends with the delivery of a system version that corrects the defects identified earlier. The transition includes updating user documentation and describing corrected defects.

Practical Tips about Post-Deployment

It is absolutely necessary to correct defects in order to satisfy valid user expectations. It is also necessary to try to satisfy their new requirements, eventually using new technologies — a piece of software that does not evolve soon becomes obsolete. To do so, it is important to focus on maintaining architectural integrity, otherwise entropy takes over — little by little, the cost of change increases, the design becomes more complex and maintenance becomes more and more difficult.

In all cases, regardless of the actions taken, the resolve displayed and the development and maintenance teams' good will, there will come a time when the software program will need to be thrown away and replaced by another. Software programs carry within themselves the reasons for their death, as well as their hopes for life...

Distribution of Activities in Relation to Phases

The importance of each development activity varies from one phase to another. There is no one to one correspondence between the phases of the support view and the classical phases of a waterfall cycle. Activities such as analysis and design are spread across many phases of the support view. The activities are distributed among the cycles, and their beginnings and endings do not correspond to the limits of the phases of the support view.

In fact, the important point is the density of activity implemented in each phase of the support view.

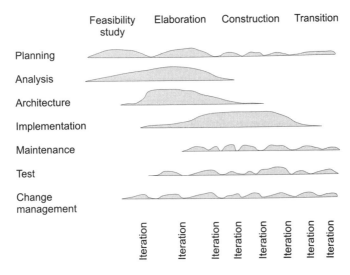

The diagram above shows that:

- Planning is performed throughout the phases

- Analysis is mainly restricted to the elaboration phase, although part of the analysis may already be performed in the feasibility study phase, and part may be refined during the construction phase

- The main part of the architecture is determined within the elaboration phase

- The implementation (which also includes unit tests) starts with the elaboration phase (for the architectural elements) and peaks within the construction phase

- Maintenance starts as soon as the first version of the software has been defined, generally in the elaboration phase

- Tests and quality measurements are spread across all the phases and apply to all the prototypes

- Change management (versions and configurations) records the history of the whole project

- There is no integration phase per se — the integration is continuous, the software is integrated by construction

Relative Effort by Activity

The following diagram illustrates a typical situation, representing an average object-oriented development project of about a year, with a small team of about five people. It describes a typical distribution of the effort with respect to the activities.

In order to spread the effort according to the various activities, the following postulates are established:

- Planning includes project piloting activities, development plans, measurement of the progress, and control of the project resources

- Analysis includes the development of object and user models, the specification of the project vision, and the description of evaluation criteria

- Architecture includes the implementation of software foundations, the general design of the whole application, and the building of common mechanisms

- Implementation groups all the detailed design activities, coding, and unit testing

- Maintenance includes the modifications made to the software once it is placed under version and configuration management

- Tests and evaluation include the activities that are necessary to prove that the software has reached the objectives established and measured by the criteria

- Change management archives the consecutive states of all the development artifacts

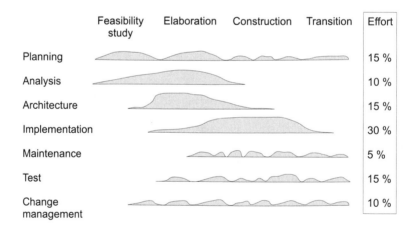

Relative Effort by Phase

The effort is spread differently with respect to the phases, and this distribution may vary widely, depending on the project characteristics. The diagram below illustrates a typical situation, representing a project of average size. The end of the transition phase is indicated by general product availability.

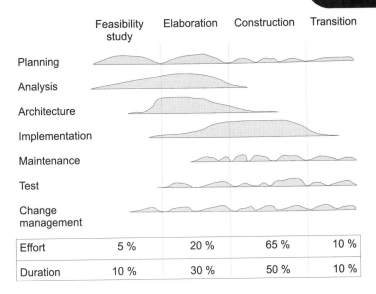

	Feasibility study	Elaboration	Construction	Transition
Effort	5 %	20 %	65 %	10 %
Duration	10 %	30 %	50 %	10 %

For a maintenance cycle, the feasibility study and elaboration phases are considerably reduced. The use of code generation or application building tools may strongly reduce the construction phase; in some cases, it may be shorter than the feasibility study and elaboration phases combined.

Phase Review Points and Decision Points

The end of each phase is marked by a planned decision that corresponds to important decisions concerning how business matters are handled. During the feasibility study phase, the economic viability and the technical feasibility of the product are established. At the end of the feasibility study, a decision must be made as to whether or not elaboration resources should be allocated. At the end of the elaboration phase, a similar decision is reached. Based on the architectural work already implemented and the evaluation of outstanding risks, it may or may not be necessary to allocate resources to complete the product.

The construction is complete when the product is sufficiently mature for users to start operating it in a reliable way. The transition terminates when the product is replaced by a new generation, either when the product reaches the end of its lifecycle, or when it stops being used.

Parallel to the progress of each phase, the end of each iteration sheds light on the technical progress and project maturity. The evaluation of iterations determines the extent of the progress and triggers, at the same time, a re-evaluation of the global cost of planning and project contents.

The table below summarizes the objectives and decision metrics with respect to the iterations of the technical view and the phases of the support view.

Iteration	Phase	Objective	Decision metrics
Preliminary	Feasibility study	Understand the problem	Allocate resources for the elaboration
Architectural	Elaboration	Understand the solution	Allocate resources for the construction
Development	Construction	Implement the solution	Product delivery
Transition	Transition	Broadcast the solution	Receipt by the customer

The final table summarizes the steps, metrics, and results of each phase.

Phase	Step	Metrics	Result
Feasibility study	Marketing plan Executable prototype	Prototype completion Risk	Effective project launch
Elaboration	Use case model Domain model Architecture	Stability Simplicity	80% of the scenarios 80% of the domain model
Construction	Prototypes Deployment plan	Delivery completion Defects percentage Defects density Stability	Complete product Complete documentation Acceptable quality
Transition	Beta versions	Users satisfaction Defects percentage Defects density Stability	Final version

Summary

This chapter has discussed in some depth the broad concepts that lie behind good organization and support of an object-oriented project. A formalized development process is not defined by UML, but it is crucial in order to manage the complexity inherent in modern applications. The process outlined in this chapter is use case driven, centered on architecture and iterative. Using an object-oriented approach in analysis and design is vital to the success of this development process. The important points covered in this chapter are:

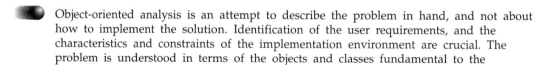

- Object-oriented analysis is an attempt to describe the problem in hand, and not about how to implement the solution. Identification of the user requirements, and the characteristics and constraints of the implementation environment are crucial. The problem is understood in terms of the objects and classes fundamental to the application, and the relationships between them.

- Object-oriented design is the expression of a solution to the problem identified in the analysis stage. Design is the determination of the software architecture — the data structures that will be used as a framework for the whole project.

- Use cases facilitate the implementation of software that satisfies the users' real requirements by bringing the focus back to the users' perspective. A use case can then be associated with a collaboration that describes objects, the relationships between them and how they interact. The implementation of the use cases using this object oriented approach marks the transition between analysis and design.

- Software architecture describes the overall form of the application, resulting from the design. It may be considered from different perspectives, and expressed as graphical projections of these different views using the notation of the UML diagrams.

- Implementation of the design is carried out using an iterative approach. This presents the advantages of identification of problems and risks at an early stage, measurable progress points and the continuing involvement of the user. It facilitates the incremental addition of requirements and functionality, with testing at every stage.

- The development process can be represented by five phases. Firstly, the feasibility study examines whether a project is financially justified. Secondly, during the elaboration phase the overall architecture of the project is determined. The development of the model, ready for the users, is then carried out during the construction phase. The transition marks the delivery of the application to the users for beta testing etc. Finally, the post-deployment phase is the stage when maintenance is performed.

The final chapter of this book comprises a realistic case study of an access control application for a building. The case study brings together all the concepts covered so far, employing the techniques of use cases and the UML notation in the analysis and design of the project.

Chapter

5

Case Study: An Access Control Application

This final chapter presents an example of using UML for the object-oriented modeling of a building access control system. The case study described in this chapter was inspired by an application deployed at the Advanced School of Applied Sciences for Engineers, in Mulhouse (ESSAIM, or *Ecole Supérieure des Sciences Appliquées pour l'Ingénieur, Mulhouse*).

The model used in this example is available on the Wrox Press web site (http://www.wrox.com), in a form readable by both Rational Rose and Microsoft Visual Modeler.

The Process

The case study begins with the analysis of requirements. The system requirements are established based on information obtained during an interview with the future supervisor of the system. These requirements are expressed as use cases, in language that the eventual users of the system would understand.

Studying use cases requires the selection of a level of granularity for the information modeled in the interactions; this often raises a problem that is sometimes expressed with the question, "Is it a small rock, or a big stone?" In the following example, use cases are intentionally considered as 'coarse' granularity elements.

Each use case encompasses many scenarios that are first described in a general way, from the actor's point of view, and then represented in a more 'computerized' way, so that the evaluation of the application's implementation costs can be as accurate as possible.

The static structure — expressed by the relationships between the objects that participate in the collaborations — is first implemented in the draft class diagrams, and then finalized in a class diagram that represents all the key domain abstractions and their relationships.

Finally, domain analysis studies the features of the hardware to be used, and facilitates the creation of a strategy for implementing the use cases. The case study ends with a description of the software and hardware architecture required for the application.

Requirements Analysis

The space to be protected is divided over 4 floors of a building with a total area of about 5000m². The building itself is divided into five areas: two research wings, an experimental wing, an administration wing, and a central section containing classrooms and the two lecture halls.

The site accommodates about 500 people every day: mostly students, but also teachers, researchers, administrative and technical staff, as well as numerous visitors.

After various items of property started disappearing, it was decided to restrict access to some of the rooms using doors with automatic locking. The opening of each door is controlled by a badge reader, located nearby.

The badges that allow the opening of these doors are only given to the people that need to access restricted areas in order to perform their duties. Access rights are distributed among groups of people and groups of doors. Each person and each door must always belong to a group, even if they are the only member of that group.

A group of doors may consist of doors distributed throughout the building, but from the point of view of controlling access, only the concept of a *group* of doors is important — routes and movement are not controlled. However, a given door cannot be a member of more than one group of doors. A given person, on the other hand, may be a member of several groups, so that his access rights correspond to the combined rights of each of the groups he belongs to.

Access rights are established by describing, for each group of people, the various groups of doors that are accessible and under what time constraints. These rights are contained in a yearly calendar that describes the schedule a week at a time. Given that there will be a small variation of rights over time, a calendar may be initialized using 'typical' weeks that describe a fixed configuration of rights. The supervisor may create as many 'typical' weeks as he wishes, and any subsequent changes made will automatically be propagated to all the calendars using them. On the other hand, changes made to a calendar directly — to take vacation days into consideration, for example — are not affected by the modification of a 'typical' week.

The following table represents a typical week. The grayed areas correspond to time periods during which access is not authorized.

		Monday	Tuesday	Wednesday	Thursday	Friday	Saturday	Sunday
00	01							
01	02							
...	...							
06	07							
07	08							
08	09							
...	...							
21	22							
22	23							
23	24							

The access control system must operate as autonomously as possible, although a supervisor is responsible for the initial configuration and the updating of the various pieces of information that define the groups of people and doors. A guard has a control screen, and is informed of any unsuccessful entry attempts. Alarms are transmitted with a slight delay: information update on the control screen is performed every minute.

The user interface must help the users to specify their requests correctly. Legal requests and input values are systematically read from lists that define the domain of correct values.

Description of Use Cases

Use cases are described in text and with interaction diagrams. At this stage of the modeling process, these interactions represent the main events that occur in the application domain. Later, during the design phase, these events are translated into the messages that trigger operations.

Use Case Identification

Analysis starts with the search for the actors (categories of users) of the access control system. An actor represents a role played by someone or something interacting with the system. It is not always easy to determine the boundaries of the system, but by definition, the actors are always outside it.

The actors are 'recruited' from the system's users and the people responsible for its configuration and maintenance. They are divided up into the following categories:

- Supervisor
- Guard
- Badge holder

Here are their corresponding graphical representations:

Supervisor

Badge holder

Guard

Actors interact with the system. The goal of the use case study is to determine what each actor expects from the system. The determination of requirements is based on the description of the interaction between the actor and the system. This approach has the advantage of forcing each user to define precisely what they expect from the system.

A use case is an abstraction of one aspect of the system's behavior. Actors instantiate a use case each time they use the system. After interviews with the users, it emerges that the functional requirements of the actors may be broken down as follows:

Actor	Use case
Supervisor	System configuration
Guard	System monitoring
User	Access request validation

The following diagram represents the use cases for the access control system. To operate the system, both the supervisor and the guard must first undergo some identification procedure, so the identification is factored out of both the configuration and monitoring use cases. This is shown by the identification use case and the stereotype «uses». Badge holders interact with the system to request access, via their badges, to predefined areas:

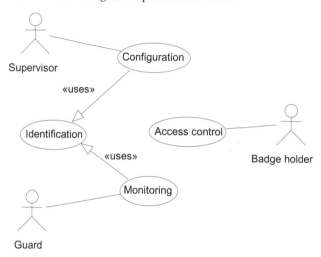

Configuration

This section describes, in words and with the graphical representation of sequence diagrams, the main scenarios associated with the configuration use case. The text takes the form of a list of simple, one-line instructions that may be converted easily to the corresponding sequence diagram. Together, the whole set of scenarios provides the functionality of the use case. The configuration use case is triggered by the supervisor:

Identification

The diagram below shows a particular scenario, in which:
The supervisor connects to the system and enters his password.
The system verifies the supervisor's identity.
The system authorizes the connection.

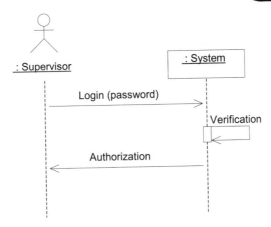

Successful identification is a precondition for the each of the remaining scenarios in this section, which may then be performed repeatedly following the identification.

Modification of Doors

The supervisor requests the list of doors.
The system displays the list of doors.
The supervisor chooses a door.
The system displays the following information:
    State (activated/deactivated)
    Duration of the period for which the door is open
    Privacy (only one person is allowed inside at a time)
The supervisor modifies the existing information.
The system records the information.

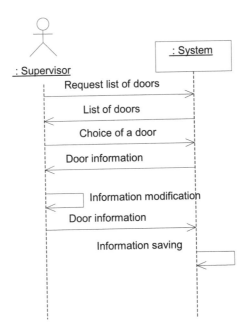

Modification of Groups of Doors

The supervisor requests the list of groups of doors.
The system displays all the groups of doors that are currently registered.
The supervisor chooses a group of doors.
The system displays the following information:
   Group name
   List of doors in the group
   List of access granted to groups of people
The supervisor modifies the existing information.
The system records the information.

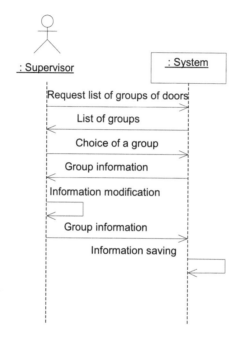

Modification of a Person

The supervisor requests the list of people.
The system displays all the people who are currently registered.
The supervisor chooses a person.
The system displays the following information about the person:
   Surname
   First name
   Phone number
   Badge number
   List of groups to which the person belongs
The supervisor modifies the existing information.
The system records the information.

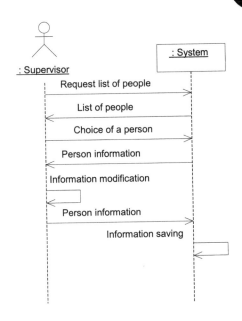

Modification of Groups of People

The supervisor requests the list of groups of people.
The system displays all the groups of people that are currently registered.
The supervisor chooses a group of people.
The system displays the following information:

Name of the group
List of group members
List of authorized access for the group

The supervisor modifies the existing information.
The system records the information.

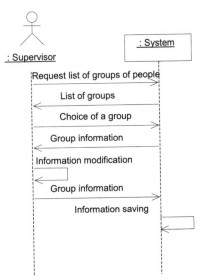

Searching for a Person Based on a Badge

The supervisor enters the badge identification number.
The system retrieves the person who has been supplied with the badge.
The system displays the following information about the person:
    Surname
    First name
    Phone number
    Badge number
    List of groups to which the person belongs

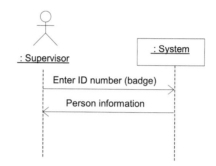

Searching for Doors Accessible by a Given Person

The supervisor requests the list of people.
The system displays all the people who are currently registered.
The supervisor chooses a person.
The system displays the list of accessible doors.
The supervisor chooses a door.
The system displays the following information:
    State (activated/deactivated)
    Duration of the period for which the door is open
    Privacy (only one person is allowed inside at a time)
    Access granted to the person

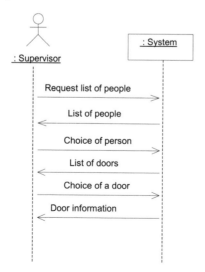

Searching for Groups that Contain a Given Person

The supervisor requests the list of people.
The system displays all the people who are currently registered.
The supervisor chooses a person.
The system displays the list of groups containing that person.

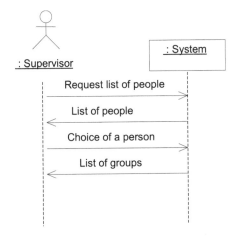

Searching for People that Belong to a Given Group

The supervisor requests the list of groups of people.
The system displays all the groups that are currently registered.
The supervisor chooses a group.
The system displays the list of people contained within the group.

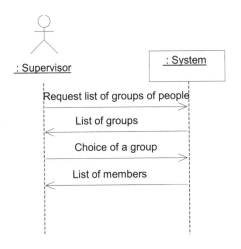

Modification of a Group of People to Access a Group of Doors

The supervisor requests the list of groups of people.
The system displays all the groups that are currently registered.
The supervisor chooses a group.
The system displays the following information:
    Name of the group
    List of people who belong to the group
    List of groups of doors and access entitlements
The supervisor chooses a group of doors from this list.
The system displays the following information:
    A default open calendar for the current week
    The authorized time periods within the calendar
The supervisor modifies the existing information.
The system records the information.

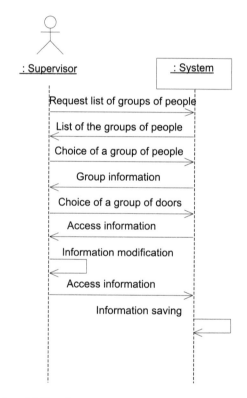

Modification of a Typical Week

The supervisor requests the list of typical weeks.
The system displays all the weeks that are currently registered.
The supervisor chooses a typical week.
The system displays the following information:
    The name of the week
    A textual description of the week
    The days of the week split into time slices
    The access validity or invalidity, hour by hour

The supervisor modifies the existing information.
The system records the information.

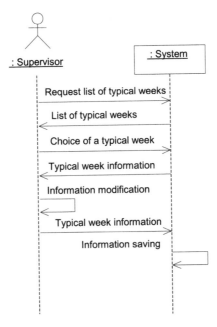

Display Access Rights for a Given Person for a Given Door

The supervisor requests the lists of all doors and all people.
The system displays all the doors and people that are currently registered.
The supervisor chooses a door and a person.
The system displays the following information:

A default open calendar for the current week
The authorized time periods within the calendar

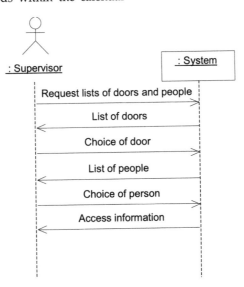

Monitoring

This section is a list of all the main scenarios identified to be part of the monitoring process use case, again using words and sequence diagrams. Monitoring is triggered by the guard:

Identification

The guard connects to the system and enters his password.
The system verifies the guard's identity and authorizes the connection.

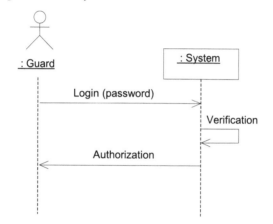

Event Report

The guard specifies the beginning and ending dates for the desired range.
For as long as the guard requires:
    The system displays the events in chronological order.
    The guard selects display filters.

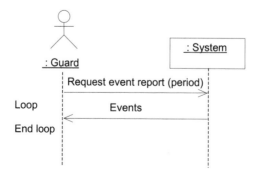

Event Purging

The guard specifies the beginning and ending dates of the period to be purged.
The system destroys the events that correspond to the period.

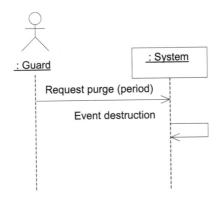

Alarm Report

The guard specifies the refresh delay (1 to 60 minutes).
Until the guard stops the detection:
    The system regularly displays any new alarms

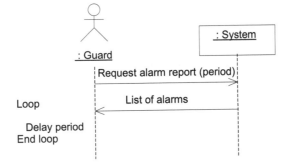

Manual Opening of Doors

The guard requests the list of doors.
The system displays the list of doors.
The guard chooses a door.
The system displays the following information:
    State (activated/deactivated)
    Privacy value (is there a person in the room?)
    The last ten events
The guard forces the door to open.
The system records the event.

[sequence diagram overleaf]

227

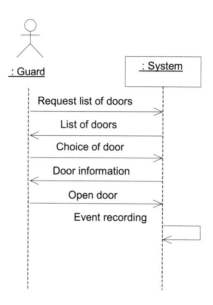

Fire

The guard triggers the fire alarm.
The system opens all the doors.

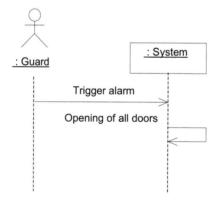

Access Control

This section lists the scenarios of the access control use case, which is triggered by the badge holder:

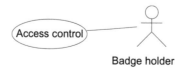

In fact, there is really only one thing that the badge holders are concerned about — gaining access.

Authorization to Pass Through

The person presents their badge.
The system determines whether access is authorized.
If the access is authorized:
    The system initiates the opening of the door

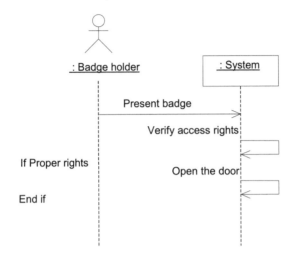

Summary Table of Use Cases and Main Scenarios

Use Case	Main Scenarios
Configuration	Identification
Configuration	Modification of doors
Configuration	Modification of groups of doors
Configuration	Modification of people
Configuration	Modification of groups of people
Configuration	Searching for a person based on a badge
Configuration	Searching for doors accessible to a given person
Configuration	Searching for groups that contain a given person
Configuration	Searching for people that belong to a given group
Configuration	Access modification for a group of people to access a group of doors
Configuration	Modification of a typical week
Configuration	Display access rights for a given person for a given door
Monitoring	Identification
Monitoring	Event report

Use Case	Main Scenarios
Monitoring	Event purging
Monitoring	Alarm report
Monitoring	Manual opening of doors
Monitoring	Fire
Access control	Entry authorization

Consistency Control

The following constraints must be taken into account by the system:

- Each badge reader is identified by a unique address
- A badge reader may only be associated with a single door
- A door must always be in a group, and only one group
- A person must always be at least one group
- A badge can only be allocated to a single person
- The time periods defined within a given day must not overlap

Description of Collaborations

The functionality described by the use cases is implemented by collaborations of domain objects.

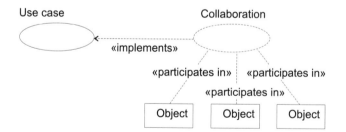

The implementation of collaborations brings in additional objects, which, although they do not belong to the application domain, are necessary for its operation. These objects generally implement the interface between the system and the user, or between the system and another system. Including these objects in the diagrams allows the proper evaluation of the cost of the application; for example, it is common to plan for a day of work to implement one screen and its associated mechanisms.

The particular nature of the classes of these objects may be suggested using the following stereotypes:

- «controller» — for direction and organization
- «device» — to manipulate hardware
- «interface» — to translate information at the boundary between two systems
- «proxy» — to manipulate objects that are outside the system
- «view» — to represent domain objects

Very often, there are three elements in the final model that correspond to just one element in the real world. This distinction can apply particularly in the case of people, where one could have:

- Actors, which represent the users of a system as seen from the outside
- Objects — class instances stemming from the domain analysis that encapsulate information describing each user (these are also known as business objects)
- Interface objects that allow manipulation, reading, and modification of the information contained within objects of the previous category

The following diagram represents this trilogy of object types. The user is shown as an actor, representing a person who is interacting with the system. Information concerning that person is stored by a substitute, and displayed by an object of an interface class, whose name is prefixed by the letter I. A given interface object may successively display the characteristics of various people.

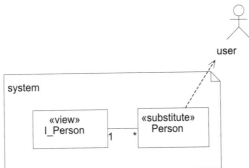

In an information system, the trustworthy information is contained *within* the system. When considering an automated system, the truth is always *outside* it. Whichever case is being dealt with, it is important to keep the three objects correctly synchronized.

Actors do not play a direct part in collaborations. Interaction with users is expressed via messages sent and received by interface objects. The level of granularity of these objects is variable, but as a general rule, the mechanisms represented as collaborating objects should avoid going too far into the details of the user interface implementation. There are two reasons for this: first, it facilitates the reading of the diagrams and second, it emphasizes the reusability of business objects. The interface is always very dependent on a given application, but business objects may often be reused by other applications.

The rest of this section examines all the main scenarios described in the last section, and shows how they correspond to collaboration diagrams. A class diagram for each scenario is then drafted, and finally, when all the scenarios have been taken into account, the draft class diagrams are analyzed to obtain a design for the application. The first three scenarios are discussed in some detail, and the remaining ones are simply displayed in terms of the appropriate collaboration diagram and corresponding draft class diagram.

Configuration

Supervisor Identification

At first, the notion of an actor may be preserved, in order to represent the user interface in a compact way.

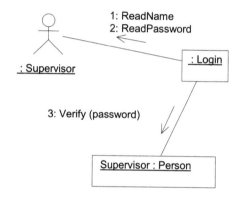

Alternatively, it is equally possible to create a **SystemLimit** class and to use it instead of the actor.

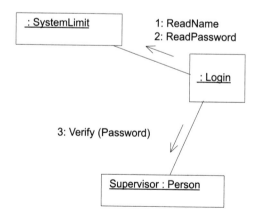

Next, the main design of the user interface may be described in terms of classes that represent it. Here, the goal is not to describe precisely the graphical classes of the interface, but rather to capture the general form of the interactions and, therefore, to quantify the workload associated with the interface development. The implementation of the interface itself is the responsibility of special tools for generating and building graphical interfaces automatically.

Each domain object is represented by an interface object of the same name, prefixed with the letter **F**. In the following diagram, the object of class **Login** is accessible via a graphical object **F_Login**

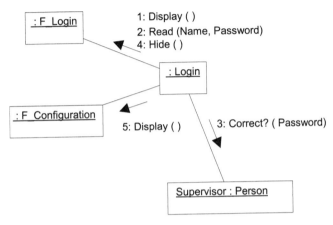

The above collaboration diagram shows objects of four different classes: two domain object classes, and two user interface classes.

The preliminary class diagram shown below is compatible with the above collaboration. Given the early stage of the modeling process, multiplicity information has not yet been fully determined.

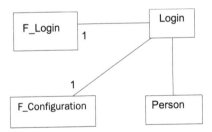

The behavior of objects of the **Login** class may be described in a general way using the state machine on the next page. The state machine shows, among other things, that the system does not specify the precise cause of a connection rejection.

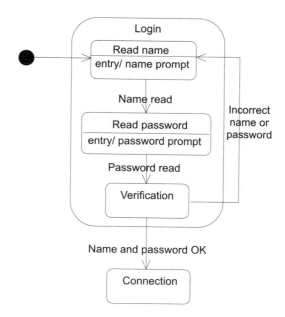

The user interface classes both derive from a **Window** class that defines the functions **Display()** and **Hide()**.

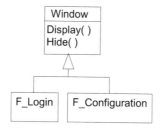

Modification of Doors

The supervisor may modify doors individually or in groups. The following two scenarios correspond to these options.

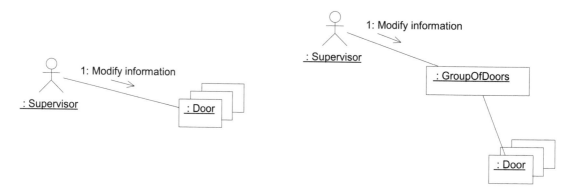

Scenario for a Single Door

The following collaboration diagram represents the modification of the information for one door.

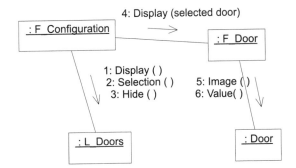

The functions **Image()** and **Value()** symbolize the writing and reading of the state of the **Door** object to and from the user interface. The **Image()** function makes it possible for an interface object to extract information contained within a domain object in order to show it to the users. Conversely, the **Value()** function allows an interface object to transfer information *from* a user *to* a domain object. These functions are inherited from the abstract class **DomainObject**.

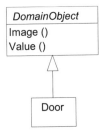

The preliminary class diagram below corresponds to the preceding collaboration diagram.

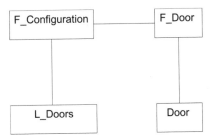

Classes whose names are prefixed with the letter **L** represent user interface classes that specialize in displaying lists of items. These classes have a **Selection()** function, so that the element selected by the user from the list may be retrieved. **List** display classes are also **Windows**, as shown in the class diagram on the next page.

Scenario for a Group of Doors

The operation for modifying doors may also be implemented more generally, to affect a number of doors gathered together into a 'group' of doors.

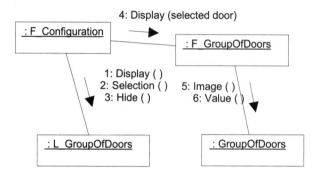

The earlier class diagram can now be extended to take into account the manipulation of groups of doors.

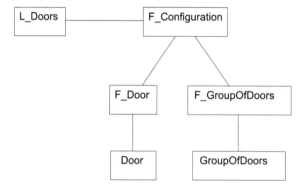

Modification of People

This section and those to come simply display the collaboration and class diagrams that correspond to each of the main scenarios detailed earlier. Firstly, the remaining scenarios of the configuration use case are displayed diagrammatically, and these are followed by diagrams for the scenarios of the monitoring and access control use cases respectively.

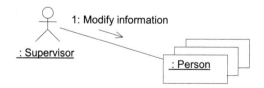

Collaboration Diagram

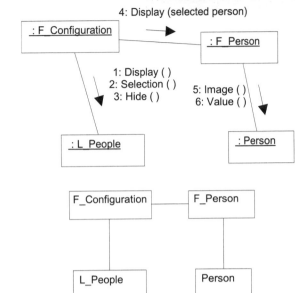

4: Display (selected person)

: F_Configuration

: F_Person

1: Display ( )
2: Selection ( )
3: Hide ( )

5: Image ( )
6: Value ( )

: L_People

: Person

Draft Class Diagram

F_Configuration

F_Person

L_People

Person

Modification of Groups of People

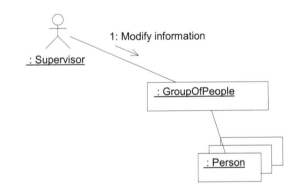

: Supervisor

1: Modify information

: GroupOfPeople

: Person

Collaboration Diagram

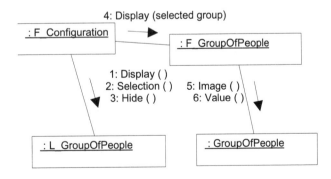

4: Display (selected group)

: F_Configuration

: F_GroupOfPeople

1: Display ( )
2: Selection ( )
3: Hide ( )

5: Image ( )
6: Value ( )

: L_GroupOfPeople

: GroupOfPeople

237

Draft Class Diagram

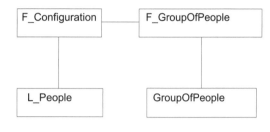

Searching for a Person Based on a Badge

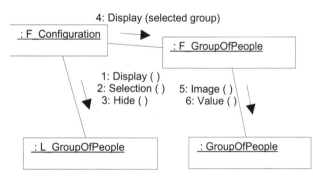

Collaboration Diagram

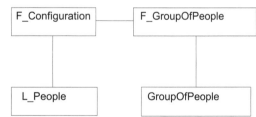

Draft Class Diagram

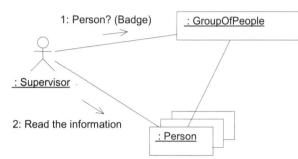

Searching for Doors Accessible to a Given Person

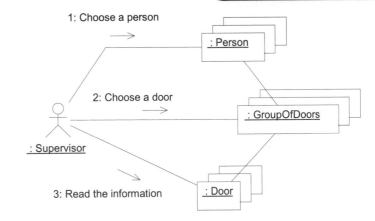

1: Choose a person

: Person

2: Choose a door

: GroupOfDoors

: Supervisor

3: Read the information

: Door

Collaboration Diagram

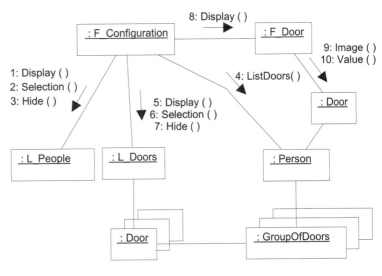

8: Display ( )

: F_Configuration

: F_Door

9: Image ( )
10: Value ( )

1: Display ( )
2: Selection ( )
3: Hide ( )

4: ListDoors( )

: Door

5: Display ( )
6: Selection ( )
7: Hide ( )

: L_People

: L_Doors

: Person

: Door

: GroupOfDoors

Draft Class Diagram

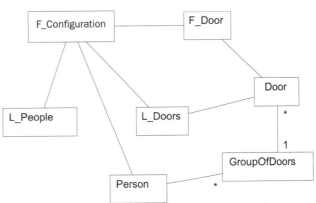

F_Configuration

F_Door

Door

L_People

L_Doors

*

1

Person

GroupOfDoors

*

Searching for Groups that Contain a Given Person

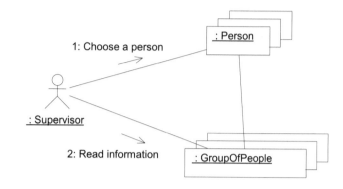

Collaboration Diagram

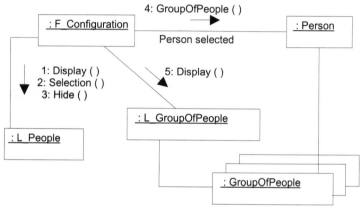

Draft Class Diagram

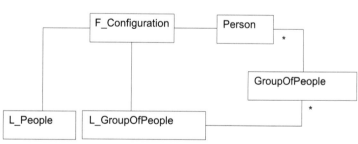

Searching for People that Belong to a Given Group

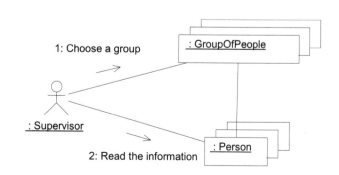

Collaboration Diagram

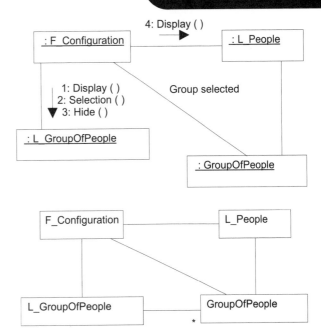

Draft Class Diagram

Modification of a Group of People to Access a Group of Doors

This is the most complicated of all the interaction diagrams, and bears further explanation. The diagram below shows how the supervisor modifies the access rights for a specific group of people. Firstly, he selects the group from the groups defined in the system (1). The information about the people in the group is retrieved, including the groups of doors to which they have access (2). The supervisor can then select the appropriate group of doors and modify the access rights for the group of people (3). Finally, he modifies the associated calendar.

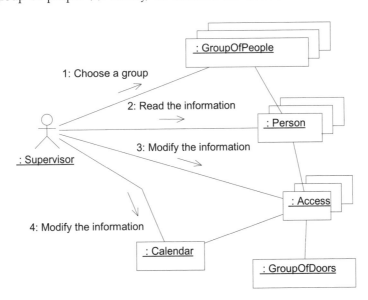

Collaboration Diagram

The following collaboration diagram shows the interactions involved when the supervisor wants to modify the information for a group of people. The diagram is the graphical representation of the list of procedures given below:

1. The system displays a list of the registered groups of people.
2. One of the groups is selected.
3. The group selection list is hidden.
4. The group of people selected is displayed.
5. The access rights of the group are retrieved.
6. The access rights window is displayed.
7. The access rights information is retrieved to populate the window.
8. The modified access rights are updated.
9. The associate calendar window is displayed.
10. The calendar information is retrieved to populate the window.
11. The modified calendar info is updated.

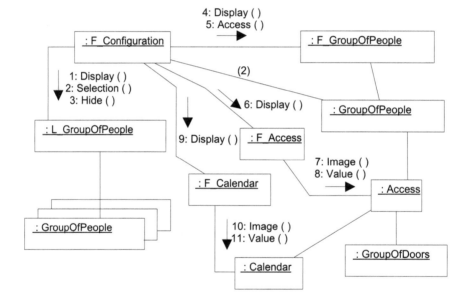

Draft Class Diagram

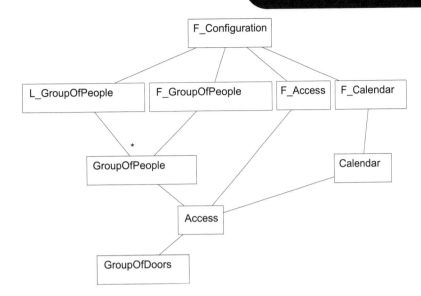

Modification of a Typical Week

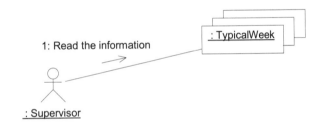

Collaboration Diagram

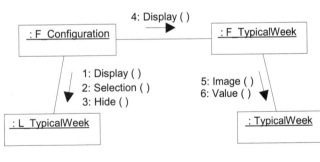

Draft Class Diagram

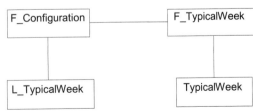

243

Searching Access Rights of one Person for a Given Door

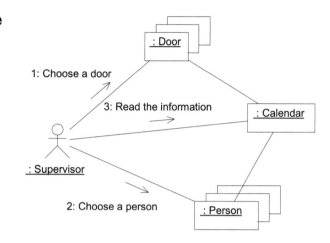

Collaboration Diagram

Links annotated with a number between parentheses were created by the operation triggered by the message with the corresponding number.

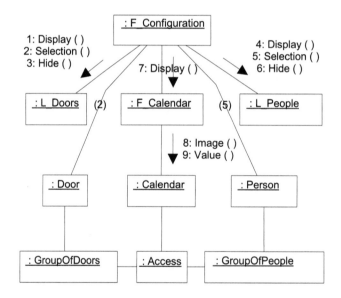

Draft Class Diagram

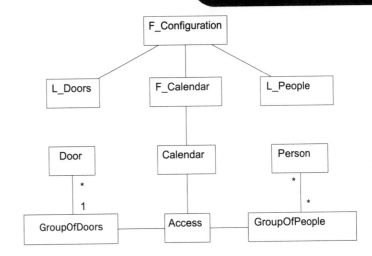

Monitoring

Guard Identification

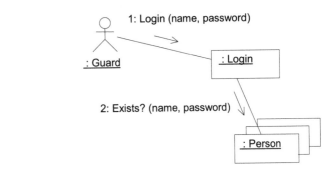

Collaboration Diagram

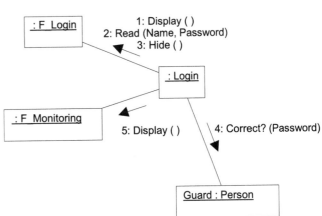

Draft Class Diagram

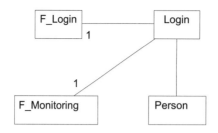

Reporting Events

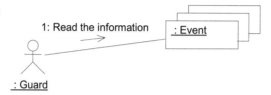

Collaboration Diagram

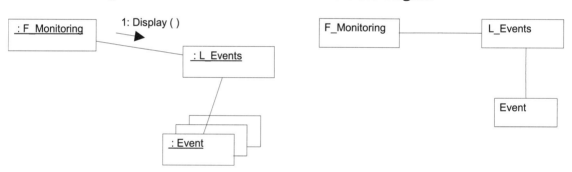

Draft Class Diagram

Purging Events

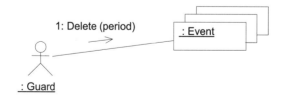

Sequence Diagram

The interaction is represented here using a sequence diagram, which is more expressive than a collaboration diagram for representing control structures.

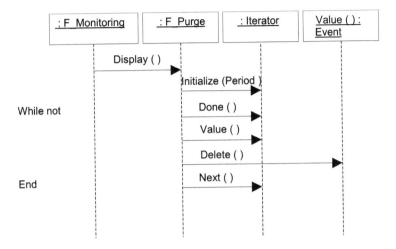

Draft Class Diagram

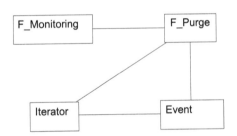

Reporting Alarms

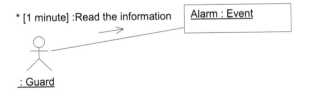

Collaboration Diagram

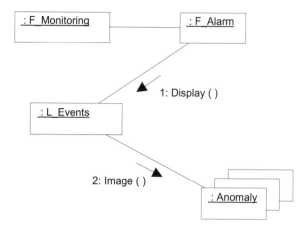

Draft Class Diagram

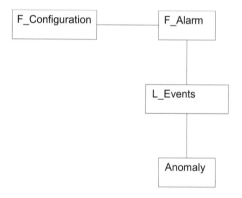

Manual Opening of Doors

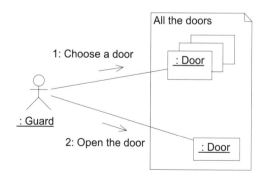

Collaboration Diagram

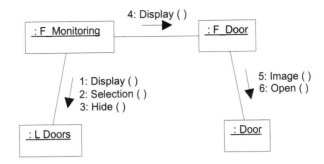

4: Display ( )

: F_Monitoring

: F_Door

1: Display ( )
2: Selection ( )
3: Hide ( )

: L_Doors

5: Image ( )
6: Open ( )

: Door

Draft Class Diagram

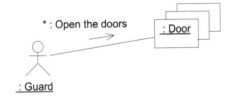

F_Monitoring

F_Door

L_Doors

Door

Fire

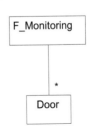

* : Open the doors

: Door

: Guard

Sequence Diagram

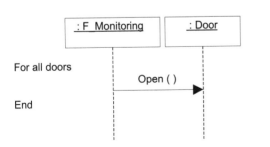

: F_Monitoring

: Door

For all doors

Open ( )

End

Draft Class Diagram

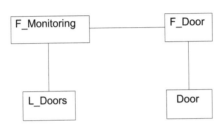

F_Monitoring

*

Door

249

Access Control

Entry Authorization

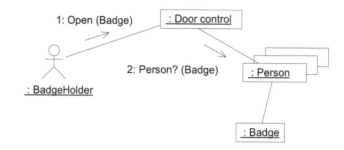

Collaboration Diagram

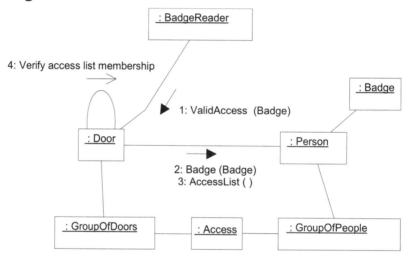

Draft Class Diagram

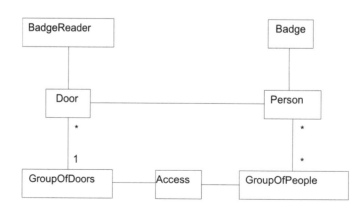

Analysis

Domain Analysis

Use cases divide up the requirements space according to the viewpoint of a single actor at a time. The description provided by use cases is purely functional, and it is important to take care not to start performing a functional decomposition instead of an object-oriented decomposition. Use cases must be seen as classes of behavior.

UML implements use cases with the help of collaborations between objects that come from the application domain. Each collaboration combines an object context and an interaction between these objects. The object context is expressed in a specific way in the collaboration diagrams, and in a general way in the class diagrams. These are the same class diagrams that were drafted in the preceding sections.

The following class diagram is obtained automatically (thanks to the Rational Rose tool) based on these various drafts. The multiplicity of **0..4000** on the association between **BadgeReader** and **Badge** results from the fact that each badge reader can memorize a maximum of 4000 badges.

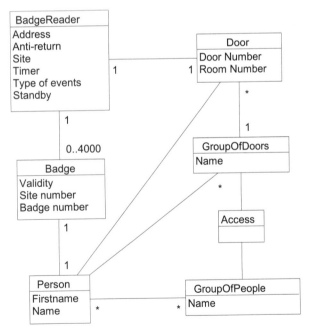

Inspection of this diagram identifies two redundant associations (between **Person** and **Door**, and **Person** and **GroupOfDoors**) that may be derived from other associations. The following diagram includes the changes that were brought about to the domain model.

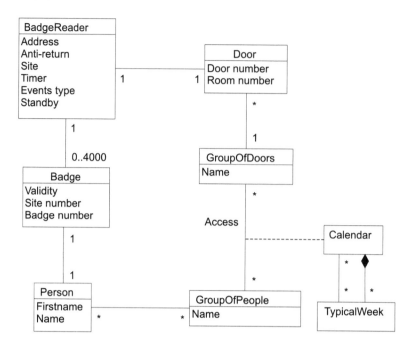

The **Access** class has been transformed into an association class, since it did not contain any particular information. The details about access rights are expressed in the association class **Calendar**. Notice that this has two different types of relationship with **TypicalWeek** class; the composition relationship represents typical weeks that have been modified locally in a given calendar.

Analysis of the Existing Setup

ESSAIM already has a number of badge readers, and wishes to reuse them in the new access control system. These badge readers can function in a completely autonomous fashion; they can be programmed in-place using special badges, or remotely via a serial connection. All the readers are slaves of the control system: a reader never originates an interaction.

Characteristics of the Badge Readers

Each badge reader has the following characteristics:

- The ability to memorize 4000 badges, with the possibility of invalidating certain ones
- The ability to memorize the last 100 events (a filter makes it possible to record only the anomalies)
- An address on the network (there may be up to 64 readers connected to the network)
- A software clock
- 8 different time periods
- A delay mechanism
- An optional anti-return function

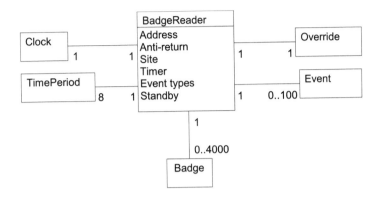

An 'override' input, connected to a push-button or a detection loop

A state that specifies whether the reader is active or on standby

Setting the Time

Each reader contains a software clock. If there's a power interruption, the reader records a special event when it is reconnected to the power line, and does not manage time segments. The clock must be reset by the control system in order for the reader to operate with time periods again. The difference between the clock's time and the real time indicates the duration of the power interruption.

Badge Management

The reader can memorize up to 4000 badge numbers. These badge numbers may be manipulated individually, or in groups of numbers in ascending order. The reader supplies the following operations:

Validation of one badge

Validation of a group of badges

Invalidation of one badge

Invalidation of a group of badges

Time Periods

A time period is associated with each badge or group of badges. A reader contains the description of 8 time periods, which make it possible to restrict access according to the day and time at which the badge is being used. The first 7 periods are configurable by the supervisor, while the last one allows access at all times. Each time period is made up of 3 sub-periods that must not overlap.

The periods are represented like this:

Sub-periods	Mo	Tu	We	Th	Fr	Sa	Su
00:00-00:00							
00:00-00:00							
00:00-00:00							

And the corresponding class diagram looks like this:

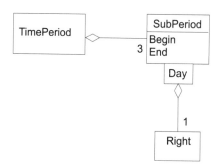

Events

Events are memorized according to the specified criteria (all the events, or only the anomalies). Each reader may record a maximum of 100 events between two interrogations by the master system. The events are erased after each interrogation. The reader's memory is organized as a circular buffer, and the oldest events are erased upon a memory overflow.

Each event includes the following information:

 Date

 Badge number

The reader records the following events:

- Badge accepted
- Power failure
- Badge rejected: reader on standby
- Badge rejected: out of range
- Badge rejected: invalid site code
- Badge rejected: not programmed

- Badge rejected and not returned
- Badge rejected: invalid time period

These event types are represented in the following diagram:

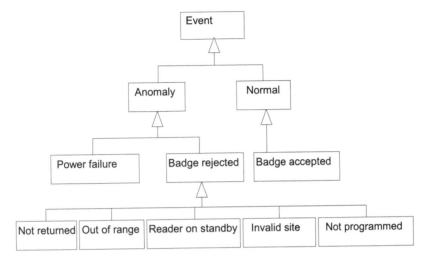

Types of Message

The communication between the badge readers and the master system is performed by messages that form three main categories:

- Simple messages that contain a header but no data
- Messages that contain fixed-length data
- Messages that contain variable-length data

These types of message are represented in the following diagram:

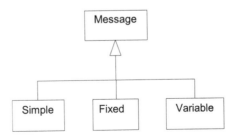

Simple Messages

Simple messages include synchronization messages, report requests, and commands.

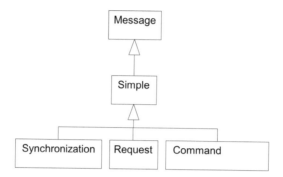

Messages received by the reader:

Acknowledgment

Non-acknowledgment

Request for events

Request for adjustment of parameters

Request for valid badges

Request for invalid badges

Request for clock

Request for site code

Standby mode command

End standby mode command

Door open command

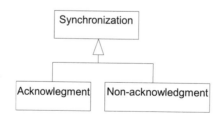

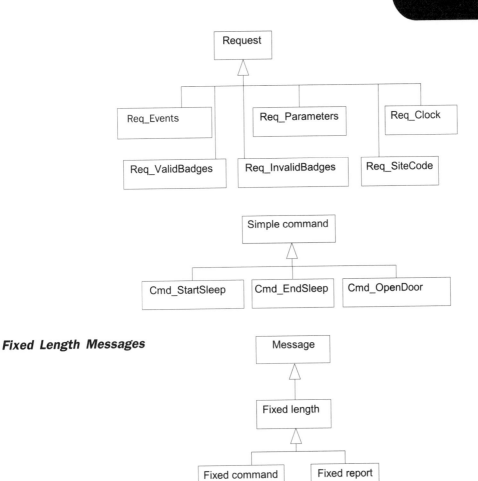

Fixed Length Messages

Messages received by the reader:

    Command to adjust parameters

    Command to validate one badge

    Command to validate a group of badges

    Command to invalidate one badge

    Command to invalidate a group of badges

    Command to set the time

    Command to transmit a time period

    Command sending a site code

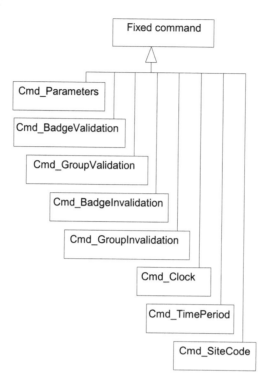

Messages sent by the reader:

Report adjustment of parameters

Report clock

Report of a time period for the reader

Report the site code

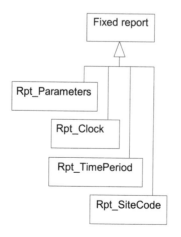

Variable Length Messages

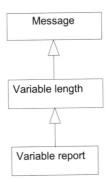

Messages sent by the reader:

Events report

Valid badges report

Invalid badges report

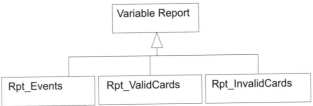

Frame Structures

Messages are encapsulated within frames that contain information for addressing and transmission checking. Each frame has the following structure:

	Begin	Address	Checksum	Data	End
Length	1 byte	1 byte	2 bytes	0 to n bytes	2 bytes
Legal Values	01H	00H to 3FH			F1H, F2H

The frame class provides the functions **Image()** and **Value()** for frame transfer. The **Image()** function transforms a frame object into a sequence of bytes that may be transmitted via the serial link that connects badge readers to the PCs. Conversely, the **Value()** function reconstructs a frame object based on a sequence of bytes coming from one of the badge readers.

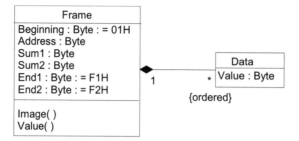

The behavior of the function **Value()** is described by the following state machine:

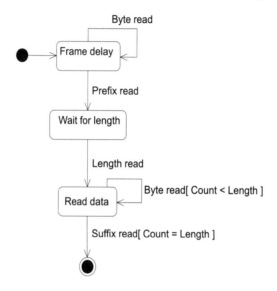

Architecture

Software Architecture

A badge reader may be represented by an actor. In the diagram below, the badge reader is represented by a stereotyped class to make clear that it is a hardware device class, rather than a class of people.

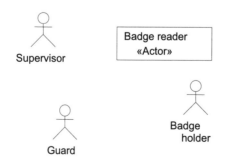

The hardware used makes it possible to shift the emphasis of the access control use case towards the badge readers. From this point of view, the badge reader acts as an actor for the whole access control system, or as an independent system with which the human badge holder interacts.

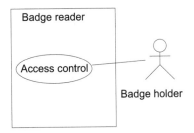

From a global standpoint, the badge readers look like actors, just like the supervisor and the guard. The system is now composed of two distinct subsystems. On the one hand, there's the custom software to be developed (for execution on PCs), and on the other hand, there's the pre-built system delivered with the badge readers.

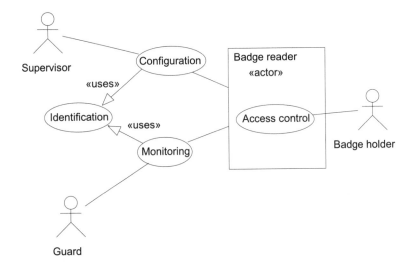

The logical view structure appears in the next diagram. Business objects are grouped in a **Domain** package. Proxy components of these domain objects are contained in the **UI** package. The lowest layer includes a **Persistence** category that encapsulates a database, a **Virtual Machine** package that isolates the application from the specifics of the hardware, and a **Physical Reader** package containing classes that allow the manipulation of badge readers and encapsulate the full complexity of the communication.

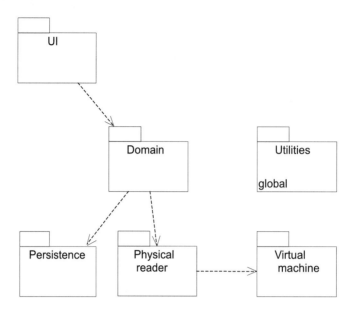

Hardware Architecture

The system is composed of software and hardware elements, which are interchangeable to a large degree.

The badge readers are connected using a dedicated network, independent of the intranet, to which the supervisor's workstation and the guard's control station are also connected. There can be up to 64 badge readers connected to the network.

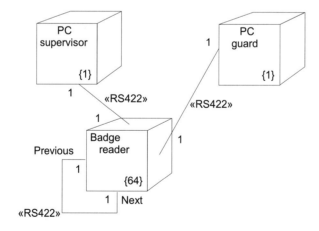

Implementation

The goal of this case study was to introduce object-oriented modeling using UML, so the implementation is not described here in great detail. The main implementation phases include:

- The automatic generation of the database schema based on the domain classes described as 'persistent'
- Screen generation using a graphical interface builder
- Manual implementation of interactions based on the collaboration diagrams

Clearly, even the extensive decomposition given here isn't exhaustive. For a complete specification, it would be necessary to be explicit about details like variable types, function return types, and multiplicities, as well as niceties like the styling of the user interface.

What the process *has* produced is a firm understanding of the users' requirements, and an object-oriented model of the system that is comprehensible to anyone who can read UML. It would be reasonable to hand the model to any number of programmers and expect them to come up with similar implementations — certainly, there should be no differences in functionality. Object-oriented analysis and design with UML has resulted in a model that is well reasoned, readily communicable, and unambiguous.

Summary

This final chapter has presented a case study in the use of UML notation to assist with the object-oriented analysis and design of a realistic software project. It began by establishing the users' requirements through the creation and study of use cases, and then built on those use cases by representing candidate objects and simple interactions in sequence diagrams.

The study then moved on to elaborate further, first by representing the interactions identified in the sequence diagrams as collaboration diagrams, and then expanding on these by taking into account the constraints on the system. At this stage, thought was given to the relationships necessary for the exchange of information between objects, and to those between application objects and user interface objects. From this base, draft class diagrams were produced. Finally, ways of incorporating existing hardware into the design were examined.

Of course, this is not the end of process: as implementation proceeds, there may well be resulting feedback into the design of the application — this is quite natural, and an aspect of the iterative nature of a good method. The important thing is not to work on design and implementation simultaneously: take a break from implementation, change the model, and then return to coding. That way, everybody involved always knows what the current position is.

As mentioned at the start of the chapter, the model developed during this case study is available for download from the Wrox Press web site, and it can be viewed in the demonstration version of Rational Rose. The full version (or Microsoft Visual Modeler) can save changes to the model as well. Good luck, and good modeling!

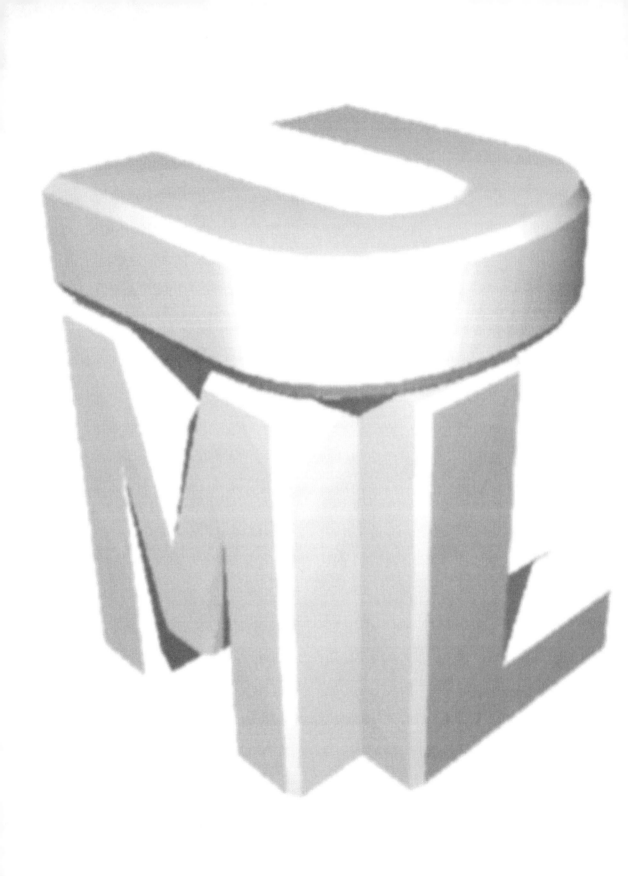

The Standard Elements

There are three standard mechanisms available to the user for extending 'core' UML: stereotypes, tagged values, and constraints.

Predefined Stereotypes

UML's predefined stereotypes are presented in alphabetical order in the following table. The three columns contain respectively the stereotype name, the model element to which it is applied, and a description of its semantics.

Name	Applies To	Semantics
«becomes»	dependency	Transformation of the characteristics of the given instance
«call»	dependency	An operation that calls another operation
«copy»	dependency	An exact copy of one instance into another
«create»	event	An event in which the instance referred to is created
«derived»	dependency	The source is derived from the target
«destroy»	event	An event in which the instance referred to is destroyed
«document»	component	A component that represents a document
«enumeration»	primitive type	A set of identifiers that make up the possible values of an instance of a type
«executable»	component	A component that represents an executable program
«extends»	generalization	The source use case extends the behavior of the target use case
«façade»	package	A package that simply references elements within another package
«file»	component	A component that represents a source file
«framework»	package	A package that consists mainly of patterns
«friend»	dependency	An extension of the visibility of a package to include the visibility of another package

Name	Applies To	Semantics
«import»	dependency	Makes the public part of a package visible to another package
«inherits»	generalization	Instances of the source subtype can be substituted for instances of the target supertype
«instance»	dependency	A relationship between an instance and its type
«invariant»	constraint	Specifies a set of conditions that must hold for all instances of the type to which it refers
«library»	component	A component that represents a static or dynamic library
«metaclass»	dependency	A dependency relationship between a type and its metaclass
«postcondition»	constraint	Specifies a set of conditions that must hold after the invocation of the operation to which it refers
«powertype»	dependency	A dependency relationship between a generalization and a type whose instances participate in the generalization
«precondition»	constraint	Specifies a set of conditions that must hold before the invocation of the operation to which it refers
«private»	generalization	Indicates private inheritance; the inherited features of a class are hidden
«process»	classifier	An active class that represents a process
«requirement»	comment	A note indicating a responsibility or obligation
«send»	dependency	A dependency relationship between an operation and a signal sent by that operation
«stereotype»	classifier	The element referred to is itself a stereotype
«stub»	package	A package that is incompletely transferred; only the public parts are provided
«subclass»	generalization	The subtype inherits the structure and behavior of a supertype, but cannot be used in its place
«subtype»	generalization	The subtype inherits the structure and behavior of a supertype, and can be used in its place
«system»	package	A package containing a number of models of the same system
«table»	component	A component that represents a table in a database
«thread»	classifier	An active class that represents a thread
«uses»	generalization	The source use case uses the behavior of the target use case
«utility»	classifier	A non-instantiable type that groups operations and attributes

Predefined Tagged Values

UML's predefined tagged values are presented in alphabetical order in the following table. The three columns contain respectively the value name, the model element to which it applies, and a description of its semantics.

Name	Applies To	Semantics
documentation	any element	A comment, description or explanation
location	classifier component	The element is part of a given component (if it's a classifier) or node (if it's a component)
persistence	attribute classifier instance	Indicates the permanence of the state of the element
responsibility	classifier	An obligation of the classifier
semantics	classifier operation	A specification of the meaning of the element

Predefined Constraints

UML's predefined constraints are presented in alphabetical order in the following table. The three columns contain respectively the constraint name, the model element to which it applies, and a description of its semantics.

Name	Applies To	Semantics
association	link-end	The corresponding instance is visible via an association
broadcast	request	The request invocation order is not specified
complete	generalization	All the subtypes have been specified
disjoint	generalization	Instances may have only one of the given subtypes as a type
global	link-end	The corresponding instance is visible because it is located within a global scope
implicit	association	The association is not straightforward, but conceptual
incomplete	generalization	Not all the subtypes have been specified
local	link-end	The corresponding instance is visible because it is located within a local scope
or	association	Mutually exclusive associations
overlapping	generalization	Instances may have several of the given subtypes as a type
parameter	link-end	The corresponding instance is visible because it is an operation parameter

267

Name	Applies To	Semantics
self	link-end	The corresponding instance is visible because it plays a role in request distribution
vote	request	The return value is chosen by majority vote among the values returned by the collection of requests

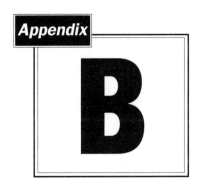

Guide for Making the Transition from Booch and OMT to UML

The goal of this guide is to ease the transition of users of Booch'93 or OMT-2 to the UML notation. The Booch, OMT, and UML notations provide three different views of object concepts that are very closely related. In fact, the Booch and OMT notations could be used to represent most of the model elements defined in the UML metamodel.

Graphically, UML is closer to OMT than to Booch, since the cloud icons were abandoned and replaced by rectangles, which are easier to draw. Beyond the graphical considerations, UML can be considered as a superset of the other two notations.

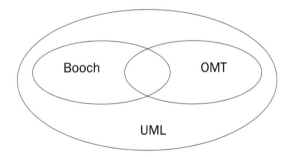

UML is a superset of Booch and OMT.

The tables in the remainder of this appendix illustrate the differences between the notations pertaining to the main object concepts.

Basic Mechanisms

Constraints

In all three notations, constraints are represented by expressions between braces.

Booch	OMT	UML
Text between braces {This is a constraint}	Text between braces {This is a constraint}	Text between braces {This is a constraint}

Notes

In Booch and UML, notes are represented by rectangles with a folded corner. In OMT, notes are represented like constraints. In Booch, the bottom left corner is folded, while in UML the top right corner is folded.

Booch	OMT	UML
This is a note	Text between braces {This is a note}	This is a note

Subsystems

In Booch and OMT, subsystems are part of the set of model elements. In UML, subsystems are implemented by stereotyping packages.

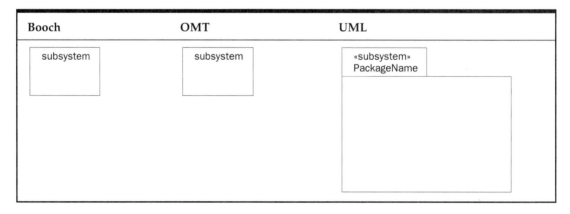

Booch	OMT	UML
subsystem	subsystem	«subsystem» PackageName

Objects

In Booch, objects are represented by clouds. In OMT, as in UML, objects are represented by rectangles. In UML, the name of the object is underlined.

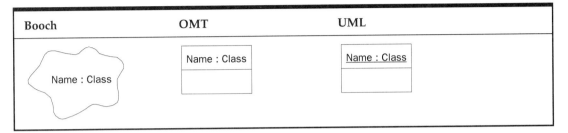

Links

In all three notations, links are represented by a continuous line drawn between the objects.

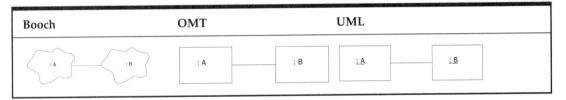

Messages

In the three notations, messages are represented using arrows located near the links. The control flow type is represented by using a particular arrowhead.

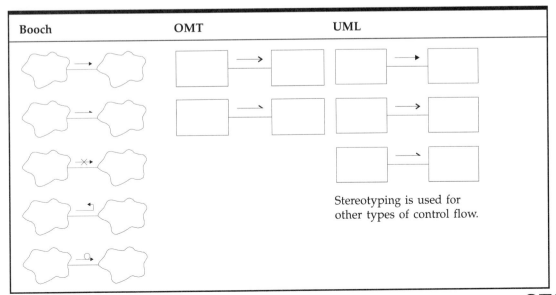

Message Labels

In the three notations, the message label is represented using an expression placed in front of the message name.

Booch	OMT	UML
Decimal notation	Pointed decimal notation	Modified pointed decimal notation
		Thread name
		Step within a thread
		*[iteration]

Data Flow

Booch and UML allow the representation of data flow as well as control flows (the messages) by using small circles connected to an arrow pointing in the direction of the data flow. This notation is optional, as it has become redundant — data flow can be represented in message labels.

Booch	OMT	UML
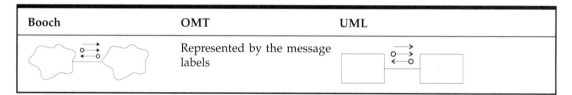	Represented by the message labels	

Classes

In Booch, classes are represented using dotted clouds. In OMT, as in UML, classes are represented using rectangles.

Simple Classes

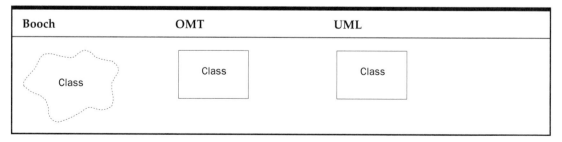

Attributes and Operations

In the three notations, attributes and operations are represented within the class icon. Some attributes and operations can be hidden for the sake of clarity of the diagrams. OMT and UML use boxes to distinguish the attributes from the operations.

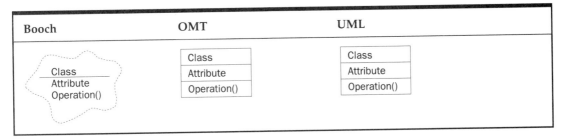

Booch	OMT	UML
Class Attribute Operation()	Class Attribute Operation()	Class Attribute Operation()

Visibility

The three notations propose public, protected, and private levels with the same semantics as the C++ language. Booch provides an additional 'implementation' level.

Booch	OMT	UML
		nothing unspecified
nothing public	+ public	+ public
| protected	# protected	# protected
|| private	– private	– private
||| implementation		

Class
  Public Attribute
| Protected Attribute
|| Private Attribute
  Public Operation()
| Protected Operation()
|| Private Operation()
	Class
	+ Public Attribute
	# Protected Attribute
	– Private Attribute
	+ Public Operation()
	# Protected Operation()
	– Private Operation()
		Class
		+ Public Attribute
		# Protected Attribute
		– Private Attribute
		+ Public Operation()
		# Protected Operation()
		– Private Operation()

Abstract Classes

In Booch, abstract classes are specified by a small triangle containing the letter 'A'. In OMT, an abstract class has zero multiplicity. In UML, the name of the abstract class is written in italics.

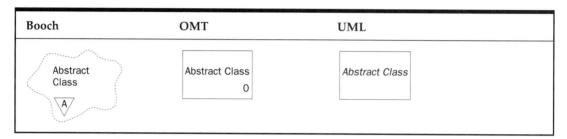

Utility Classes

In Booch, a utility class is represented as a simple class augmented with a grayed boundary. OMT does not propose any particular graphical attribute other than constraints, and UML uses the «utility» stereotype.

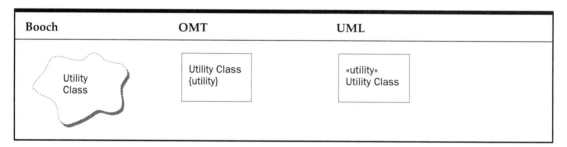

Template Classes

Booch and UML propose a special notation, derived from the representation of simple classes augmented by a small dotted rectangle containing the formal parameters. OMT adds the formal parameters as a suffix of the name of the template class.

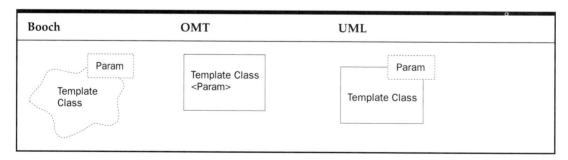

Bound Elements

The instantiation of a template class produces a bound element. Booch proposes an icon like the one for the template class, but this time the rectangle is drawn with solid lines. OMT and UML represent bound elements just like simple classes, adding the values of the parameters as suffixes of the class name.

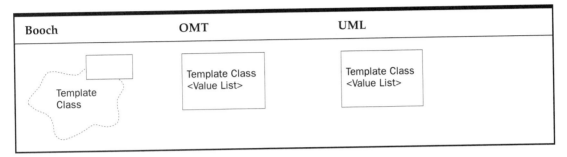

Metaclasses

Booch represents a metaclass by using a grayed cloud. OMT does not provide any particular graphical attribute other than constraints. UML uses the «metaclass» stereotype.

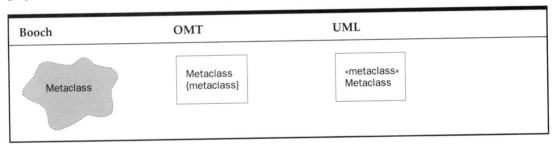

Relationships

Associations

In all three notations, an association is represented by a continuous line drawn between the classes that participate in it.

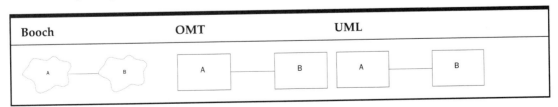

Roles

In the three notations, the rolename is placed at the end of the association line closest to the class to which it refers.

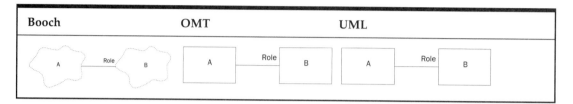

Multiplicity

Booch and UML are identical apart from the 'unlimited' value, which is represented by **N** in Booch and ***** in UML. OMT proposes a graphical representation based on circles. Take care not to confuse these circles with those meaning *has* and *uses* in Booch, as there is no relationship between these two representations.

Booch	OMT	UML
1	**1** by default	**1**
0..1		**0..1**
N	0..N / 0..1	*****
3..5, 7, 15	1+ / 3..5	**3..5, 7, 15**
3..N		**3..***

Qualifiers

Qualified associations are represented in Booch using an attribute placed between brackets. In OMT and UML, a qualifier is represented using a rectangular box. The qualifier is represented on the source side in OMT and UML, and on the target side in Booch.

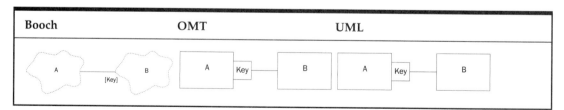

Association Classes

In all three notations, an association class is represented using a class connected to an association.

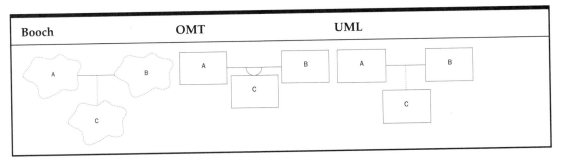

Aggregation

There is no strict equivalence between Booch on one hand, and OMT and UML on the other. As far as aggregations are concerned, Booch is closer to the design phase, OMT is closer to the analysis phase, and UML covers both. The following table represents the two most common situations: aggregation by reference and aggregation by value ('composition' in UML). It is important to note that in the case of OMT, the graphical representation does not distinguish the type of aggregation.

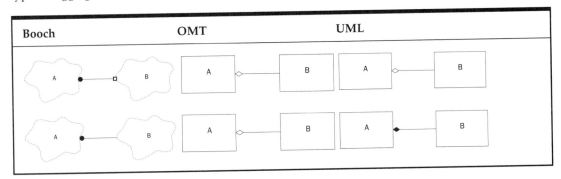

Dependency

Booch represents a dependency using an association labeled with a small circle placed on the client side. OMT represents a dependency using a dotted arrow with a filled head. UML uses a dotted arrow with an open head. In OMT and UML, the arrow points to the supplier — the element being depended on.

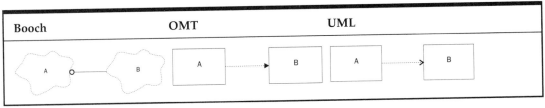

279

Inheritance

In all three notations, inheritance is represented using an arrow that points from the subclass to the superclass.

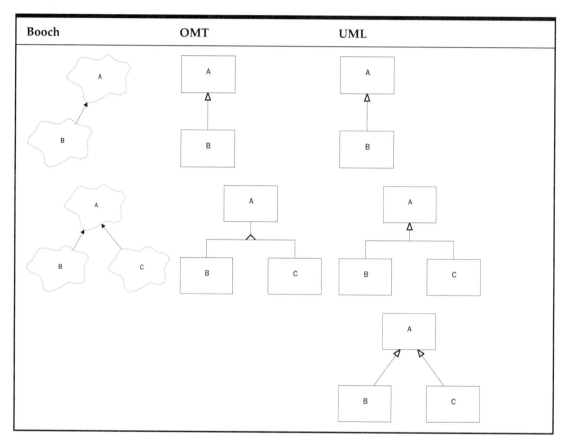

Metaclass Instantiation

Booch uses a grayed arrow to represent the relationship between a class and its metaclass. OMT does not supply a specific notation other than constraints. UML stereotypes a dependency relationship.

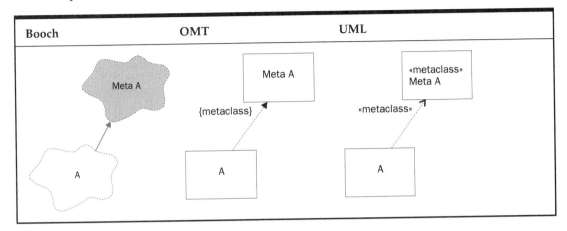

Template Instantiation

Booch proposes a dotted arrow to represent the relationship between parameterized classes and template classes. OMT uses a dependency relationship. UML stereotypes a dependency relationship.

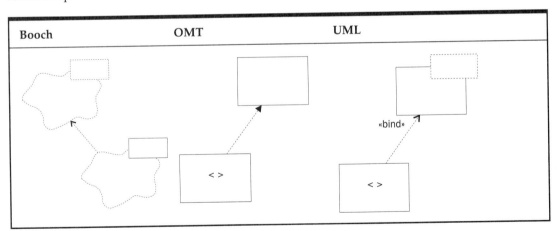

Derived Elements

Associations and derived attributes are prefixed by the '/' character in OMT and UML. The concept does not exist in Booch.

Booch	OMT	UML
	/	/

281

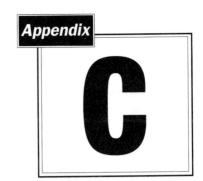

C++ Code Generation

The following code samples were generated automatically by Rational Rose from UML models. These examples do not illustrate the whole range of Rose code generation capabilities, but they *do* describe the overall correspondence between UML and the C++ language.

Classes

Empty Class

The code generator was configured to generate a constructor, a copy constructor, a destructor, an assignment operator, and two equality operators.

The operations in this table are not represented in the following tables for the sake of clarity of the examples.

Model	Code
| A | ```
#ifndef A_h
#define A_h 1
class A
{
public:
    //## Constructors (generated)
    A();
    A(const A& right);

    //## Destructor (generated)
    ~A();

    //## Assignment Operation (generated)
    const A& operator = (const A& right);

    //## Equality Operations (generated)
    int operator == (const A& right) const;
    int operator != (const A& right) const;
};
#endif
``` |
```

Class with Attributes and Operations

Model	Code
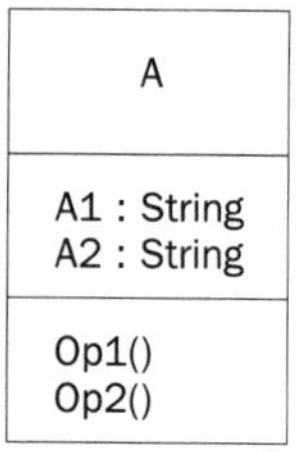 A A1 : String A2 : String Op1() Op2()	(see code below)

```
class A
{
public:
   ...
   //## Other Operations (specified)
   void Op1();
   void Op2();

   const String get_A1() const;
   void set_A1(const String value);
   const String get_A2() const;
   void set_A2(const String value);

private:
   String A1;
   String A2;
};

inline const String A::get_A1() const
{
   return A1;
}

inline void A::set_A1(const String value)
{
   A1 = value;
}

inline const String A::get_A2() const
{
   return A2;
}

inline void A::set_A2(const String value)
{
   A2 = value;
}
```

Template Class

Model	Code
| 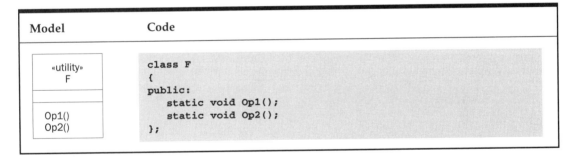 | ```
template <argtype Att>
class D
{
public:
    D();
    D(const D<Att>& right);
    ~D();

    const D<Att>& operator = (const D<Att>& right);

     int operator == (const D<Att>& right) const;
     int operator != (const D<Att>& right) const;
...
};
``` |

Utility Class

All the operations of a utility class are prefixed by the keyword **static**.

Model	Code
| «utility» F — Op1() Op2() | ```
class F
{
public:
    static void Op1();
    static void Op2();
};
``` |

Associations

1 to 1 Association

If the association is by reference, the code generator implements the association using pointers located in the private sections of the classes that participate in the association.

```
class A
{
    ...

    const B* get_Rb() const;
    void set_Rb(B* const value);

private:
    B* Rb;
};

inline const B* A::get_Rb() const
{
    return Rb;
}

inline void A::set_Rb(B* const value)
{
    Rb = value;
}
```

```
class B
{
    ...

    const A* get_Ra() const;
    void set_Ra(A* const value);

private:
    A* Ra;
};

inline const A* B::get_Ra() const
{
    return Ra;
}

inline void B::set_Ra(A* const value)
{
    Ra = value;
}
```

N to 1 Association

The code generator implements the association using pointers located in the private sections of the classes participating in the association. The multiplicity **0..*** is implemented using a set of unrestricted size.

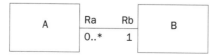

```
class B
{
    ...
    const UnboundedSetByReference<A> get_Ra() const;
    void set_Ra(const UnboundedSetByReference<A> value);

private:
    UnboundedSetByReference<A> Ra;
};

inline const UnboundedSetByReference<A> B::get_Ra() const
{
    return Ra;
}

inline void B::set_Ra(const UnboundedSetByReference<A> value)
{
    Ra = value;
}
```

N to 1 Association with a Constraint

The code generator implements the association using pointers located in the private sections of the classes that participate in the association. Due to the constraint **{Ordered}**, the multiplicity **0..*** is implemented using a list of unrestricted size, rather than the set we had in the last example.

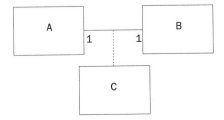

```
class B
{
    ...
    const UnboundedListByReference<A> get_Ra() const;
    void set_Ra(const UnboundedListByReference<A> value);

private:
    UnboundedListByReference<A> Ra;
};
```

Association Class

287

```
class A; class B;

class C
{
    ...
    const B* get_the_B() const;
    void set_the_B(B* const value);

    const A* get_the_A() const;
    void set_the_A(A* const value);

private:
    A* the_A;
    B* the_B;
};
```

```
#include "C.h"
class A
{
    ...
    const C* get_the_C() const;
    void set_the_C(C* const value);

private:
    C* the_C;
};
```

```
#include "C.h"
class B
{
    ...
    const C* get_the_C() const;
    void set_the_C(C* const value);

private:
    C* the_C;
};
```

N to N Association Class

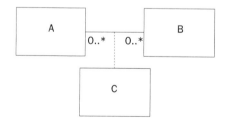

```
#include "C.h"
class B
{
    ...
    const UnboundedSetByReference<A> get_the_C() const;
    void set_the_C(const UnboundedSetByReference<A> value);
```

```
private:
    UnboundedSetByReference<A> the_C;
};
```

Aggregation

1 to 1 Aggregation

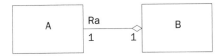

```
#include "B.h"
class A
{
    ...
    const B* get_the_B() const;
    void set_the_B(B* const value);

private:
    B* the_B;
};
```

```
#include "A.h"
class B
{
    ...
    const A* get_Ra() const;
    void set_Ra(A* const value);

private:
    A* Ra;
};
```

Aggregation with Restricted Navigation Capabilities

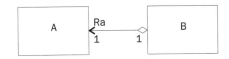

```
class A
{
    ...

private:
};
```

```
#include "A.h"
class B
{
```

```
   ...
   const A* get_Ra() const;
   void set_Ra(A* const value);

private:
   A* Ra;
};
```

Composition

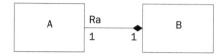

```
#include "B.h"
class A
{
   ...
   const B* get_the_B() const;
   void set_the_B(B* const value);

private:
   B* the_B;
};
```

```
#include "A.h"
class B
{
   ...
   const A get_Ra() const;
   void set_Ra(const A value);

private:
   A Ra;
};
```

1 to N Composition

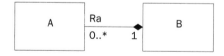

```
#include "A.h"
class B
{
   ...
   const UnboundedSetByValue<A> get_Ra() const;
   void set_Ra(const UnboundedSetByValue<A> value);

private:
   UnboundedSetByValue<A> Ra;
};
```

Inheritance

Single Inheritance

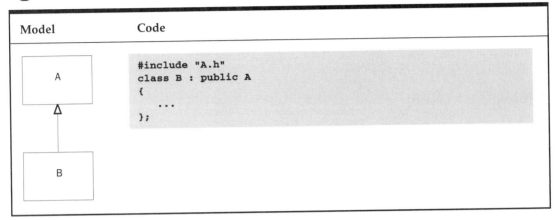

Model	Code

```cpp
#include "A.h"
class B : public A
{
    ...
};
```

Multiple Inheritance

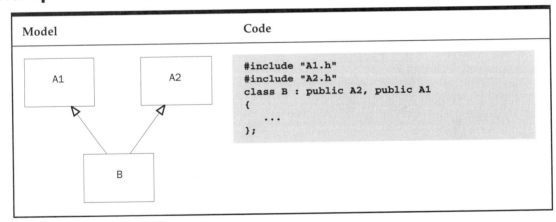

Model	Code

```cpp
#include "A1.h"
#include "A2.h"
class B : public A2, public A1
{
    ...
};
```

Java Code Generation

The following code samples were generated automatically from UML models by Rational Rose. These examples do not illustrate the whole range of Rose code generation capabilities, but they *do* describe the overall correspondence between UML and the Java language.

Classes

Empty Class

The code generator was configured to generate a constructor and a destructor. These operations are not represented in the tables after this one for the sake of clarity of the examples

Model	Code
| A | ```java
public final class A {

    public A() {
        super();
        ...
    }

    protected void finalize() throws Throwable {
        super.finalize();
        ...
    }
    ...
}
``` |
```

Class with Attributes and Operations

Model	Code
| A<br><br>A1 : String<br>A2 : String<br><br>Op1()<br>Op2() | ```java
public final class A {

    private String m_A1;
    private String m_A2;

    public void Op1() {
    ...
    }

    public void Op2() {
    ...
    }
    ...
}
``` |

Abstract Class

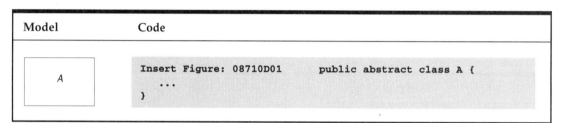

Model	Code

A	Insert Figure: 08710D01 public abstract class A {
	    ...
	}

Interface

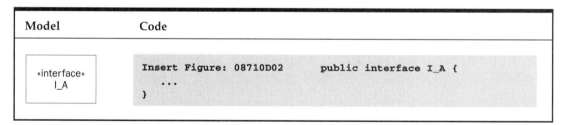

Model	Code

«interface»
I_A
	Insert Figure: 08710D02 public interface I_A {
	    ...
	}

Associations

1 to 1 Association

```

```
public class A {

    public B m_Rb;
    ...
}
```

```
public class B {

    public A m_Ra;
    ...
}
```

1 to N Association

```
┌──────────┐ Ra     Rb ┌──────────┐
│    A     │           │    B     │
│          │ 0..*    1 │          │
└──────────┘           └──────────┘
```

```
public class B {

    public Vector m_Ra = new Vector();
    ...
}
```

```
┌──────────┐ -Ra    Rb ┌──────────┐
│    A     │           │    B     │
│          │ *       1 │          │
└──────────┘           └──────────┘
```

```
public class B {

    private Vector m_Ra = new Vector();
    ...
}
```

When the multiplicity is limited, the association is implemented using an array.

```
┌──────────┐ -Ra    Rb ┌──────────┐
│    A     │           │    B     │
│          │ 5       1 │          │
└──────────┘           └──────────┘
```

```
public class B {

    private A[] m_Ra = new A[5];
    ...
}
```

Aggregation

1 to 1 Aggregation

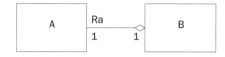

```
public class A {

    public B m_B;
    ...
}
```

```
public class B {

    public A m_Ra;
    ...
}
```

Aggregation with Restricted Navigation Capabilities

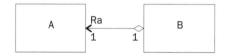

```
public class A {

    ...
}
```

```
public class B {

    public A m_Ra;
    ...
}
```

Inheritance

Single Inheritance

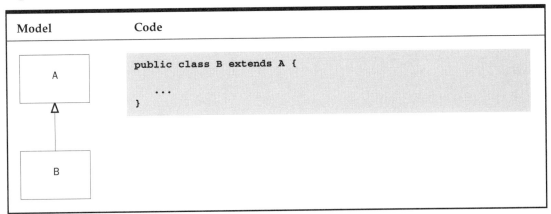

Model	Code
| A ▲ B | ```
public class B extends A {

    ...
}
``` |

Inheritance between Interfaces

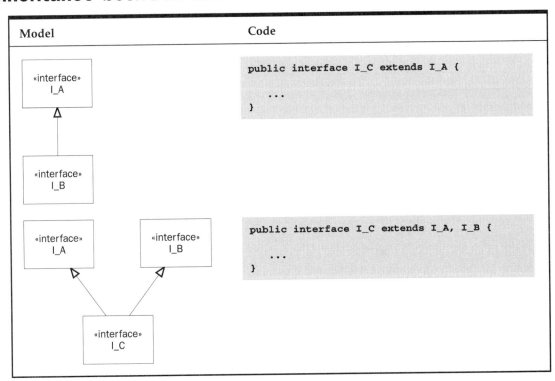

Model	Code
| «interface» I_A ▲ «interface» I_B | ```
public interface I_C extends I_A {

    ...
}
``` |
| «interface» I_A    «interface» I_B ◁    ◁ «interface» I_C | ```
public interface I_C extends I_A, I_B {

    ...
}
``` |
```

Implementation of an Interface by an Abstract Class

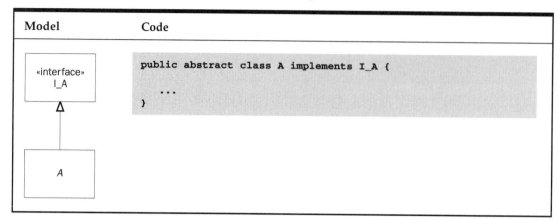

Model	Code

```
«interface»
I_A
        △
        |
        A
```

```java
public abstract class A implements I_A {

    ...
}
```

Implementation of an Interface by a Class

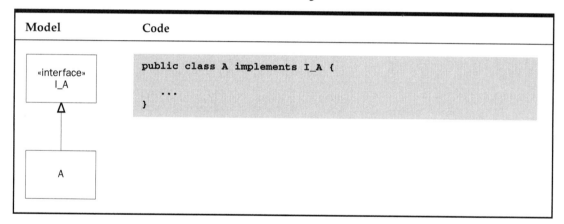

Model	Code

```
«interface»
I_A
        △
        |
        A
```

```java
public class A implements I_A {

    ...
}
```

Implementation of Several Interfaces by a Class

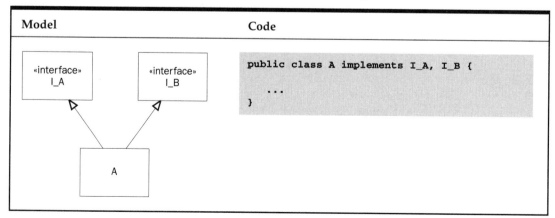

Model	Code

```
«interface»    «interface»
I_A             I_B
        △      △
         \    /
           A
```

```java
public class A implements I_A, I_B {

    ...
}
```

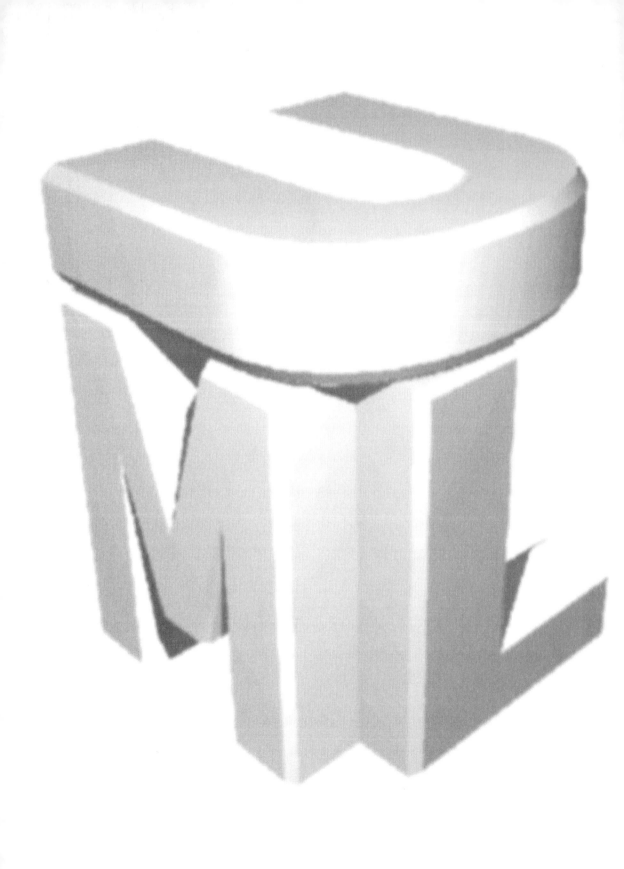

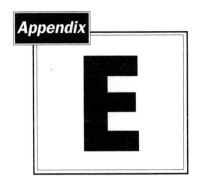

IDL Code Generation

The following code samples were generated automatically from UML models by Rational Rose. These examples do not illustrate the whole range of Rose code generation capabilities, but they *do* describe the overall correspondence between UML and IDL.

Classes

Empty Class

A class is translated into an IDL interface.

Model	Code
A	```interface A { ... }; ```

Class with Attributes and Operations

Model	Code
A A1 : String A2 : String Op1() Op2()	```interface A { attribute String A1; attribute String A2; void Op1(); void Op2(); }; ```

Associations

1 to 1 Association

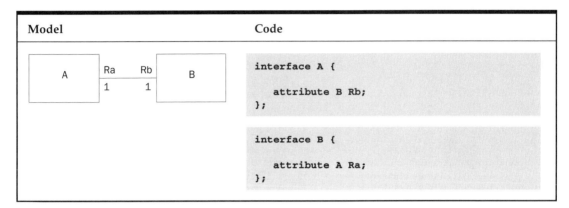

Model	Code
| | ```
interface A {

    attribute B Rb;
};
``` |
| | ```
interface B {

    attribute A Ra;
};
``` |

N to 1 Association

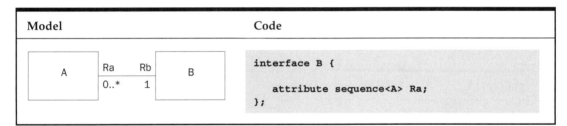

Model	Code
| | ```
interface B {

    attribute sequence<A> Ra;
};
``` |

5 to 1 Association

Model	Code
| | ```
interface B {

    attribute sequence<A,5> Ra;
};
``` |

Aggregation

1 to 1 Aggregation

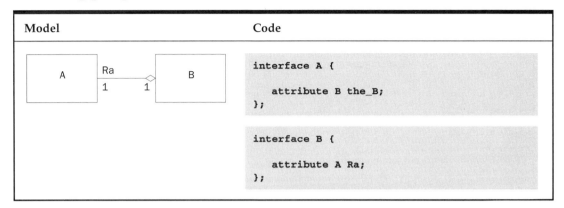

Model	Code

```
interface A {

    attribute B the_B;
};
```

```
interface B {

    attribute A Ra;
};
```

Aggregation with Restricted Navigation Capabilities

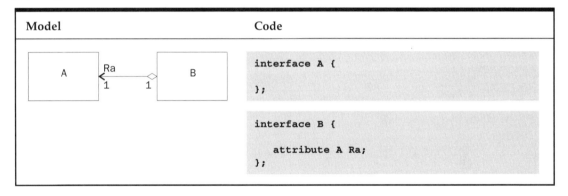

Model	Code

```
interface A {

};
```

```
interface B {

    attribute A Ra;
};
```

303

Inheritance

Single Inheritance

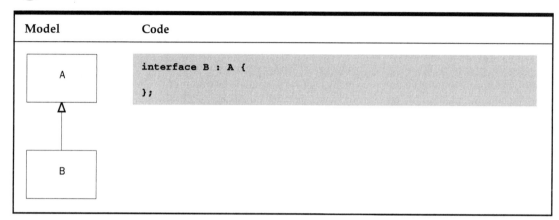

Multiple Inheritance

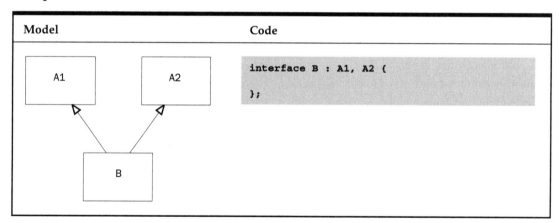

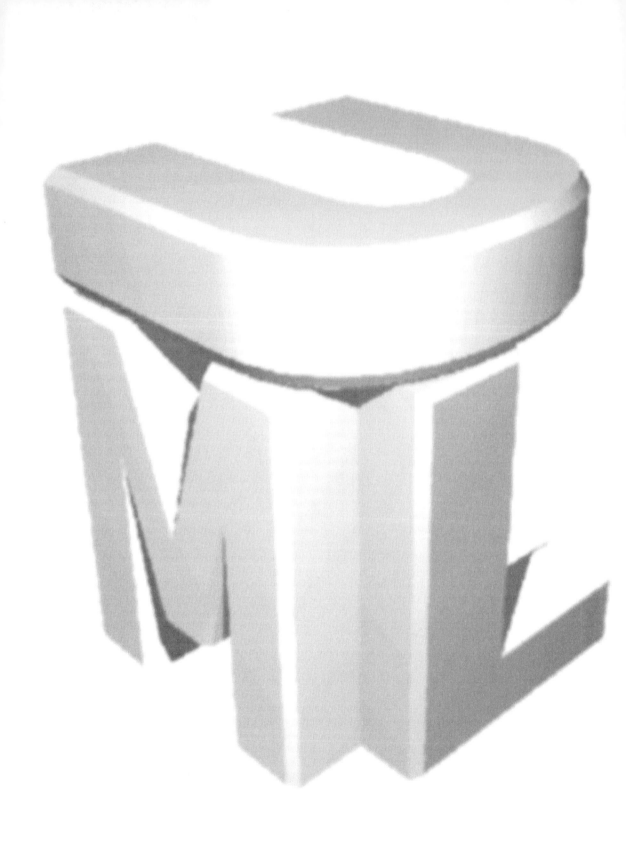

Visual Basic Code Generation

The following code samples were generated automatically from UML models by Rational Rose. These examples do not illustrate the whole range of Rose code generation capabilities, but they *do* describe the overall correspondence between UML and the Visual Basic language.

Classes

Empty Class

Model	Code
| A | ```
Option Base 0

Private Sub Class_Initialize()
End Sub

Private Sub Class_Terminate()
End Sub
``` |

Class with Attributes and Operations

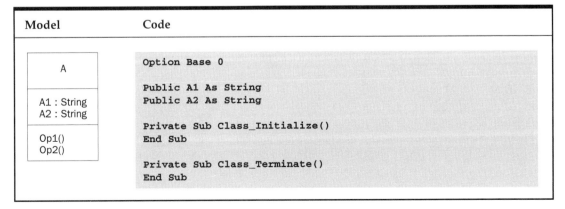

Model	Code
| A<br><br>A1 : String<br>A2 : String<br><br>Op1()<br>Op2() | ```
Option Base 0

Public A1 As String
Public A2 As String

Private Sub Class_Initialize()
End Sub

Private Sub Class_Terminate()
End Sub
``` |

Model	Code

A
 	
A1 : String
A2 : String
 	
Op1()
Op2()
	``
	Public Sub Op1()
	   On Error GoTo Op1Err
	   ...
	
	   Exit Sub
	
	Op1Err:
	   Call RaiseError(MyUnhandledError, "A:Op1 Method")
	
	End Sub
	
	Public Property Get Op2() As Boolean
	   On Error GoTo Op2Err
	   ...
	
	   Exit Property
	
	Op2Err:
	   Call RaiseError(MyUnhandledError, "A:Op2 Property")
	
	End Property
	``

Utility Class

Model	Code
«utility» **F** Op1() Op2()	``` Option Base 0 Private Sub Class_Initialize() End Sub Private Sub Class_Terminate() End Sub Public Sub Op1() End Sub Public Property Get Op2() As Boolean End Property ```

308

Associations

1 to 1 Association

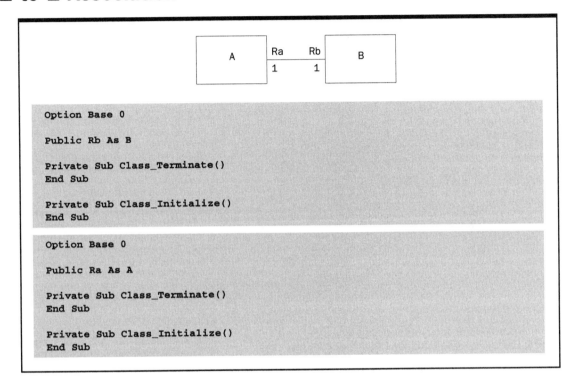

```
Option Base 0

Public Rb As B

Private Sub Class_Terminate()
End Sub

Private Sub Class_Initialize()
End Sub
```

```
Option Base 0

Public Ra As A

Private Sub Class_Terminate()
End Sub

Private Sub Class_Initialize()
End Sub
```

1 to N Association

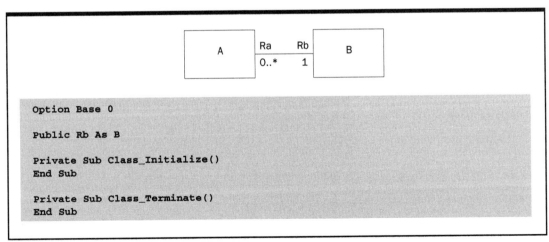

```
Option Base 0

Public Rb As B

Private Sub Class_Initialize()
End Sub

Private Sub Class_Terminate()
End Sub
```

Table contnued on following page

```
Option Base 0

Public Ra As Collection

Private Sub Class_Initialize()
End Sub

Private Sub Class_Terminate()
End Sub
```

Inheritance

Single Inheritance

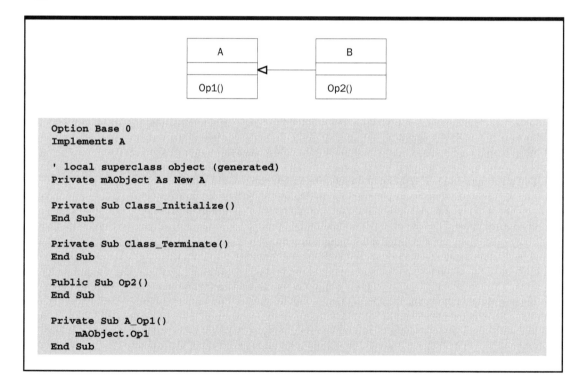

```
Option Base 0
Implements A

' local superclass object (generated)
Private mAObject As New A

Private Sub Class_Initialize()
End Sub

Private Sub Class_Terminate()
End Sub

Public Sub Op2()
End Sub

Private Sub A_Op1()
    mAObject.Op1
End Sub
```

SQL Code Generation

The following code samples were generated automatically from UML models by Rational Rose. These examples do not illustrate the whole range of Rose code generation capabilities, but they *do* describe the overall correspondence between UML and the ANSI SQL language.

For more details concerning SQL code generation from a class diagram and the various possible strategies, the reader is referred to Chapter 17 of *Object-Oriented Modeling and Design*, (see appendix I).

Classes

Empty Class

Model	Code
| A | ```
CREATE TABLE T_A (
    A_Id NUMBER (5),
    PRIMARY KEY (A_Id)
)
``` |

Class with Attributes and Operations

The generator builds the static structure; operations are ignored.

Model	Code
| A<br>A1 : String<br>A2 : String<br>Op1()<br>Op2() | ```
CREATE TABLE T_A (
    A_Id NUMBER (5),
    A1 VARCHAR (),
    A2 VARCHAR (),
    PRIMARY KEY (A_Id)
)
``` |

Associations

1 to 1 Association

```
CREATE TABLE T_B (
    B_Id NUMBER (5),
    PRIMARY KEY (B_Id)
)
```

```
CREATE TABLE T_A (
    A_Id NUMBER (5),
    B_Id NUMBER (5) REFERENCES T_B (B_Id),
    PRIMARY KEY (A_Id)
)
```

N to 1 Association

```
CREATE TABLE T_B (
    B_Id NUMBER (5),
    PRIMARY KEY (B_Id)
)
```

```
CREATE TABLE T_A (
    B_Id NUMBER (5) REFERENCES T_B (B_Id),
    A_Id NUMBER (5),
    PRIMARY KEY(A_Id)
)
```

N to N Association Class

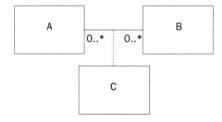

```
CREATE TABLE T_A (
    A_Id NUMBER (5),
    PRIMARY KEY (A_Id)
)
```

```
CREATE TABLE T_B (
    B_Id NUMBER (5),
    PRIMARY KEY (B_Id)
)
```

```
CREATE TABLE T_C (
    A_Id NUMBER (5) REFERENCES T_A (A_Id) ON DELETE CASCADE,
    B_Id NUMBER (5) REFERENCES T_B (B_Id) ON DELETE CASCADE,
    PRIMARY KEY (A_Id, B_Id)
)
```

Inheritance

In the following examples, each class is implemented by a table. Within the class hierarchy, object identity is preserved by using a shared identifier.

Single Inheritance

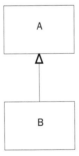

```
CREATE TABLE T_A (
    A_Id NUMBER(5),
    PRIMARY KEY (A_Id)
)
```

```
CREATE TABLE T_B (
    A_Id NUMBER (5) REFERENCES T_A (A_Id),
    PRIMARY KEY (A_Id)
)
```

Multiple Inheritance

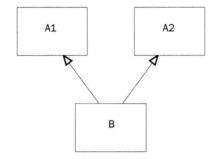

```
CREATE TABLE T_A1 (
    A1_Id NUMBER (5),
    PRIMARY KEY (A1_Id)
)
```

```
CREATE TABLE T_A2 (
    A2_Id NUMBER (5),
    PRIMARY KEY (A2_Id)
)
```

```
CREATE TABLE T_B (
    A1_Id NUMBER (5) REFERENCES T_A1 (A1_Id),
    A2_Id NUMBER (5) REFERENCES T_A2 (A2_Id),
    PRIMARY KEY (A1_Id ,A2_Id)
)
```

Glossary

abstract class	A *class* that cannot be directly instantiated and is only used for specification purposes. Contrast *concrete class*.
abstraction	The main characteristics of an entity, rather than the details. Sometimes used as a synonym for *class*.
abstract data type	The description of a piece of data in operational terms.
abstract operation	An *operation* defined in one *class* while its implementation is deferred to a *subclass*.
action	A procedure that results in a transition from one state to another. An action cannot be interrupted.
active class	A *class* whose instances are *active objects*. See *active object*.
active object	An *object* that owns a thread and can initiate control activity; an instance of an *active class*. See *active class*.
activity	A procedure executed within a state. An activity can be interrupted. Contrast *action*.
actor	A class of people or systems that interact with a system.
agent	An object that can be the origin and destination of an *interaction*.
aggregation	A form of asymmetric *association* that specifies a whole-part relationship between the aggregate (whole) and a subordinate part. Contrast *composition*.
algorithm	The chain of actions necessary to make up a task.
analysis	The formulation of the 'what' and 'what to do' of an application. Contrast *design*.
ancestor	A synonym of *superclass*.
application	A software system implemented with a precise goal in mind.
architect	An *architecture* specialist.
architecture	1) The art of building. In computer science, it refers to the art of building software. 2) The organizational structure of a piece of software.

artifact	A piece of information produced or used during software development activities.
association	A relationship between classes that describes a set of *links*.
association class	An *association* promoted to the level of a class.
asynchronous	A form of non-blocking communication without acknowledgment.
attribute	A named property of a *type*.
automatic transition	A *transition* triggered as soon as the ongoing state activity terminates.
base class	A *root class* in a class hierarchy.
big bang	A way of describing the integration methodology when it is concentrated at the end of the development cycle.
bound element	A class resulting from the specification of parameters in a template class. See *template class*.
category	A form of *package* in the logical view; a category encapsulates classes.
class	An abstract description of a set of *objects*; the implementation of a *type*. See *type*.
classification	The act of ordering to facilitate understanding.
class method	An operation which is specific to the class rather than to its *objects*.
class variable	An *attribute* that pertains to the class rather than its *objects*.
client	An *object* that initiates a request.
collaboration	1) A term used to specify an *interaction* between *objects* that is implemented in order to satisfy a user requirement. 2) A UML structuring element used to describe the *context* of an *interaction*. See *interaction*.
collection	A generic term that refers to any assembly of objects without specifying the nature of the assembly.
component	A physical entity that is part of an application and is usually represented in the implementation view.
composition	1) A form of organization that complements *classification*. 2) *Aggregation* by value.
concrete class	The opposite of an *abstract class*; a class that can be instantiated to generate *objects*. Contrast *abstract class*.
configuration management	Definition of relationships between system components intended to ensure consistency.
constraint	An expression that focuses the role or the scope of one or more *model elements*.
construction	The phase of the development process that encompasses the implementation of software and its transition to a mature state that is sufficient for delivery to end users.

constructor	The class operation that instantiates objects.
container	A data structure that contains *objects*.
context	A set of *model elements* that serves as the infrastructure for an *interaction*.
contract	An agreement between classes that is put together according to the provider's specifications.
coupling	A dependency between *model elements*.
CRC	An abbreviation for Class/Responsibility/Collaboration.
cycle	A complete loop through the four phases of the development process.
data flow	The description of data transferred from one object to another.
decomposition	A division into smaller elements meant to reduce complexity.
delegation	A communication mechanism between *objects* that allows a provider object to have some tasks handled by a subcontracting object while keeping the client object unaware of it.
dependency	A relationship between two *model elements* in which a change to one model element (the independent element) will affect the other model element (the dependent element).
derived association	An *association* that results from other associations.
derived attribute	An *attribute* that results from other attributes.
design	The determination of the 'how' of an application.
destructor	The class operation that deletes objects.
diagram	A graphical representation of a *collection* of *model elements*.
discrete	The opposite of continuous.
display element	The graphical projection of a collection of *model elements*.
documentation	The textual description of *models*.
domain	A synonym for application scope.
domain analysis	The part of the *analysis* that focuses on the application environment.
dynamic classification	A form of *classification* in which an object may change its *type* or *role*.
dynamic linking	The association between an object name and a class implemented during execution.
elaboration	The phase of the development process during which the architecture is defined.
element	A building block of a *model*.
entity	A term borrowed from data-centered modeling methods; it is used as a synonym for a domain object.
enumeration	A list of named values; the definition of the domain of a *type*.
error	An unexpected *event*.

event	An occurrence that results in a change of *state*.
exception	An exceptional condition that results from an execution flaw.
export	To make part of a package visible. See *visibility*.
expression	A string that evaluates to a value of a particular type.
extension	A kind of programming activity that facilitates the encompassing of new requirements.
extends	A relationship from one *use case* to another specifying how the behavior defined for the first use case can be inserted into the behavior defined for the second use case.
factorization	The process of finding and extracting similarities between classes.
feasibility study	A phase of the development process during which the product vision is defined.
framework	A generic micro-architecture.
function	The expression of a need in imperative terms, as a set of tasks to execute.
generalization	The name given by UML to the *classification* relationship used to build class hierarchies; although it is a more abstract concept, generalization is often used as a synonym for *inheritance*.
hierarchy	A class hierarchy ordered by a *generalization* relationship.
identity	A fundamental characteristic of an *object* that distinguishes it from all other objects.
idiom	A construct that is specific to a given language.
implementation inheritance	The inheritance of the interface and implementation of a more general element. Contrast *interface inheritance*.
import	A *dependency* relationship between *packages* that shows the exports of one package within another. Contrast *export*.
inheritance	A relationship between classes that allows the sharing of properties defined within a class; the main implementation technique for *generalization*. See *generalization*.
instance	A synonym for *object*; an object is an instance of a class.
instance method	An *operation* that is specific to an object.
instance variable	An *attribute* of an *object*.
integration	A feature of the interdependency between *model elements*.
interaction	Description of behavior in the context of a *collaboration*.
interface	The visible part of a class or a group of objects. Sometimes used as a synonym for *specification*.
interface inheritance	The inheritance of the interface of a more general element without its implementation. Contrast *implementation inheritance*.

interrupt	A change in the normal execution flow which results from sensing a hardware condition.
invariant	1) A Boolean expression whose change in value triggers an exception. 2) A criterion for detecting objects; an *object* is a domain invariant.
invocation	The *mechanism* through which a *message* triggers an *operation*.
iteration	1) The act of traversing an object collection. 2) The sequence of activities in the technical view that leads to the delivery of an executable *prototype*.
iterator	The *object* or *mechanism* that allows the visiting of all the elements of a *collection* without exposing its internal structure.
layer	Horizontal division of *models* that supports the grouping of *packages* in a model at the same level of abstraction.
lifecycle	The development stages and the ordering of such.
lifeline	The representation of the existence of an object in a sequence diagram.
link	The semantic connection among a set of objects through which one object can communicate with another object. An instance of an *association*. See *association*.
link attribute	An *attribute* that belongs to a *link* between objects rather than to the objects themselves.
maintenance	The lifecycle phase that follows development; maintenance groups activities related to defect fixing and the handling of enhancement requests.
maturity level	The description of the quality of a development process.
mechanism	A synonym for the *collaboration* between objects.
member	The C++ terminology used to designate an *attribute* or an *operation* contained within a class.
message	A communication element between objects that triggers activity in the target object; the receipt of a message is normally considered an *event*.
metaclass	A *class* whose instances are classes; it contains data and operations that are specific to a class rather than its instances.
metamodel	A *model* that describes *model elements*.
metamodeling	The recursive modeling of *model elements* from themselves.
method	1) Often used as a synonym of *operation*. Sometimes used to distinguish the specification of an operation from its multiple implementations — the methods — that exist in the subclasses. 2) A set of reasoned steps intended to achieve a goal.
mode	Characterizes parameters based on *data flow* direction: input, input and output, and output.
model	A descriptive representation of a system based on *model elements*.
model element	The representation of an *abstraction* drawn from the problem domain.

modeling	A synonym of *analysis*. By extension, it refers to the elaboration of models, including conceptual models.
modifier	An operation that modifies the internal state of an object.
modularity	The characteristic of an implementation environment that allows partitioning.
module	The lexical space within which other constructs may be declared.
monomorphism	A concept drawn from type theory according to which a name can only reference objects of one class.
multiple generalization	A form of generalization in which a class may be derived from multiple ancestors. Although it is a more abstract concept, multiple generalization is often used as a synonym for *multiple inheritance.*
multiple inheritance	A relationship between classes that allows the sharing of properties defined in several classes.
multiplicity	Specifies the number of objects that may participate in a relationship.
namespace	A part of a *model* in which names may be defined and used. Within a namespace, each name has a unique meaning.
navigability	The feature of a relationship that allows transfer from one class to another.
node	A piece of hardware that is capable of executing a program.
notation	The set of signs and symbols that constitute a language. In the case of the UML, it corresponds to the set of graphical and textual representations that make up the diagrams.
note	A piece of textual information that can be associated with any *model element* or combination thereof; a note belongs to a view and does not carry any semantics.
object	An atomic entity composed of state, behavior, and identity.
operation	The behavioral component of objects, defined globally within a *class*.
overloading	The use of an identical name to designate different constructs; overloading is resolved statically by compilers based on the *context* and *signature* of operations.
package	A mechanism for organizing elements into groups within *models*.
partition	A vertical division of models. By extension, a subset of a *model*.
pattern	A micro-architecture; a recurring design (or analysis) element.
persistence	The ability of an object to exist after the *process* or *thread* that created it has ceased to exist.
phase	A set of activities between two checkpoints within a development process.
polymorphism	A concept drawn from type theory according to which a name can reference objects that are instances of several classes grouped in a *generalization* hierarchy.

postcondition	A Boolean condition which must be true after the completion of an operation.
precondition	A Boolean condition which must be true when an operation is invoked.
primitive type	A predefined UML basic type.
private section	The part of a class specification that groups properties which are invisible from the outside.
process	1) A thread that can execute concurrently with other threads. 2) A sequence of steps, more or less ordered, which pertain to satisfying an objective.
projection	A relationship between a set and a subset.
property	A characteristic of a *class*.
protected section	The part of a class specification that groups properties which are only visible to subclasses from the outside.
prototype	The result of an *iteration*; a partial version of a system.
pseudo-state	Specifies particular states such as the initial state, the final state, or the history.
public section	The part of a class specification that groups properties which are visible from the outside.
qualifier	An attribute of an association that partitions the set of objects being referred to.
real time	The characteristic of a piece of software whose response time is compatible with the dynamics of a system.
recursivity	The application of a rule to its own results in order to generate an infinite sequence of results.
reflexive	Qualifies a relationship in which the *roles* pertain to the same class.
reification	The act of treating a concept or a function as an entity.
requirements analysis	An assessment of user needs.
responsibility	The obligation of a *class*; a part of its raison d'être.
reuse	The continued or repeated use of a development *artifact*.
reverse engineering	The rebuilding of *artifacts* from activities pertaining to earlier stages, based on artifacts from activities in the later stages.
review	A formal revision of documentation or a *model*.
risk	An element that may interfere with proper development execution.
role	The 'end' of an *association*; by extension, it refers to the way in which class instances view instances of another class through an association.
root class	The root class of a class hierarchy.
scenario	A simple *interaction* between objects. See *interaction*.

SEI	Software Engineering Institute.
selector	1) An operation that gives information concerning the internal state of an object without modifying it. 2) Within a navigation expression, it refers to an association that partitions a set of objects given a key value.
server	An object that never originates an interaction.
signal	A named event that can be invoked ('raised') explicitly.
signature	An unambiguous operation identifier, built from the name and parameters of an operation.
specialization	A descendent (heir) viewpoint applied to a *classification*.
specification	A declarative description of a model element. Contrast *implementation*.
state	The condition of an object or system at a given point during its lifetime.
state space	The set of all possible states.
static classification	A form of classification in which an object may not change its type or role. Contrast *dynamic classification*.
static linking	The association between an object name and a class implemented during compilation.
stereotype	An extension of the semantics of a metamodel element.
structure	Static relationships between *model elements*.
structured	Describes a decomposition technique based on the concept of *modules* and the description of the data flow between such modules.
subclass	A specialized class connected to another more general class through a *generalization* relationship. Contrast *superclass*.
substate	A *state* which is part of a *superstate*.
subsystem	A form of package in the component view. A subsystem contains implementation elements; it results from the category defined in the logical view. Contrast *system*.
superclass	A general class linked to another more specialized class through a *generalization* relationship. Contrast: *subclass*.
superstate	A state containing *substates*.
synchronization	The expression of the type of communication existing between two objects.
synchronous	A form of blocking communication with implicit acknowledgment.
template class	A class that serves as a model for building classes. See *bound element*.
test	The set of measures and activities meant to ensure proper software operation.

topology	Describes the organization of modules and their associated data and operations within an application.
transition	1) The phase of the development process during which the software is transferred to its users. 2) The move from one *state* to another.
type	A description of a set of instances that share the same operations, abstract attributes, relationships, and constraints.
typing	In a programming language, a way of supporting the concept of a *type*.
uninterpreted	A placeholder for a type whose implementation is not specified by the UML. Every uninterpreted value has a corresponding string representation.
use case	A specification technique for functional needs as perceived by a category of users.
utility class	A degenerate class reduced to the concept of a *module*.
version management	The recording of the history of an element.
view	A way to observe model elements that may be drawn from different models.
visibility	An encapsulation level for attributes and operations within classes.
vision	The definition of a product and its scope.

327

References

To Learn More

References

A Pattern Language
Alexander, Ishikawa, Silverstein, Jacobson, Fiskdahl-King, Angel
Oxford University Press, 1977. 0195019199

A Practical Handbook for Software Development
Birrel, Ould
Cambridge University Press, 1985. 0521347920

Object-Oriented Analysis and Design with Applications, 2nd edition
Booch
Addison-Wesley, 1994. 0805353402

Object Solutions: Managing the Object-Oriented Project
Booch
Addison-Wesley, 1995. 0805305947

The Mythical Man-Month: Essays on Software Engineering, anniversary edition
Brooks
Addison-Wesley, 1995. 0201835959

Pattern-Oriented Software Architecture: A System of Patterns
Buschmann, Meunier, Rohnert, Sommerlad, Stal
Wiley, 1996. 0471958697

Object Oriented Analysis, 2nd edition
Coad, Yourdon
Yourdon Press, 1991. 0136299814

Quality, Productivity, and Competitive Position
Deming
Massachusetts Institute of Technology, 1982. 0911379002

Object-Oriented Systems Analysis: A Model-Driven Approach
Embley, Kurtz, Woodfield
Yourdon Press, 1992. 0136299733

Design Patterns: Elements of Reusable Object-Oriented Software
Gamma, Helm, Johnson, Vlissides
Addison-Wesley, 1995. 0201633612

Object-Oriented Methods, 2nd edition
Graham
Addison-Wesley, 1993. 0201593718

Managing the Software Process
Humphrey
Addison-Wesley, 1989. 0201180952

Object-Oriented Software Engineering: A Use Case Driven Approach
Jacobson, Christerson, Jonsson, Overgaard
Addison-Wesley, 1994. 0201544350

The Object Advantage: Business Process Reengineering with Object Technology
Jacobson, Ericsson, Jacobson
Addison Wesley, 1995. 0201422891

Software Reuse: Architecture, Process and Organization for Business Success
Jacobson, Griss, Jonsson
Addison-Wesley, 1997. 0201924765

Object-Oriented Methods: Pragmatic Considerations
Martin, Odell
Prentice Hall, 1996. 0136308643

Object-Oriented Software Construction, 2nd edition
Meyer
Prentice Hall, 1997. 0136291554

Object-Oriented Modeling and Design
Rumbaugh, Blaha, Premerlani, Eddy, Lorensen
Prentice Hall, 1991. 0136298419

Object-Oriented Systems Analysis: Modeling the World in Data
Shlaer
Yourdon Press, 1989. 013629023X

Clouds to Code
Liberty
Wrox Press, 1997. 1861000952

Useful Internet Addresses

UML 1.1 Specification (Rational Software)
http://www.rational.com/uml/
Documents available in Word, HTML and PDF formats, and composed of five sections:

- *UML Summary:* Introduction to UML.
- *UML Notation Guide:* Description of the unified notation with illustrative examples.
- *UML Semantics:* Description of the metamodel that is the basis for the UML semantics.
- *UML Glossary:* Glossary of UML terms.
- *UML Process-Specific Extensions:* specific extensions to represent development processes.

Rational Rose (Rational Software)
http://www.rational.com/pst/products/rosefamily.html
Modeling tool supporting the Booch'93, OMT-2 and UML notations.

General information on UML (author's site)
http://w3s.essaim.univ-mulhouse.fr/~uml/webuml/index.html
ESSAIM is the Advanced School of Applied Sciences for Engineers (*Ecole Supérieure des Sciences Appliquées pour l'Ingénieur, Mulhouse*).

Index

B

behavior, objects 20
big bang effect 179, 184
Booch, Grady 8, 9, 141
Booch method 8
  Booch '93 8
  message flows 8
  notation example 16
  OMT, closing the gap with 8
Boolean data type 70
branching
  conditional 105, 114
broadcasting
  messages 26, 109
    categories of 26
  objects 21
bugs and debugging 144
business software 142

C

C++
  classes 34
  inheritance 51
«category» stereotype 70, 162, 173
characteristic property
  of classes 45
  of sets 43
child classes 51
class
  abstract 90
  active 91
  association 81
  representation 31, 73
  template 76
  utility 77
class diagram 73
classes, object-oriented methods and 30
  abstract classes 45
  abstraction 30
  aggregation 38

associations 36, 39
  roles 37
encapsulation 34
  coupling 34
  levels of 34
  visibility rules 35
hierarchies 40
  classification 47
  generalization 40
  inheritance 50
  polymorphism 55
  specialization 40, 41
implementation 33
instantiation 30
objects, comparison with 39
see also sets 43
specification 33
classification, class hierarchies 47
  covariance 47
  covariant decomposition 47
  inheritance, classification implementation 50
  multiple generalization 48
clients, object intercommunication 22
collaboration 158
  diagram 28, 102
  implementation of patterns 171
  metamodel 107
  representation of behavior 165
  use case implementation 158, 204
collaboration diagram 28, 102
collection
  multiplicity 79
  templates 76
complexity
  iterative cycle 184
  management 100, 153
  requirements 154
  risk 197
  software development 142
  transfer 149
component 133
  diagram 133
  integration 179, 196
  metamodel 91
  reusable 76, 205
  topology 174
component diagram 133

G

generalization 40, 87, 93
  class hierarchies 40
    classification 48
    superclasses 40
  constraints 89
  sets 44
  state 122
  state machine 115
generation 189, 211
generic
  association description 80
  class 76
  collaboration, pattern 107
  mechanism 204
  name 18, 74
guard 119, 130

H

Harel diagrams, OMT 8
hierarchy
  of classes 40
  of categories and subsystems 168
  of packages 70
history
  state machine memory 124

I

identity
  collaborations 107
  objects 21
idiom 172
implementation, classes 33
implementation view 162

import, packages 71
inheritance
  to implement classification 88
inheritance, class hierarchies
  classification implementation 50
  composition 51
    private 51
    public 51
  delegation 53
  multiple inheritance 52
  parent and child classes 51
  substitution 54
initial state 117
instantiation, classes 30
integer, data type 70
integration
  phase 178
  scheme 148
  test 178
  with development environments 135
integration, object-oriented methods 17
interaction 107
  organization of use cases 154
  representation 102, 108
intercommunication, objects 22
  agents 22
  clients 22
  messages 24
    message categories 24
    message synchronization 25
  servers 22
interface 76
  of a project 201
  package 72
  type 76
internal event 120
interrupt 109
iteration
  clause 105
  evaluation 186
  lifecycle 153, 180
  message broadcast 103
iterator
  accessing a collection 57
iterators, messages 24

J

Jacobson, Ivar 8, 9
Java, classes 34
   multiple inheritance 53

L

layer
   architecture 173
   prototype 195
lifecycle
   iterative and incremental 176
   sequence diagram 109
   use case 95
   waterfall 177
lifeline 108
link
   association instance 73
   communication 137
   instance of a ternary association 82
   representation 99
linking
   dynamic 149
   static 59
links, object representation 18, 20, 36, 39
logic gates, classes 33
logical view 161

M

maintenance 95, 148, 184
   cycle 211
   deployment 208
   post-deployment 196
management
   risk 192
   versions and configuration 135, 188, 206, 210

mechanism
   common 67
   execution 129
   generic 204
   partitioning 70
member
   class 72
message
   asynchronous 109
   broadcast 102
   communication mode 148
   creation 111
   deletion 111
   flow 97
   parameters 106
   procedure call 111
   recursive 112
   reflexive 110
   representation 104
   synchronization 104
   synchronous 109
messages, object intercommunication 24
   broadcasting 26
   message categories 24
   message synchronization 25, 27
metaclass
   stereotype 74
metamodel 11, 90, 128
   specialization 67
method
   development 152
   implementation of operations 90
methods, need for in modern programming
      5
   see also analysis and design methods 5
mockup 190, 202
mode
   control 112
   synchronization 148
model 11, 67
   4 + 1 views 161
   CMM (Capability Maturity Model) 152
   complexity 172
   of classes 76
   organization 163
   partitioning 70
   see also modeling languages 11

P

341

U

V

Beginning Java 1.1

Author: Ivor Horton
ISBN: 1861000278
Price: $36.00 C$50.40 £32.99
Available May 97

If you've enjoyed this book, you'll get a lot from Ivor's new book, Beginning Java.

Beginning Java teaches Java 1.1 from scratch, taking in all the fundamental features of the Java language, along with practical applications of Java's extensive class libraries. While it assumes some little familiarity with general programming concepts, Ivor takes time to cover the basics of the language in depth. He assumes no knowledge of object-oriented programming.

Ivor first introduces the essential bits of Java without which no program will run. Then he covers how Java handles data, and the syntax it uses to make decisions and control program flow. The essentials of object-oriented programming with Java are covered, and these concepts are reinforced throughout the book. Chapters on exceptions, threads and I/O follow, before Ivor turns to Java's graphics support and applet ability. Finally the book looks at JDBC and RMI, two additions to the Java 1.1 language which allow Java programs to communicate with databases and other Java programs.

Beginning Visual C++ 5

Author: Ivor Horton ISBN: 1861000081
Price: $39.95 C$55.95 £36.99

Visual Basic is a great tool for generating applications quickly and easily, but if you really want to create fast, tight programs using the latest technologies, Visual C++ is the only way to go.

Ivor Horton's Beginning Visual C++ 5 is for anyone who wants to learn C++ and Windows programming with Visual C++ 5 and MFC, and the combination of the programming discipline you've learned from this book and Ivor's relaxed and informal teaching style will make it even easier for you to succeed in taming structured programming and writing real Windows applications.

The book begins with a fast-paced but comprehensive tutorial to the C++ language. You'll then go on to learn about object orientation with C++ and how this relates to Windows programming, culminating with the design and implementation of a sizable class-based C++ application. The next part of the book walks you through creating Windows applications using MFC, including sections on output to the screen and printer, how to program menus, toolbars and dialogs, and how to respond to a user's actions. The final few chapters comprise an introduction COM and examples of how to create ActiveX controls using both MFC and the Active Template Library (ATL).

WROX

Register Instant UML
and sign up for a free subscription
to The Developer's Journal.

A bi-monthly magazine for software developers, The Wrox Press Developer's Journal features in-depth articles, news and help for everyone in the software development industry. Each issue includes extracts from our latest titles and is crammed full of practical insights into coding techniques, tricks, and research.

Fill in and return the card below to receive a free subscription to the Wrox Press Developer's Journal.

Instant UML Registration Card

Name _____

Address _____

_____

_____

City _____ State/Region _____

Country _____ Postcode/Zip _____

E-mail _____

Occupation _____

How did you hear about this book? _____

☐ Book review (name) _____

☐ Advertisement (name) _____

☐ Recommendation _____

☐ Catalog _____

☐ Other _____

Where did you buy this book? _____

☐ Bookstore (name) _____ City _____

☐ Computer Store (name) _____

☐ Mail Order _____

☐ Other _____

What influenced you in the purchase of this book?

☐ Cover Design

☐ Contents

☐ Other (please specify) _____

How did you rate the overall contents of this book?

☐ Excellent   ☐ Good

☐ Average   ☐ Poor

What did you find most useful about this book? _____

What did you find least useful about this book? _____

Please add any additional comments. _____

What other subjects will you buy a computer book on soon? _____

What is the best computer book you have used this year?

_____

Note: This information will only be used to keep you updated about new Wrox Press titles and will not be used for any other purpose or passed to any other third party.

WROX PRESS INC.

Wrox writes books for you. Any suggestions, or ideas about how you want information given in your ideal book will be studied by our team. Your comments are always valued at Wrox.

Free phone in USA 800-USE-WROX
Fax (312) 397 8990

UK Tel. (0121) 706 6826   Fax   (0121) 706 2967

Computer Book Publishers

NB. If you post the bounce back card below in the UK, please send it to:
Wrox Press Ltd. 30 Lincoln Road, Birmingham, B27 6PA